Praise for *Gravitas*

"*Gravitas* challenges the one-note version of confidence society has written for women and demonstrates that confidence comes in many forms. Discovering your own unique version of it—your confidence language—is an authentic and powerful route to self-belief. Simply put, it's self-worth on your own terms."

— **Mika Brzezinski**, *New York Times* best-selling author of
Know Your Value and co-host of MSNBC's *Morning Joe*

"*Gravitas* is a must-read for anyone who wants a deeper understanding of themselves and their superpowers. Lisa Sun's research, relatable examples, and firsthand personal experience, along with the brilliant quiz and explanation of what true confidence and leadership looks like, provide a road map for how we can be our best selves, not just at work, but in all facets of life. This is a guide I want to reread and give as a gift to everyone I care about to boost their confidence and help them understand what will make them shine in a joyful and sustainable way."

— **Vicky Nguyen**, NBC News anchor and senior consumer investigative correspondent

"In *Gravitas*, Lisa Sun shares lessons that will transform your life as she guides you through every step of your journey to claim your confidence. If your best friend, your mother, and your mentor had a baby, it would be this book."

— **Schele Williams**, Broadway director and
author of *Your Legacy: A Bold Reclaiming of Our Enslaved History*

"In her fascinating new book, *Gravitas*, former McKinsey & Company consultant, entrepreneur, and glass-ceiling crasher Lisa Sun argues that self-confidence is an innate gift inside each of us to own, hone, and celebrate. Sun explains with great passion and precision how this singular manifestation of wellness, character, and faith radiates outward like a force multiplier. And through a step-by-step approach, Sun helps expand society's definition of confidence to meet the challenges of modern life."

— **John Gerzema**, *New York Times* best-selling co-author of *The Athena Doctrine: How Women (and the Men Who Think Like Them) Will Rule the Future*
and CEO of The Harris Poll

"You have to have ultimate belief in yourself because why should someone believe in you if you can't believe in yourself? *Gravitas* answers that question with a powerful, practical guide to discovering and unlocking inner confidence. Lisa Sun offers her unique blend of down-to-earth warmth and well-researched insight to help us navigate through the minefields that chip away at our self-belief. If you want to block out the noise and tap into your own signature form of confidence, *Gravitas* is an essential companion."

— **Mindy Grossman**, partner at The Consello Group and
former CEO of WW International and HSNi

"*Gravitas* is a playbook for confidence! Through her research-backed tools, Lisa empowers women to identify our unique gifts and shows us how to amplify them as our superpowers. She coaches us to examine areas where we aren't naturally fluent and delivers powerful solutions to face challenges head-on. This is a book about seeing yourself, loving yourself, and realizing how truly spectacular you are."

— **Julie Neimat**, Warner Bros. Discovery EVP of Talent + Culture

"*Gravitas* is a compelling read and road map all-in-one that blasts through the real challenges women face at work and outside it. Lisa Sun is an inspiring storyteller, and her eight strengths are a powerful, practical, and creative way to gain self-awareness and self-acceptance—the first steps toward tremendous success in the work we choose to do. This is a book you'll earmark and come back to regularly for practical advice and tools, and WWLD (what would Lisa do) will become your mantra!"

— **Joanna Barsh**, McKinsey & Company senior partner emerita and best-selling author of *How Remarkable Women Lead* and *Centered Leadership*

"Lisa Sun makes a clear case for redefining confidence in the modern era. She reexamines outdated notions of what it means to be self-assured and creates a new vocabulary and practical guide we all can use to be truly confident in our personal lives and at work. It is a must read for anyone looking to find their voice and present themselves with true power."

— **Deepa Purushothaman**, author of *The First, The Few, The Only*

"After I took the Gravitas Superpower Quiz, I knew author Lisa Sun was onto an important idea that would improve women's lives through rocket-boosting self-awareness. I was excited to find out my own confidence language and, through this extraordinary book, discover how to tap into its power. It has been a joy to apply what I learned to my personal and professional lives. I can't wait to share the quiz with friends and compare results!"

— **Dana Cowin**, founder of Speaking Broadly

"Lisa Sun's genuine desire to teach, support, and empower women is nothing short of magical, and in *Gravitas* she gives us a precision toolkit for identifying our unique strengths. Lisa taught me how to strategically harness my confidence as a business owner and entrepreneur, and I am thrilled that a larger audience will now have access to her powerful approach."

— **Anna Kaiser**, renowned wellness expert and founder of Anna Kaiser Studios

GRAVITAS

GRAVITAS

The 8 Strengths
That Redefine
Confidence

LISA SUN

with Kathryn Huck

HAY HOUSE, INC.
Carlsbad, California · New York City
London · Sydney · New Delhi

Published in the United States by: Hay House, Inc.: www.hayhouse.com®
Published in Australia by: Hay House Australia Pty. Ltd.: www.hayhouse.com.au
Published in the United Kingdom by: Hay House UK, Ltd.: www.hayhouse.co.uk
Published in India by: Hay House Publishers India: www.hayhouse.co.in

Project editor: Melody Guy • *Indexer:* J S Editorial, LLC
Jacket design: Shubhani Sarkar • *Interior design:* Claudine Mansour Design
Photo of Lisa Sun in Introduction: Courtesy of McKinsey & Company

Cataloging-in-Publication Data is on file at the Library of Congress

Hardcover ISBN: 978-1-4019-7253-0
E-book ISBN: 978-1-4019-7254-7
Audiobook ISBN: 978-1-4019-7255-4

10 9 8 7 6 5 4 3 2 1
1st edition, September 2023

To my mother, my first and forever role model
for what it means to live with gravitas.

May I grow up to be just like you.

我愛妳. 謝謝妳為我做的一切.

CONTENTS

INTRODUCTION

Discovering My Own Gravitas

Lisa's McKinsey & Company ID photo, September 2000

"Lisa comes across as young and overly enthusiastic at times. She should seek to have more gravitas."

I didn't know it then, but these two lines, written by my boss in my first annual review as a business analyst at the global management consulting firm McKinsey & Company, would change my life. In fact, when I first read this, I thought it was the end of my career at McKinsey. It was a Friday afternoon in 2001 as I sat on a plush gray couch opposite my development group leader, Diane, in her corner office that overlooked the White House.

"Why don't you take a minute to read it?" she said to me as she handed me a copy of my review. Her copy was in her lap.

I tried to read the rest of the review, but my eyes kept creeping back to that line. Gravitas. I didn't actually know what that word meant, but at 22 years old, recently sprung from college, I was too intimidated and overwhelmed to ask. The review was a blur, because I didn't hear a word Diane said as I spiraled. The positive points in her review didn't register: People enjoy working with you. You're great with clients; you go above and beyond for them. You're a distinctive problem-solver. While the review was 99 percent positive, all I took away was the negative. (Sound familiar?)

After our meeting, I went back to my desk and looked up gravitas in the dictionary: "dignity, importance, depth of substance." Ah, she was right. I didn't have any gravitas. *How do I get that?* I thought.

Later in the day, I caught Diane heading to the ladies' room, and I naively thought it was as good a time as any to nail her down for an explanation.

"Diane, how do I get gravitas?" I asked.

"Go buy a new dress, big shoes, and great jewelry," she replied, and she kept walking down the hallway.

Is she asking me to buy new clothes? I thought.

Later, I stirred up the courage to ask her to elaborate. She replied, "Every morning when you wake up, you are the first person you see. You should look in the mirror and like yourself. I can teach you how to be great at this job, but I can't teach you to like yourself."

When I still looked doubtful, she drew on a classic children's story. "Do you remember Dumbo, and how he thought his magic feather gave him the ability to fly? He could always fly, but the feather reminded him that he could. A great dress does that for me—it reminds me to see the best in myself. It's not about the dress or how others see me, it's about the reminder to believe in myself. If you like what you see, you're going to take that confidence with you throughout the day."

It turned out that her feedback was not about my clothes as much as it was about reminding myself to feel good about myself on the inside, even before I stepped foot into the office. It took me 11 years to decode the feedback from that fateful day, but eventually I knew I had to make the choice toward self-confidence. I needed to understand my unique gifts so that I could believe in those gifts and then others could see them too. We cannot give what we do not know we have. Diane could help me be better at my job, but she couldn't give me self-worth. Only I could do that. When I did finally figure it out, I named my company after it.

Owning my own business was in my blood. I started my life in the company of entrepreneurs, as the daughter of Taiwanese, college-educated immigrants. Before I was born, they came to the United States, arriving in California with no money and knowing very little English. My mother took a job working on a hamburger truck, and my father worked on a loading dock. With their grit and perseverance, they eventually went on to own and run a small family business. I saw firsthand what it takes to be an entrepreneur, often working shoulder to shoulder with my parents when they needed help. This is what is expected of a firstborn, second-generation daughter, so it was never a question that I would step in to help. My parents were the first to teach me how to be relentlessly self-reliant, resilient, and kind, all in the service of visionary belief.

My education was a gateway to a better life. It opened up a landscape of possibilities: law school, medical school, English grad school. Yes, I studied for every standardized test possible (my mom was a tiger mom before tiger moms were a thing!). Eventually, I got that job at McKinsey & Company. I spent 11 years there, a considerable amount of time given the average tenure of a management consultant is 18 to 24 months. In my 20s and 30s, I was humbled and honored to work with the world's leading thinkers and solve Fortune 500 executives' critical problems in compressed time frames. To this day, I am still in awe of the C-suite offices and boardrooms that I frequented. This was where I learned the power of client service ("It is my job to help others succeed"), where I was mentored by the very best in business, and where I learned to become a leader and a coach.

After more than a decade of being on the road as a consultant, I was burned out. The 20-hour workdays, the constant travel, the pressures of being on call for clients and teammates alike, and the rigorous performance metrics for promotion had finally gotten to me. For the first time in my life, I hit the pause button. I took more than a year off, a luxury that I decided was worth tapping into my life savings for. I had racked up thousands of frequent-flier miles and points that I was able to use for travel, and during the last two months of this time off, I spent time with my parents, who had retired to their hometown in Taiwan. During my last week there, my mother said, "Lisa, home is nice, but you cannot live here. You must find job."

I looked at her and said, "I have this idea I've been working on. . . ." I had recently read Walter Isaacson's biography of Steve Jobs, and it had reminded me of Jobs's Stanford commencement speech, in which he advocated "connecting the dots" by looking back at how specific life experiences had shaped his path. For example, dropping out of college meant he didn't have to take required courses and could audit a calligraphy class, which led to the Macintosh computer being the first to have beautiful typefaces; or being fired from Apple led to him founding Pixar and falling in love. I was particularly inspired by this portion of the speech:

"You can't connect the dots looking forward; you can only connect them looking backwards. So you have to trust that the dots will somehow connect in your future. You have to trust in something—your gut, destiny, life, karma, whatever. This approach has never let me down, and it has made all the difference in my life."

With this in mind, during my year off, I looked back at the dots of my life, literally jotting down memories, ideas, and thoughts on a cloth napkin I had picked up in my travels.

One of those memories was when I was told I didn't have gravitas. Another idea came from how I had mastered looking my best at various sizes (I've been a size 22, a size 8, and a size 12). I knew what silhouettes worked on my body, how accessories could be my ally, and how to assemble outfits cohesively. I enjoyed doing it so much that I helped friends and colleagues in my free time with wardrobe reviews. Going into their closets and editing, styling, and completing outfits for them became an unofficial hobby. I'd never thought much of it. But in the context of the dots of my life, I realized how much I enjoyed advising women on what to wear.

I showed my mother the napkin with the dots of my life scrawled all over it (each dot written in whatever pen or marker was most accessible at the time when I recalled the memory!). She replied, "Napkin is not job. How much money you save?" I told her how much money I had saved while working for over a decade, and she said, "Oh good. Bet on yourself." The next morning, I woke up to 10 e-mails in my inbox from my lawyer and my accountant, ranging from company formation documents to bank account applications. My mom had e-mailed them, informing them that I would be starting my own business. I got out of bed and went into the kitchen, where my mother was eating breakfast. I asked her, "Mom, what did you do last night?" And she said, "You not have guts. I have guts. I go on the Internet and start company last night."

And so, in 2013, realizing the transformative power that clothing can have, I founded Gravitas, a company with a mission to catalyze confidence. Through our products and services, I would give women the gift of embodying their best selves. When I first started out, it was all about the perfect dress, patented with built-in shapewear and made with luxury fabrics and flattering details for every shape and in sizes 0 to 24W.

Once I launched the company, however, I quickly learned that what I was offering was more than the dress. Within a few months of the company launch, I started to receive e-mails and handwritten letters from women that were windows into their lives: An airline attendant had been laid off and, with her last paycheck, she bought a dress to wear to her mother's funeral and to interviews for a new job. A lawyer who had sold her home to run for a district superior court judgeship won with over 60 percent of the vote and shared with us a video of her two sons putting her judge's robe on her over her Gravitas dress. A full-time parent going through a divorce bought a dress to attend her son's high school graduation and to interview for a job to go back to work for the first time in nearly two decades. An executive wrote saying that she was presenting for the first time to her company's steering committee and that she felt stronger because the word *gravitas* was literally emblazoned on the label in her dress.

These stories became a rallying cry for me to get to know the women I serve directly, so I created the Confidence Closet, a pop-up shop experience where I personally style any woman. The Confidence Closet is where I've earned my stripes as the dress whisperer. What I have learned over thousands of sessions with women all over the country is that the dressing room is an analogy for how we are all taking on the day. Many women, myself included, come into a dressing room setting themselves up to fail. Before we've even started the fitting, she'll likely reveal everything she hates about her body: "I don't like my arms [or hips, thighs, bust]," "I am going to lose 10 pounds," "I am oddly shaped with a long torso," "I just had a baby and am still carrying the weight". She will tell me how she's tried every dress out there, and none of them work for her. She blames herself. Think about it: standing there, in your underwear, in front of a mirror—it's one of the toughest, most self-reflective moments an adult woman can undergo.

It is in this moment of vulnerability that I have found the opportunity to make the greatest difference. Before we even look at the clothes I've selected for her, I change the chemistry of the fitting room from a place of negativity to a platform for positive energy. I ask her to remember what it was like to be a young girl shopping for a new dress, when all she wanted was a dress that twirled in her favorite color. Before words such as *skinny, fat,* and *size* were ingrained in our fitting-room vocabulary. I start every fitting with a few questions that have nothing to do with clothing, because inevitably what happens in that room has little to do with actual pieces of fabric. I ask the woman about her accomplishments, what she's the best at in the world (this stumps every woman because we can't pay ourselves a compliment, which is why it's so hard to receive them!), what she wants to do in this dress, what she wants the dress to do for her. We take stock of what she loves about herself. Because it's not about fitting into the dress, it's about finding a dress that finally fits her. That's my job, not hers.

When we're done, she looks in the mirror and often thinks I've doctored the mirror—"This mirror has to be wrong. It's a skinny mirror, isn't it?" She's dubious as she looks at herself: "How did you do that?" I tell her that it's not a magical dress (and that the mirror is from Bed Bath & Beyond, so definitely not a doctored skinny one!). I've found something that brings out the best in her.

More often than not, in the dressing room, we've unbottled more than just the physicalities, we've discussed all the ways in which she has felt "stuck" in her life. While the specific circumstances may differ, the emotions are universal, whether she is going through a divorce, works at a job that has limited opportunities, or is a full-time parent who feels unfulfilled or has grownup kids and is at a crossroads about the next chapter of her life. I get that vulnerable spot because I am the same woman as that customer in the dressing room. The firstborn daughter of immigrants, I grew up as an outsider with parents who lived paycheck to paycheck. I have experienced the ups, downs, and up agains of dress sizes. I have felt held back and undervalued in the workplace. I have seen my fair share of romantic disappointments. We share the most intimate space possible, and we quickly get to the most vulnerable places we can go.

I end every fitting by asking the woman to tell me something she loves about herself—not a physical quality, but an emotional quality. If she can't come up with it, I will share what I see in her: "I am inspired by how much you take care of everyone in your life," "I'm amazed by how you've achieved what you have," or "I've learned so much about something that you're the expert on!" Most of the time we can't see it in ourselves; someone else has to ask us or tell us. All those hours in the Confidence Closet with our customers proved that while women think our dresses are somehow "magical," the dress is only the reminder of our distinctive talents. I tell them to embrace their strengths, to shut out doubt and fear, and to share their talents with those around them. I spur them to action. Real confidence is the outward expression of an inner belief, and that belief translates into action. We see the final result only from the outside, but most of the work is happening on the inside.

This book will be an extended stay in that fitting room. No one lives without insecurities, and it's the choice to be self-confident that will change your life. Once you've made the choice between being self-conscious and self-confident, I am going to show you how to see the best in yourself, to let go of the insecurities that haunt you, and to deftly navigate situations and relationships. That's the power of gravitas; it is a total approach to living life with self-assurance.

The Roots of Gravitas

Society is full of unwritten rules that hold women back. The system was not built by us, nor was it built for us, so we are still finding our way in the fight for our equal rights (work in progress), equal pay (still trying), and racial justice (eyes are opening). On top of all of this, it's *really hard* to use our own individual voices in our daily lives. We still get hung up on what other people will think, hold back on asking for that raise or bank loan, stay silent when someone takes our idea or cuts us off or speaks over us, and doubt ourselves when we are given that promotion. And if we do get up the nerve, many of us still apologize for asking for what we deserve. If we can each master gravitas in our own lives, we have a chance to make a contribution to the collective.

One of the biggest things I have seen hold women back is not know-ing their worth. And so before you can go out busting rules and getting what you want, you need to fully understand your own value. The question is, HOW do we fix this once and for all? One woman at a time.

This is my inspiration for painting a more complex picture of gravitas. For most of us, the word conjures up an outward presence; we think of world leaders and heads of companies as having it, mostly framed by patriarchal notions of what it means to be confident. What I've learned in thousands of conversations is that we feel genuinely confident when we value and deploy our strengths. Those strengths come in many forms, not just in a singular ideal. Much like how we can understand and appreciate differences in people's personalities—how we relate to people, how we soak up information, how we make decisions, and how we organize our lives (or, if you're like me, don't organize it)—I saw that the strengths that form the basis of self-confidence come in many forms. In dressing rooms, Zoom calls, boardrooms, and event ballrooms alike, I began to ask women a simple question: "What is your superpower—what are you the best at in the world?" as a way to have them articulate their strengths. Every time a woman answered this simple question, I could see the start of her journey toward gravitas, rooting her sense of self-worth in her strengths. Over the years, I have captured thousands of answers to this question, and I noticed that several characteristics kept recurring. I realized there would be power in codifying these superpowers, correlating them to how confident and capable women felt, and creating a vocabulary women could use to value, and therefore believe in, themselves. To fully develop this methodology, my company's team conducted qualitative and quantitative research with thousands of women to dive deeper into what it means to truly have gravitas.

Through this work, we identified eight strengths: **leading, performing, achieving, giving, knowing, creating, believing, and self-sustaining**. Each of us is strongest in at least one or two of these qualities—our superpowers—while there are other qualities that you may demonstrate sometimes or not at all. Think of it like languages. There may be a language in which you are fluent, one in which you are proficient, and others which sound like gibberish to you. Your unique combination of superpowers is your "confidence language"— the strengths that are the basis of your self-confidence, the language in which you are fluent.

Discovering your confidence language is an important step on the journey toward gravitas. Belief in oneself comes from within; getting to an unbreakable belief in yourself starts with knowing what makes you uniquely you, making the unconscious conscious. The next step is understanding how your superpowers are helping (or hurting) you, so that you can fully embrace the foundation of your self-belief. But that's not enough to be a master of gravitas. We face challenging situations and other people with different confidence languages, so we may need to develop other skills, navigate outside of our comfort zones, or decide when a situation doesn't serve us. Once you know what you are best at and acknowledge where you would like to grow, you can fully realize gravitas. Mastering all eight strengths will always be a work in progress, but I am here to tell you that the process will make you stronger, wiser, happier, and more self-actualized.

Expanding the definition of gravitas creates space for all of us to own our power and get what we want in life. I have never been an advocate of slogans like "fake it until you make it" because there is a difference between performative confidence and real gravitas. Real gravitas is a deep-in-the-bones belief in yourself rooted in your strengths, so much so that you need to share it with the world, along with the ability to navigate anything that comes your way. Our external lives are mirrors of what is happening on the inside.

This is what this book is all about. I want women to master their own ideal of gravitas like I did (and still do, every day). I want women to turn moments of self-consciousness into bursts of self-confidence. I want women to understand that the strengths that underpin their self-belief can come in many versions: extroverted or introverted, reassuring or swaggering. Sometimes confidence can even come from making other people look or feel good, from letting others shine.

And now, what this book is NOT: This is not a book about getting people to like you. This is not a primer on how to successfully climb the corporate ladder (although it will help you do that). This is not about performative positivity with platitudes such as "be a boss." It is about loving yourself. Loving how you interact with others. Loving how you act and react in difficult or stressful situations. This is about deeply getting to know who you are, about appreciating your strengths and learning how to lean into them, and becoming proficient, much like with a language, in the other traits that make up gravitas.

This is going to be real work. Work that needs to undo what the sociologists Shani Orgad and Rosalind Gill call "confidence culture" in their book of the same name. "To be self-confident is the imperative of our time. As gender, racial, and class inequalities deepen, women are increasingly called on to *believe in themselves*," read the first lines of the text. It criticizes the confidence messages pushed by corporations to "believe in yourself" or "just be more confident" because they ignore structural and systemic barriers, and they minimize or fail to acknowledge the immense work self-love requires.[1] I want you to *think* differently about yourself—to discover how special you really are and tap into that. And part of what this book is going to do is give you the language to understand what confidence really means for you. This book isn't theoretical—it's interactive and practical. And it's not performative, it will be transformative. I offer exercises to try and real takeaways for personal and professional advancement.

In short, this is the book that I would have wanted to give to my 12-year-old self when I first learned what the word "chubby" meant; my 22-year-old self after my first professional review; my 32-year-old self when I was fired for the first time; and my 41-year-old self who was on the verge of giving up during the COVID-19 pandemic. It's the book I want to give every woman I am with in the dressing room when she tells me about her life wins—a step-up promotion, a skill mastered—and her struggles—a divorce, an office setback, a sick parent or child. It's the book that I want you to be able to turn to when you need to look in the mirror and fall in love with yourself all over again. And it may be the first time you fully understand what makes you tick.

Gravitas is not about pretending or putting on a smile. This is so much more than that. It's about making the choice toward self-confidence and believing in your superpowers as the basis of that choice. By believing in your strengths and building on them, you will become the best version of yourself, with the ability to navigate whatever comes your way. Ultimately, you will become who you want to be. That's the journey I want to take you on in this book. In Part I, we will explore the underpinnings of this new approach to confidence, and I will show you why confidence is a choice and how to make that choice. In Part II, you will take a quiz to discover your confidence language and understand the superpowers you naturally exhibit as the basis for your inner strength. In Part III, I will show you how to harness the power of your confidence language, learn new skills to get what you want in life, and, ultimately, how this work can make a difference for others.

Now let's get started.

Do any of these resonate? If so, this book is for you.

- I want to show up, I mean really show up, and not just be in the room.

- I want the power to step forward when it's easier to stand still.

- I want to be seen and recognized.

- I want to be resilient when challenges come my way. Because they will come.

- I want to get to that next milestone and not doubt myself.

- I want to be able to communicate better with others.

- I want to have more meaningful connections with family, friends, and colleagues.

- I want others to better understand me.

- I want to better understand others.

- I want to use my unique strengths to make a difference in my life and for others.

- I want to accomplish those things that will fulfill me, but fear has stopped me from doing.

- I want to hold myself in high regard on my own terms and not settle for less than I deserve.

- I want to feel in charge of my life.

Part I

CHOOSE CONFIDENCE

REDEFINING GRAVITAS

The simplicity of the Gravitas Confidence Closet belies the magic that happens inside it. I typically construct my pop-up shops at a conference or speaking engagement, and we try to make it feel as much like a real fitting room as possible. In the back of a hotel ballroom, we fill dressing rooms with hanging racks brimming with clothes, and at the entrance we place a sign that reads: PAY YOURSELF A COMPLIMENT. CHANNEL YOUR SUPERPOWER. STEP IN AND LET YOUR CONFIDENCE TAKE SHAPE. This is where so many connections are formed and transformations happen.

For example, Susan is a longtime Gravitas customer who is adept with numbers and at the helm of the finance team at a major health care company. She had been there for a decade, yet she felt she wasn't getting the recognition she deserved. As she was getting undressed, she told me, "This fitting could not have come at a better time. My boss just told me I don't have gravitas." (Yes, he used the very same word that Diane did with me!) She added, "And I don't know what to do about it."

We talked, and she told me more about her boss's personality. While she is an intellectual to the core who takes care of her team in a soft-spoken style, her boss, the CEO, is highly extroverted; he commandeers a room with a charm offensive, which he honed as he rose up through the sales division.

"Are you getting credit for the contributions you're making? For the strengths you bring to the table every day?" I asked.

"I don't think so. . . . I have never been one to toot my horn," she replied.

"Are you kidding me? He would be nowhere if you weren't doing the numbers and keeping that team engaged. Can I suggest something? Schedule 15 minutes on his calendar every week. Sit in front of him and make sure he understands all of your team's successes. On top of that, let's give you some new leadership tools to get you where you want to be."

I role-played with her a few times what conversations she could have with her boss, and she executed my advice. Every week she was in front of him, ensuring that he was aware of her team's accomplishments, showing him the skills she hadn't been recognized for, and demonstrating new ones around leading. By engaging with the CEO and speaking up more, Susan was eventually promoted to chief financial officer.

Susan's scenario may sound familiar to you—it's certainly not uncommon to have different work styles. But more important, her boss's version of confidence was different from hers. His was swaggering and extroverted, and her style was quietly supportive, which can be an equally high-impact way to lead a team. As I thought through how Susan could best navigate her way within the parameters of her job, a light bulb went off for me that day: we have been living with a singular, reductive version of confidence. Her boss's version of gravitas is what we as a society have defined it as for centuries—an outward self-assuredness that, as we'll share in later chapters, is relevant for only some people and situations and excludes most of us. Susan's struggle, similarly to what you may be experiencing in your work or personal life, was trying to fit into the mold of that singular definition of confidence.

As I reflected on this aha moment, I began to see many recent events through a different lens. In 2013, Janet Yellen was nominated to be the chair of the U.S. Federal Reserve System. While possibly one of the most qualified candidates for the role, she didn't look or act like any of her predecessors. She had a steep climb to getting confirmed, one likely made steeper because she was soft-spoken. The pervasive view of gravitas did not stretch to include her. In a July 2013 op-ed by then *Washington*

Post reporter Ezra Klein, he wrote: "I've had a surprising number of discussions that follow the same pattern: 'Yellen is great,' my interlocutor will say. 'But . . . ' The 'but' is a variation on a theme. She lacks 'toughness.' She's short on 'gravitas.' Too 'soft-spoken' or 'passive.'"[1] He goes on to see right through these naysayers: "What the complaints share is an implicit definition of leadership based on stereotypically male qualities. They aren't qualities that all men have, or all women lack, but they're qualities that tend to be more rewarded in men than in women, and thus more prevalent among men than women." Although she went on to be confirmed—by the narrowest margin ever and as the first woman to hold the position—the perception of women in leadership roles hasn't gotten much better in the decade since she took the helm.

Yellen and accomplished women like her still have an uphill battle because they don't look and act like most of the people in the room. A few of us have been paying attention: McKinsey's *Women in the Workplace* report of 2021 covers how female leadership blossomed throughout the COVID-19 pandemic as the typically female traits of compassion and empathy were welcomed in companies working remotely worldwide, yet women are the ones who are experiencing the most burnout as we exit the worst of it. Those who step into the role of nurturer continue to be undervalued because traditionally, the workplace has not recognized giving as a form of confidence all its own. At least not yet. As pointed out in the 2013 landmark book *The Athena Doctrine: How Women (and the Men Who Think Like Them) Will Rule the Future*, which is based on a series of surveys, in-depth research, and interviews from around the world, social theorist John Gerzema and author Michael D'Antonio show that more feminine-leaning traits such as nurturing, cooperation, communication, and sharing are finally starting to be recognized for their significant value.

So let's make room for more types of confidence beyond the sharpest-elbowed, loudest-voice-in-the-room style that has been the marker for leadership for so many years. We should not have to "fake it until we make it" and be performative about being confident. Let's recognize all these other forms of confidence that have been undervalued for way too long, especially those more feminine strengths. Repeat after me: confidence is a plural, not a singular construct.

Don't take just my word for it—the very definition of *confidence* from the *Oxford English Dictionary* is: "a feeling of self-assurance arising from one's appreciation of one's own abilities or qualities." No mention of performative swagger there. But a search for the word *confidence* or *gravitas* online yields hundreds of books on the subject; most, if not all, of them use a very narrow, old construct of the leadership ideal. I want to change that. I want to change this outmoded way of thinking into one with a more inclusive definition of *confidence*, one that we can use every day, in every situation. We need to expand the traditional views of competence—along with what is recognized and rewarded—to create room for everyone to have it. That's where a lot of these confidence books are incomplete: they force us into a specific prototype without recognizing our unique gifts as a foundation. They tell us to speak up, be gregarious, get noticed—to perform.

I love Dale Carnegie—the dog-eared 99-cent copy of *How to Win Friends and Influence People* that my dad bought me at a garage sale changed my life. Growing up as a second-generation immigrant who started high school at 12 years old with parents who were not equipped to help me be social in the American landscape, it was up to Dale to do it. His book taught me to smile and remember other people's names, to make an effort in conversation, and to not be afraid on a stage. I wouldn't be the person I am today if I hadn't read it. Since then, I've realized that Carnegie's ideal of confidence is one-note. Smile, shake hands, remember people's names—all are great fundamental techniques most commonly associated with a traditional definition of confidence. Yet these characteristics appear in only a small percentage of the population. (As you will see later, a mere tenth of the population.) But for centuries we have been told that this sociable form of confidence is the thing that we all need to have. Do we all really need to be leaders and performers? Nothing would get done if that were the case.

I believe we can all be powerful in our own skin without being extroverted leaders; there are so many other qualities that can lead to confidence. For example, in Taiwan, where my parents are from, quiet stoicism, not attention-demanding bravado, is celebrated as a marker of confidence. Self-promotion and hubris are looked down upon. The strengths that Yellen and most other women possess—high achieving and self-effacing—are the same as those celebrated in the East (I am an anomaly in my own culture!). As an example, during the COVID-19 pandemic, introverts felt more successful at work because they did not need to play into the likability norms of a traditional office; their contributions could be more fairly evaluated, seen, and promoted without the office chit-chat that historically has defined belonging.[2]

We can learn something here: you don't have to conform to our society's definitions of confidence. When I launched my company, I didn't want to play into the performative elements of the body positivity movement by simply showing many different sizes and body types in imagery. I tapped into a deeply personal place, having myself been many sizes and confronted internal and external weight bias and fat-shaming. It was important that we designed our first collection inclusively from the woman back, meaning that we didn't design a dress and then retrofit larger sizes for that one pattern. We started with different female body types, sizes, and needs and built the dress around her; we thought about the woman first before the product. We used five different fit models, all with various sizes and body types ranging from athletic to hourglass, whereas most brands use a single fit model (this is why there are some brands that fit you and others that just never will). The goal was not that every style would work for every body, but at least two styles would in sizes 0 to 24W (and we continue to work on expanding that size range further). Some dresses don't work for my own pear-shaped body type, but I don't beat myself up about it when a style doesn't fit me; I wear the ones that do. I believe everyone deserves to end the negative thinking that we beat ourselves up with about not fitting into something and to start finding something that finally fits us. We actively acknowledge and celebrate the existence of multiple ideals, just as we accept other forms of confidence as a way to empower people in embracing their own unique beauty.

In the same way that many of us look for happiness in all the wrong places, we've been taught to search for confidence in a room we can't access. So, when someone tells you to be more confident or you read an Instagram post that says, "Be a boss lady today," this may be a false ideal that may not come naturally to you. Yet if I tell you about a trait that makes you really special—that you are generous with your time or

you execute a to-do list like no one else can—that is much more insightful and meaningful. Giving credit to other forms of confidence can help
women feel relieved they don't have to "be a boss" in the traditional
sense. Feel free to scroll past all those Instagram posts that command
you to RISE & SPARKLE or HUSTLE LIKE A BOSS, LIVE LIKE A
QUEEN. Those are one-note, and there are so many other forms of confidence that we can celebrate—especially those that are more aligned
with who we really are.

When I do a speaking engagement, I often ask the audience my
superpower question, "What are you the best at in the world? No one in
the world is better than you at this." Most people struggle to answer the
question, and many women come up to me afterward to tell me, "Oh,
my superpower is so boring."

"Like what?" I ask.

"I am super organized and a planner."

"Oh, you mean you get shit done!" I reply. "Please come work with
me. I admire that superpower. I'm a procrastinator and disorganized. I
can't get anything done. And I surround myself with people who can get
things done. I need people like you!"

We can easily dismiss our own strengths for many reasons: lack
of self-awareness, defaulting to only seeing our flaws, or perhaps it's
because society has not deemed them valuable or worthy of notice. No
wonder it's so hard to recognize our own self-worth when we've been
conditioned to find some traits lacking in value.

What Are You the Best at in the World?

Write down the first thing that comes to mind. Are you the best listener?
Perhaps you are the best at taking abstract concepts and making them a
reality. Or you get the work DONE. Was it hard to think of it right away? Think
of a time when you were firing on all cylinders. What did you bring to the
table at that moment? Maybe it will be easier once you see the descriptions
of all eight superpowers in Chapter 4. A participant in one workshop told
me that she struggled to come up with something until I shared the eight
superpowers. And that in and of itself was a lesson for her: it wasn't something she could call on ASAP.

While confidence has been singularly defined up until this point, it doesn't mean we have to continue to live this way. If we want to build truly inclusive and strong workplaces, friendships, and families, we have to recognize that confidence comes in many forms and that our superpowers are the basis of self-belief. We have to honor our strengths and build on them. We've identified eight superpowers, so we can know what we're the best at before others see it too. We cannot be recognized for, or give, what we do not know we have.

Jung and Me

To identify these eight superpowers, I didn't have to start from scratch—I researched past philosophers and psychologists who recognized the diverse and complementary strengths we humans have. Carl Jung, for instance, acknowledged that there are lots of different types of personalities and created a language for how to understand ourselves and others. Fundamentally, my methodology stems from Jung's theories. He categorized human traits into archetypes that make up our collective (and subconscious) psyche. And there have been many takes on these archetypes over the years, from the Myers-Briggs personality test to Gallup's *CliftonStrengths*.

My aim is to be a part of this body of knowledge and to build on it through the lens of self-confidence. Because when I'm in the dressing room with a woman, I want to give her the vocabulary to know and value her inner strength; this interaction gives the encounter deeper meaning far beyond trying on clothes together. We study everyone and everything but ourselves. We need to celebrate the source of our strengths, whatever they look like, and not let them be ignored or diminished. This is not pretending or changing who you are to emulate someone else—this is about discovering the root of your self-belief. My part is to help you zero in on the capabilities or skills that are going to help you go from self-doubt to self-confidence, as the basis for courage and action-taking in our lives.

My superpowers framework is also rooted in my work experience. At McKinsey & Company, a core principle was to deeply understand what made our colleagues and clients tick, so we could take great care in how we could best be of service. I had this ingrained in me as I started my clothing line, Gravitas. As I helped 21st-century women find that perfect dress, I started seeing similarities in women's strengths and vulnerabilities as I dressed them in our Confidence Closet. We conducted focus groups and one-on-one interviews with women at different stages of their lives, all with different backgrounds and different careers. As we heard their stories, we came to deeply understand their unmet needs and their strengths, from the full-time parent to the executive. Through numerous focus groups, thousands of hours of dressing room consults, hundreds of hours in workshops with executives across industries, and then through an unbiased, U.S. general population quantitative study of 1,000 women, we were able to validate and further describe the eight superpowers. With that data at the ready, we refined what these characteristics are and how we can double-click on our own confidence language—our unique combination of these superpowers—to redefine traditional notions of confidence. Not confidence as a corporate slogan, but as a personal journey and source of power. You have your version of confidence; I have mine. Oh, and it can evolve!

I'm a real-life practitioner, and much of what you will find in this book was experiential, lived on the job and in life, supported by our own proprietary qualitative and quantitative research. And so the best advice I can give you is inspired by you all, in your real lives. While the research we did has elements that are rigorous and academic, much of what you will read here was gleaned from the many, many hours in dressing rooms and focus groups, individual interviews, coaching sessions, and workshops conducted to help women find their best traits and act on them to live bigger, more fulfilling lives. These hours helped me unlock that ability to see ourselves differently, acknowledge blind spots that stop us from being fully self-actualized, and, most important, take action.

Your Confidence Language
(Or *Parlez-Vous . . . Vous?*)

Through all of this work, I've created a new vocabulary to define what it means to be confident. Of the eight strengths, only one or two are dominant in most of us. Where you are strongest is your confidence language, the combination of superpowers that is the basis for your self-belief. Having gravitas—living life with self-assurance—requires knowing what you are the best at and what your superpowers are, and channeling the power that comes with them (which is what you will be doing in Part III of this book). This is not toxic positivity, because that ignores the realities and pressures of our lives. This is an in-depth understanding of your distinctive capabilities that have powered, are driving, and will continue to fuel you through the best and worst of times. Understanding your superpowers roots your self-belief in tangible strengths; your confidence language shines light on your talents.

Beyond knowing your unique confidence language, growth comes from being aware of and understanding all eight superpowers. Because life happens, and we are constantly facing people who have different confidence languages than ours and encountering situations where our own set of superpowers aren't enough to get us through. Think of these eight superpowers as a "confidence language dictionary" or a decoder ring to better read others and situations, so you can navigate the world with mastery and progression. Just as it is handy to know a bit of a foreign language when traveling in another country, knowing the language of yourself and others will help you navigate any situation in life.

The eight superpowers are the building blocks of this approach, and once you are familiar with the vocabulary, you'll be better able to identify how you see yourself and others, articulate your needs and wishes to others (and vice versa), and see where you might want to further develop to get what you want in life. In fact, we found that as women age or advance into more senior roles at a company, the number of superpowers they have on average grows from two to three or more, showing that we can evolve our confidence language.

Being proficient or knowledgeable in superpowers outside of your own can help you navigate through all sorts of situations, from how to be confident going into a first date to how to advocate for a raise, get credit for something, or deal with loss. This new vocabulary is designed to clearly identify your gifts, help you understand any gaps that you may have, and interpret feedback to learn how to grow and be empowered in anything you do. I hope to hold up a mirror that helps you see deeper connections with others, but more important, that transforms how you see yourself.

The Three Cs

What's in it for you? How can my inclusive understanding of confidence impact your everyday life? This is the exciting part. Once you discover your unique fingerprint of confidence, you can build on your own confidence language and engage in life with a stronger, growth-oriented mindset. This mindset is what I call the Three Cs, which together have the power to embolden you.

COURAGE

My equation for courage is having self-belief that spurs us to take action, and then interpreting the results of those actions from a viewpoint of our strengths and with a desire to learn, grow, and do it all over again. This equation doesn't work if the first part—self-belief—is replaced with self-doubt, because then there is no action. And self-belief is rooted in a deeply held sense of why you're amazing.

Consider the reverse. While it's unfashionable to admit that we crave validation from outside sources—tell me you don't refresh an Instagram post or story to see the number of likes or views—external praise says that my choices are validated. There is science behind this: external validation releases our feel-good neurochemical, dopamine. It can act like a drug, and we can get addicted—or not. For courage to be lasting and become effortless, we need to start with validating ourselves first. We can't receive a compliment until we can acknowledge it in ourselves first. On my speaking circuits, I do an audience exercise where I ask women to pair up and share their superpower. I then ask pairs to compliment each other in front of the audience. The typical reaction? When she is complimented by another person in front of others, she is embarrassed and visibly shrinks, even though she shared her superpower just minutes before to her partner. I ask her to throw back her shoulders and hear the compliment again—and this time to believe it! Audiences cheer.

We can create a pattern of lasting internal validation that powers courage. The concept of neuroplasticity tells us that our brains are always evolving new connections, learning new habits, beliefs, and traits. One piece of research showed how participants' confidence increased over time by stimulating their brain activity. Neuroscientist Mitsuo Kawato said, "How is confidence represented in the brain? Although this is a very complex question, we used approaches drawn from artificial intelligence (AI) to find specific patterns in the brain that could reliably tell us when a participant was in a high or low confidence state. The core challenge was then to use this information in real-time, to make the occurrence of a confident state more likely to happen in the future." Coauthor Aurelio Cortese added, "Surprisingly, by continuously pairing the occurrence of the highly confident state with a reward—a small amount of money—in real-time, we were able to do just that: when participants had to rate their confidence in the perceptual task at the end of the training, they were consistently more confident."[3] We can train ourselves to believe in ourselves.

From here, we can take action—and sometimes that action takes the form of the courage to realize when we need to move on to a better environment. Take Theresa. Well established in her career as a partner at a major consulting firm, she was at a crossroads. "The constant pressure of meeting ridiculous revenue targets and the responsibility of managing hundreds of staff is more than I want to do for the next twenty years," she confided to me one day. "I value my family and friends so much more than work, and because of that I rarely work on the weekends. But I'm surrounded by competitive high achievers and sometimes feel like I'm not working hard enough." We found that her strengths of optimism and giving were fighting against what was unnatural to her; that kind of pressure-cooker atmosphere stressed her out. And mind you, all of this was during a pandemic, when compassionate, empathetic female leadership was paramount to success, but still undervalued.

This realization gave her the power of knowing that it wasn't her, it was about her not being like the culture of her firm. Unlike Susan, she decided that it wasn't worth it to her to try to shore up the qualities her firm valued. Now the question was, does she, knowing what her strengths are, lean into them, hoping they will work within the confines of her job, or does she move on to something that better matches her profile? Now that she has the tools, she has better self-awareness of what she's striving for to courageously make that decision.

As for me, I didn't have a choice. When I was at McKinsey, I tried to get promoted six times over the course of three years, and ultimately the firm offered me a senior expert position without the compensation of partnership but with the possibility of getting onto the partnership track later, or to leave ("up or out"). I took more than a year off and reflected on the conversations I had had with mentors over the years. One comment stuck out: one mentor told me that I wasn't a good fit with what the firm valued. While I was on leave, she e-mailed me three questions:

- What are you good at? (My answer: problem-solving, analytics, process)

- What do you love to do? (My answer: generate new ideas, lead teams, inspire others)

- What are you passionate about? (My answer: fashion as a tool to empower and help others)

She was helping me navigate the very vocabulary that I have since developed for this book. If I had had our confidence language to pinpoint it back then, I would have seen that what I was good at was what the firm wanted, but did not align with what I truly loved to do. My strengths and passions could be best deployed in a different context.

This is the power we get in knowing our version of confidence. We can sift through what we want, what we value, what our gifts are. We can articulate, "This is how I operate. This is what makes me strong." We can make decisions. We can be courageous. Susan acknowledged the differences between her and her boss and did the work to get credit for her style while also recognizing that she needed to grow with more commanding attributes—that was what was important to her. Theresa, on the other hand, demonstrated courage in that once she became aware of her strengths, she had the power of choice. Theresa put herself into a position of power to consider the next stage of her career while also being a mentor and shaping a pathway for associates with her profile to obtain success. She leaned into where she was strongest and what came most naturally to her; she became more aware of and confident in her own distinctive abilities.

COMPASSION

I am a big basketball fan, and I particularly love a highlight video that the NCAA March Madness tournament makes every year called "One Shining Moment." (While I'm at it, please consider this my formal request in writing for the NCAA to do the same highlight reel for the women's tournament, perhaps with Jennifer Hudson singing the iconic song!) There are 68 teams in the tournament every year, but only 1 gets to hoist the trophy. Yet the three-minute video is dedicated to highlighting all of the teams, including the 67 teams that didn't win. There are always two or three clips where a player misses the basket, he crumples to the ground as the buzzer sounds and the game is over; his teammates rush over and comfort him. Because it wasn't about missing the shot, it was about the sweat and tears of those teammates who gave it their best. If you are more of a Broadway fan, think of it as one of my favorite lines from *Hamilton*: "I'm not throwing away my shot."

Learning your confidence language allows you to replay highlight reels like these in light of your superpowers, not from a viewpoint of disappointment. We can beat ourselves up over setbacks, or we can view moments of distress in terms of how they made us stronger. Your confidence language gives you an inventory of your strengths and others' contributions; that insight helps you build compassion for yourself and others. After all, compassion is defined as "a consciousness of another's 'distress' and a desire to alleviate it." In other words, compassion is empathy plus action. There's a negative version of events, and there's a positive way to rewind the tape every single time. So when you rewind the tape, don't be so tough on yourself and review it with this newfound compassion and vocabulary, because it will show you how strong you really are. I'm not saying not to have high standards, but rather to look at events with a discerning eye: Are there any teachable lessons there? Was there something that you did that demonstrated or tapped into your strengths, even if the result was disappointing?

Compassion is universal. We should practice it for ourselves as well as others. The COVID-19 pandemic had a horrible effect on my company— actually, all fashion companies (or really, all companies in general!). Everyone has their own story, and mine was that no one was buying work clothes when every company in the world was in lockdown. NO ONE. We were in the red for two years. Every time I think about it, I still beat myself up. One day when I was giving myself another bruising, my dear friend the entrepreneur Jane Park said to me, "Lisa, are you serious? You think this is your fault? Tell me who else made personal protective equipment like hospital gowns and face masks for the frontline. Tell me who kept people in New York City's garment district employed when you had no money in the bank account." Her highlight reel was completely different from what ran through my head.

Ambitious and smart, my friend Erica was more successful in her career than her husband at the age of 29, but she made the decision to become a full-time parent after the birth of her second child, which happened at the start of the pandemic. She traded in her career as a corporate lawyer to be the default parent—a position she signed up for in what she calls "a traditional structure," and she knowingly accepted the rules. Yet it still sucks when she is cleaning baby spittle out of her hair while her husband is celebrating his latest work triumph. When I helped her discover that her confidence language was centered around achievement, it became clear why she was unhappy at times. She shared, "This all makes sense. In my job, I was so confident because the ladder, rewards, and validation were so clear. As a parent, there are no external metrics for success until it's too late. I won't know if I've done a good job until after our kids are grown and out of the house." She discovered she missed the thrill of success—making goals and achieving them. She gave herself grace for how she was feeling and, beyond that, she did something with this newfound insight. She partnered up with another mom and started a baking company so that she would have something that she could accomplish every day outside of her children. She gave herself the compassion to do something for herself that would satisfy her natural need for achievement.

CONNECTION

While courage and compassion are about seeing ourselves, this new vocabulary of superpowers helps us see people for who they are, and that is where connection comes in. One of the reasons systemic bias persists is because connection has often been based on demography: where you grew up, your ethnicity, your age. These are all demographic factors over which we have zero control. A white male is born with unearned privilege, regardless of whether or not he chose to be a white male. Same for any woman—African American, Asian, Latinx (all without the unearned privilege!). Demography is not given to us by choice, and yet historically it has been one of the easiest markers for establishing connection with one another. When we start seeing people for their strengths—whether they're the same or different from ours—we have the opportunity to celebrate them for what they bring to the table beyond who they are demographically. We see people not in our own image, but in their image. And that connection becomes really, really powerful.

This is the foundation of allyship, which starts with seeing another's story through their lens, not yours. It's seeing the other's strengths, even when they're different from yours. One of my most important mentors, Andrew, is a British man whose upbringing was quite different from mine; we have no demography in common. When we first met, his first question in getting to know me wasn't about where I was from or where I went to school (he could look up my entire CV in the HR system), it was: "Tell me a story about your childhood. Something you're really proud of." I shared a story about working in my parents' restaurant and how I learned what it takes to build something from nothing. It was a connection built on something important to me and an opportunity to see my worldview through my story. In that moment, he gained real insight into my values and how to best promote me in my career. With this new skillset of connection, we can be better equipped to help each other rise. The McKinsey *Women in the Workplace 2022* report reinforces this point: "When women of color feel like they have strong allies at work, they are happier in their jobs, less likely to be burned out, and less likely to consider leaving their companies."[4]

Connection is also about getting rid of unhealthy comparisons. Let's use this language to finally see ourselves and others for their strengths, not to look at people with envy. My friend Vanessa has twin daughters in their twenties. Both have the double whammy of being smart and beautiful, inside and out. When one of the twins was getting married, the other one was single and was frustrated by it. After Vanessa told me what Phoebe was going through, I told her, "You know what? She needs to be Lady Edith and not Lady Mary," referring to the often-dueling sisters of the television show *Downton Abbey*. "Lady Edith spent four seasons comparing herself to Mary. At some point, she said, 'Screw it, I had a kid out of wedlock, I've already lost the respect of my family, I am just going to live my life.' And she jumped into the next phase of her life as a working woman leading a newspaper, secured her own apartment in London, and was unapologetic for her life choices. Guess what—she ends up having the happiest ending of all."

It took a while for Lady Edith to get to that place to see that she was never going to be Lady Mary, but she finally did. And it was when she stopped trying to compare herself to Mary and embraced her unique strengths that she became one of my favorite characters. Similarly, with Vanessa's help, Phoebe was able take stock of all the incredible things going on in her life, like starting her own consulting firm and spending time with her tight circle of friends, and no longer felt compelled to match her twin sister's milestones.

"Win the battle or perish. This is a woman's resolve." This mantra was to have been said by Celtic warrior Boudica, who led a rebellion against Roman rule in A.D. 61. Let's emulate this fierce femme who made a connection with her community to lead them into battle and combat systemic bias a little at a time, where we can build genuine connections off of values and strengths, not just demography, and create stronger, more resilient friendships, families, and workplaces.

When we redefine gravitas with this new vocabulary of superpowers as a foundation, we can go into the world with greater courage. We can go into the world with greater compassion. We can connect with those around us like never before and stop unfairly comparing ourselves to others. Because this is what truly confident people do.

Core Concepts

Self-belief, self-confidence, self-assurance, self-worth: A feeling of trust in and appreciation of your abilities, character, and judgment. Used inter-changeably in this book.

Superpowers: Strengths, characteristics, and traits that provide the basis for self-belief.

Confidence language: Your unique combination of superpowers.

Gravitas: A total approach to living life with self-assurance—choosing con-fidence, owning and deploying your superpowers, evolving your confi-dence language, and deftly navigating every situation and relationship.

GRAVITAS
IS A CHOICE

Someone once asked me, "What would you tell your ten-year-old self?" I answered her, but I then went on to say, "The more important question is what would your ten-year-old self say to you?"

Because if your 10-year-old self was anything like mine, she was fearless and curious, and she believed she was on track to be the first female Asian chief justice of the Supreme Court and/or president of the United States (the latter of which is still in my option set!).

Why was I like that? Because we are all born fully self-confident. Ask any child what they're the best at in the world, and you'll get a long list of responses, ranging from giving hugs to playing soccer. But there's a moment in our lives when we become self-aware and self-conscious. For me, it was when I was 12 years old and looking in the mirror and worrying if I was pretty or ugly, skinny or fat. Words that, prior to that moment, I had never considered in relationship to myself. I crossed the line from being self-confident to being self-conscious. That's the doubting preteen you see in the photo who didn't want her photo taken, along with my six-year-old brother who at that age hadn't been hit with self-consciousness yet. He's hanging upside down, smiling, and unabashedly himself.

Lisa, 12, with her 6-year-old brother.

I was lucky enough to grow up surrounded by parents and an extended family who loved me unconditionally and saw only possibility for me. When I stumbled as a toddler, someone was always there to encourage me to stand back up and try again. When I fell off my bike with training wheels, I was told to get back on again, because my family knew with full certainty that I could. When I was asked, "What do you want to be when you grow up?" every answer to that question was praised (including Supreme Court justice and president), fully supported, and never shot down. This may not have been your exact childhood, but many of us can recall similar experiences. This unabashed belief you have in yourself as a child is the purest and simplest form of gravitas. It's a quality that we can carry with us throughout our adult lives; psychologist Carl Jung described it as an "inner child" that, in its best form, could be a source of strength, wonder, and optimism to bolster well-being (the reverse is true, though, if you had a traumatic childhood).

But something happens when we hit a certain age at which we obtain an awareness about ourselves, others, and our environment. In early childhood, we are protected by our parents or a sibling, but then when we step onto that school bus, our circle of influence expands and our worldview changes. For me, it was magnified by being a person of Asian descent growing up in the middle of the Southern California desert, where I was definitively an outsider.

It is an age when this growing self-awareness often leads to self-doubt as we experience our own disappointments, oftentimes reinforced by systemic challenges. Each setback can create or reinforce a limiting belief, or highlight a flaw previously unseen. These flaws begin to out-weigh the light and power of the inner child's robust sense of self, kick-ing off a cycle of "fixed" or "deficit" thinking (more on this a bit later). We become weighed down by our flaws and default to what has worked before or retreat back into our comfort zones, creating our own ceil-ings, opting out, and living smaller lives than we deserve. Add to that persistent systemic bias that may reinforce and diminish how we see ourselves. A simple example: how many times do women say "Sorry" as a default response, whether or not they've done something wrong? It's second nature to assume that the fault or flaw lies with us, that we are less-than.

When a woman tells me she's "stuck," I imagine concentric circles within which she has shrunk her world to the smallest circle possible. It's safe within that circle, where so many other priorities and demands swirl around her, distracting her from her power to the point where she no longer can see or imagine the outer concentric circles of her life. In that situation, we become less courageous in wanting a bigger life and taking leaps with our gifts. Because what is courage, after all? It's self-belief that leads to action, and then interpreting the results of those actions from a place of strength and a desire to do it all over again. If our self-belief is diminished and replaced with self-doubt, there is no possibility for action. This paralysis becomes a self-perpetuating loop, where we lose out and the world does not benefit from our gifts. It's sim-ilar to the peril of perfectionist exhaustion: perfectionists believe that they are inherently flawed and are caught in a doomed loop of exertion to measure up.

Can we break this cycle? Can we sit in the midst of our flaws and still hold ourselves in high regard to live bigger, fuller, more fulfilling lives? I can tell you firsthand, without hesitation, that the answer is yes. But before we get there, we must understand the six forces holding us back.

1. The Deficit Mindset: Viewing life through the lens of weaknesses or what is missing; a focus on problems rather than potential.

I do not allow mirrors inside the fitting rooms of our Gravitas Con-fidence Closet. Why? As soon as a woman undresses and sees herself semi-naked in front of a mirror, she sees everything she does not like about herself, and it prevents her from even wanting to try on the first dress we've selected for her. Why are we so hard on ourselves? It is built into us. Research has shown that 8 out of 10 women are dissatisfied with their reflection, and half of them may see a distorted image.[1] A mirror in a dressing room is a setup for failure. It's a trigger for the deficit mindset.

We take that self-criticism everywhere we go, like an alter ego in our head, an inner critic overshadowing everything we experience. We may see a new opportunity, but before we can get excited, that voice starts with the criticism and the warnings of failure until finally we think, "Yeah, no, I can't do that." On top of that, women may also worry about being unlikable or unattractive, or about seeking too much attention. Isn't it ironic that members of the gender that tends to be more nurturing and giving to others are the hardest on themselves?

Add to this an increasingly image-conscious social media landscape that has amplified the already insufferable scrutiny of women. We are constantly bombarded with images of unrealistic standards. It is a heady time for us, one in which mixed messages and cultural paradoxes abound, and standards are impossible to meet. (Oh to go back to the days when we had cameras that relied on film, and you weren't obliged to take multiple shots and crowd around a phone to select the one for posting on social media! With film, we guarded our 24 frames of film carefully, taking only one shot at a time without editing or judgment. Physical photos that you could touch, pass around, and frame—today it seems so precious and intimate. It was about capturing a memory and not an opportunity to evaluate ourselves harshly in the moment!)

While it is human to compare ourselves to others, social media has significantly exacerbated this practice. While social media was initially created to inspire connection, community, conversation, and compassion, that morning scroll through any form of social media kicks off a litany of comparison and envy: *I wish I had that. Oh, I wish I looked like that. I wish I had the money to do that. How is their life so perfect?* You may not even be doing it consciously, but in frame after frame, you are comparing yourself to others. Next thing you know, you encounter an associate or friend humblebragging about an accomplishment. While comparing ourselves to others can fuel some to act proactively, it can also drain us of energy and distract us from seeing our own potential. And worse, it can become very dangerous to our psyche by focusing us on what we perceive to be missing from our lives. No wonder we struggle with self-image—79 percent of women suffer from self-esteem issues.[2] It's been reported that approximately 10 percent of our thoughts can involve comparisons of some sort,[3] which can affect that already fragile sense of self, fueling more anxiety.

2. The Shrinking Effect: Underestimating one's own abilities; the act of diminishing or shortchanging oneself.

One of my favorite pieces of writing is from Marianne Williamson in her seminal book *A Return to Love*:

> Our deepest fear is not that we are inadequate. Our deepest fear is that we are powerful beyond measure. It is our light, not our darkness that most frightens us. We ask ourselves, "Who am I to be brilliant, gorgeous, talented, fabulous?" Actually, who are you not to be? You are a child of God. Your playing small does not serve the world. There is nothing enlightened about shrinking so that other people won't feel insecure around you. We are all meant to shine, as children do.

This image of shrinking to make ourselves smaller in the midst of others has always stuck with me because we default naturally to underestimating ourselves. Studies indicate that men overestimate their abilities and performance, while women underestimate both.[4] Example: men will apply for a job or promotion when they meet only 60 percent of the qualifications, but women apply only if they meet 100 percent of them, according to a Hewlett-Packard internal report.[5] Layer on additional pressure for women of color, who feel the need to be "'perfect' to reach their seats," leading to "hypervigilance and extreme self-criticism."[6] Simply put, women don't think they have the right to apply if they don't check off all the boxes.

While helping to prepare my friend Eva for an interview for a highly competitive job as the chief medical officer at a major hospital, I noticed that she undercut herself right off the bat by saying, "I know you're probably wondering why I'm even in the running because I'm not an academic, but let me tell you why I should be considered." It took a lot of rehearsing with her to flip the narrative around to "I have run an esteemed, full-time clinical practice for 20 years and have still found the time to fund and lead nationally recognized academic research. I'm the only candidate to be both an academic and a practitioner." Her default was to diminish her narrative from the start; she didn't even hear it until I pointed it out.

Professor and author of *Women Don't Ask*, Linda Babcock reported that men will initiate salary negotiations four times as often as women do, and that women ask for 30 percent less money than men do if they do in fact negotiate.[7] All the while, women's actual performance does not differ in quality or quantity. In her second job out of college, one of my closest friends, Monica, found on the office photocopier a print-out of the bonuses for every member of her team. She discovered that while she had been given the top rating in her finance analyst class, her bonus was half that of a similarly tenured male colleague who had received a lower rating than hers. She did nothing with that information, in part because she was concerned that she was never supposed to see that printout. A few years later, in another job, Monica experienced the same pay gap issue. This time, she compiled an extensive list of her accomplishments at the company to present to her boss and asked to be compensated the same as her male colleagues. While she was successful at negotiating the pay increase, I wonder why she felt she had to prove that she deserved it.

As women, we often struggle to value our own worth—and the pandemic didn't help. Newly released research shows that the pandemic contributed to 70 percent of women feeling less financially secure. Worse, most men over 55 don't think that gender imbalance is an issue, which only adds to the problem.[8] And yet, multiple studies have shown that women are better managers and handle stress better than men do, while also, in many cases for women with families, being the "she-fault" parent at home. (We really didn't need studies to tell us what we already knew.)

3. The Satisfaction Conundrum: Chasing external markers of success (achievement, money, more stuff) and never feeling fully satisfied.

As adults, and especially as American adults, we are on a lifelong search for happiness. Whether it's in the form of money, love, or success, we all have a different idea about what happiness means. Buying things or attaining goals we think will give us happiness really just leaves us wanting more. We get more, but often not in ways we truly want: first, the constant chase for more and more of what we think will make us happy is stressful, and second, that stress only drives more dissatisfaction. The adage of getting an inch works here—you get the inch, but then you want a mile. Arthur C. Brooks describes this as a "hedonic treadmill" in which "success is relative. Satisfaction requires that you not just continuously run in place on your hedonic treadmill, but also that you run slightly faster than other people running on theirs." He continues by sharing, "The insatiable goals to acquire more, succeed conspicuously, and be as attractive as possible lead us to objectify one another, and even ourselves. When people see themselves as little more than their attractive bodies, jobs, or bank accounts, it brings great suffering."[9]

I see this satisfaction chase play out every time I dress a woman who says, "I will be happy when I lose some more weight, so I don't see the point of trying on anything before I do." "Happy when" is a telling phrase, because it means she doesn't value herself today, in the present, in this moment. Furthermore, she is delaying the opportunity to feel good about herself now and to make the journey more enjoyable. World renowned leadership coach Marshall Goldsmith calls this paradox the "Happy When" trap, in which we mistakenly believe our happiness depends upon an external event in our lives: "I'll be happy when I get married. I'll be happy when I get a raise. I'll be happy when I buy a house. I'll be happy when I win an award." While goals are admirable, attaining them doesn't necessarily change our degree of happiness or self-worth, because while they provide external validation, they don't change our internal feelings about our place in life. In a fitting room, I refocus every woman on not the destination, but on finding a way to enjoy her current place today versus expending energy chasing the future.

My last three years as a McKinsey & Company consultant were some of the toughest, because I attached my happiness and self-worth to attaining partnership. It was an elusive brass ring, an external metric of success, that I never attained. And at every stage of the highly evaluative and ego-crushing process, I became more anxious and insecure, missing out on fully experiencing the joy of being with the world's best executives, teammates, and thinkers. When I finally left the corporate world and all of its external markers of success (the thick embossed business card, the designer suits, the car, the house), it was as if I had been stripped of my identity. It took me a full year of not working to realize the unique gifts I brought to this world outside of the material, to embrace my own value outside of the corporate ladder, and to embark on founding my own company. When we strip external metrics of success away, we are left with the quality of our character and the journey itself.

4. The Superwoman Façade: Maintaining the illusion that all aspects of one's life are in order.

While the women's movement forged a path for women into corporate America, the 1980s concept of "having it all" has tortured women every step of the way. Women have had to contend with living up to a broad front of expectations and commitments, some societal and some self-imposed, but all of which most certainly conflict with each other at some point. Helen Gurley Brown's seminal book introduced the term "having it all" to represent ambition beyond what women could access at the time, but it became an unnecessary mantle for us to be all things to all people and an illusion that we have everything under control. Shonda Rhimes admitted correctly in her 2014 Dartmouth University commencement speech, "Whenever you see me somewhere succeeding in one area of my life, that almost certainly means I am failing in another area of my life."

Equating success with being the ideal colleague, partner, friend, or family member simultaneously is a struggle for women at all life stages. Working mothers may navigate the motherhood penalty, the measurable negative impact of motherhood on a woman's earnings and status in her career, while also having to muster the energy to devote to their households. Single women may be anxious about finding a significant other, especially if much of their time is spent at work or thinking about work. Full-time parents may believe they've made a choice to professionalize parenting and exert tremendous effort in being all-in and perfect to validate their choice, but feel underappreciated or exhausted. And the decision of whether or not to have children? It's a double-edged sword: we may have regrets or be judged if we decide not to embrace the perceived moral imperative of parenthood, and we're penalized on status and income if we do. There is often a crushing list of competing priorities and demands that absorb our energy, making it easier to default to our comfort zones.

Women feel the pressure to live up to expectations for these many, at times thankless, roles. A 2018 United Nations report found that "women are shouldering nearly three times more of the work associated with the home than men—childcare, elder care, cooking, cleaning, transportation—and usually for zero pay."[10] This burden may be amplified in the face of small daily upsets or higher-stake events such as a sick family member or their own health issues. With all of this pressure come pangs of guilt when we feel that we've let others down or not lived up to the expectations of these multiple roles. When we conducted focus groups for this book, one telling quote from a working mom really stuck with me: "It's hard to break ingrained traditions of the woman being the default parent. The school only calls the mom. I love my children, but it seems everyone and everything else is the priority but me. Even when I'm crushing it at work, I'm failing at making dinner." We can't have it all at once, but it doesn't mean we don't beat ourselves up trying.

Let's call this superwoman ideal out for what it really is—a façade—and have the power to let it go. As Lauren Smith Brody, founder, CEO, and author of *The Fifth Trimester* and cofounder of the Chamber of Mothers, shared with me, "Guilt should not be one more thing on your list that you feel bad about. Mom guilt is a sexist, classist construct once we acknowledge the systems working against us. Instead, this should be about having agency and choice." That is, we can reframe "having it all" as having all the choices—choosing what we want and don't want to have, being open about what's not going right, feeling strong even when one part of our life is off. Because loss of balance is a fact of life. We have the freedom to separate out all of these roles and decide the most important commitments to uphold for ourselves. Leave Superwoman to the DC Comics universe.

5. The Setback Spiral: Negative thoughts, feelings, or actions that arise from criticism, setback, or disappointment and have the potential to get progressively worse in the face of shame or embarrassment.

When we face disappointments and setbacks, many of us replay those moments in terms of what we did wrong and even extend their impact to reframe the narrative about our whole self: *It's not just that this person criticized me; I'm going to lose my job and that means I'm probably a horrible spouse/mother/friend/sister/daughter and I'm a terrible person in general.* As the author of *How Remarkable Women Lead*, Joanna Barsh, shares, "Women tend to think more holistically. If one aspect of the day isn't going too well, they tend to enlarge that picture to envelop everything. Hence, the downward spiral."

The impact of this setback spiral? It can hold us back from seizing opportunities. A major media executive once told me that in their company's annual employee survey, most employees scored the organization low on courage. As my friend dug into this, she found that one possible contributor was how people handled failure. When people experienced failure, they were afraid to take risks in the future, defaulting to what had worked in the past and acting slowly on consensus so as to deflect blame, thereby losing out on opportunities. To add to the issues, there was no postmortem on lessons for the future and recognition of strengths in the process.

My friend Jane Park often says to me: "Life doesn't get easier, we just get stronger. There is no light at the end of the tunnel, just skylights along the way that remind us of blue sky above and why we are doing it." And it made me think about how we evaluate failed experiences: Do we penalize ourselves for what we did wrong? Do we get stuck in a doom loop of negativity? Do we give up on trying again? Or can we recycle the experience into growth and redemption, becoming more capable of handling the next challenge? Each setback can hold us back from taking the next opportunity, silencing our potential to step out, step up, and be remarkable. Or it can be a chance to understand what we did well, find new approaches, come away with lessons learned for the future, and build on our strengths and capabilities.

I have my own fair share of setbacks. In the fashion business, every season we wrestle with whether to play it safe or take risks. At Gravitas, my team is mostly of Asian descent, and in 2022, the design team came to me with the idea of honoring our Asian heritage by celebrating one of the most important holidays of the year, Lunar New Year. I eagerly approved the project, and my team passionately brought it to life with a Year of the Tiger collection. (After two years of the COVID-19 pandemic, it was nice to have something to be excited about!) To this day, it is one of the most beautiful collections we've ever created. But on financial metrics, it was a disaster. It did not pay back on the investment. And yet I was so proud of our team. Instead of beating ourselves up, I asked my team in the debrief, "What did we learn and what were our strengths?"

We learned that after years of working with solid colors, we could design beautiful prints, and our core customers welcomed them. We discovered a local New York City print house that could create beautiful fabrics on demand, and that we had seamstresses in our factory who were adept at sewing these delicate fabrics. Our team was energized by creating opportunities for local workers and giving back to our community with a donation to Stop Asian American Pacific Islander (AAPI) Hate. We realized that when we did something with purpose, it energized us and reinforced why we do what we do. So next question: What can we do better next time?

Well, we were late in product marketing and that put us behind our competitors in a time-sensitive buying season. So what did we do with this information? We took the good with the bad and rolled out the next product; we had the courage to go out and do it all over again. We allowed ourselves to build upon our strengths and embrace risk once more. The setback can diminish you or make you stronger.

There is beauty in celebrating the hard work, passion, and guts that go into every play, even if you don't win each time. It's about *taking* the shot, not necessarily *making* it. In the words of hockey legend Wayne Gretzky, "You miss a hundred percent of the shots you don't take." It's a reminder about how setbacks can be constraining or empowering. It is all in how you look at them.

6. Systemic Bias: Structural constructs that underpin asymmetrical power dynamics; system-wide barriers to progress and change.

The system wasn't built by us, or for us. In 2013, why did everyone question if Janet Yellen had the gravitas to lead the U.S. Federal Reserve when she was more than qualified for the job? Because as Ruchika Tulshyan and Jodi-Ann Burey wrote in their *Harvard Business Review* article debunking imposter syndrome, "Many of us across the world are implicitly, if not explicitly, told we don't belong in white- and male-dominated workplaces," and "As white men progress, their feelings of doubt usually abate as their work and intelligence are validated over time. They're able to find role models who are like them, and rarely (if ever) do others question their competence, contributions, or leadership style."[11] The standard for what is praiseworthy is framed by a cultural bias, and even when we try to play by these rules, we're often penalized for it. And it is not just gender, but also cultural bias. A mentee of mine, Jennifer, who grew up in Taiwan and went to business school in the United States, came to me a few years ago lamenting the fact that she had been overlooked for a promotion in the Chicago office of the global company she worked at. She described a series of white male supervisors who did not seem to understand her. When I gave her the advice to move back to the Taipei office where she would not be in the minority, she was taken aback. She did move back and was promoted to senior manager in less than a year.

It has taken me nearly two decades to realize this: the myth of meritocracy ends after we are graded for performance in school. There is no "fair" grading system in the real world. Demography is the easiest indicator of connection, and it fosters systemic bias, trumping objective merit and values at times. In the workplace, this bias sometimes leads a quiet existence, but once you see it, you will notice it everywhere, whether it's a male colleague taking that promotion you deserved or taking credit for a great idea that you suggested. It reminds me of a famous *Punch* cartoon where five men and one woman sit around a conference table, and one man says, "That's an excellent suggestion, Miss Triggs. Perhaps one of the men here would like to make it."

While it is more subtle these days, long-standing stereotypes are hard to get rid of, and so we can often still feel underestimated, underappreciated, and undervalued. The Geena Davis Institute on Gender in the Media highlights that this bias starts at a young age; in evaluating the media children consume, they found that 75 percent of the speaking roles are male. A more recent example? The McKinsey & Company *Women in the Workplace* 2021 report revealed that women and their innate leadership capabilities—empathy, compassion, relationship orientation—were one of the primary reasons companies weathered turbulence of the pandemic.[12] However, traditional performance evaluations may not necessarily recognize these skills, because the systems were not originally designed to capture these attributes. To back this up, Yale professor Kelly Shue and her colleagues studied the assessment and promotion records for nearly 30,000 workers and found that women received higher performance ratings than men, but were consistently and incorrectly judged to have less leadership potential—and that pattern continued even when women exceeded performance expectations going forward. Shue continues,

> What is commonly talked about in terms of management and potential are characteristics such as assertiveness, execution skills, charisma, leadership, ambition. These are, I believe, real traits. They're also highly subjective and stereotypically associated with male leaders. And what we saw in the data is a pretty strong bias against women in assessments of potential. . . . Women get progressively lower potential scores relative to their actual future performance as we rise up the corporate ladder. So this is going to contribute, I think, to a stronger and stronger glass ceiling the higher up we go.[13]

Shue and her colleagues estimate that the lower potential ratings explain up to 50 percent of the gap in promotions for women and 70 percent of the gender pay gap as women are shut out of more senior roles.[14]

Let's go back to my friend Eva. Now in her 50s, she has worked at one of the nation's best cardiology centers for more than 20 years. We were on the phone catching up one day when she shared a frustration with me: "I keep getting passed over for the chief medical officer position. And every time a white male gets promoted over me, I don't understand why. I want to be the CEO of the group someday. I'm treated like the manager in a restaurant, always running back and forth and making sure everything and everyone is working, but I am not seen as deserving of the top job."

She is smart and talented, has given her life to what she does, and is loaded with superpowers (she took our quiz to discover her confidence language, so I know this to be true). But—and we have all done this—she assumed that because she's smart and talented, she'll get recognized for it. She worked herself to the bone. She devoted her life to her profession and assumed she would get recognized for it. But no matter what she did, her CEO promoted only those who looked like him. I told her, "In life, after school, no one's handing out first-place ribbons. No one's handing out grades. You can do everything to improve yourself, but you have to decide if you can change the system you're working within or find one that values your talents."

This was all new to her. But in our call, it finally clicked for her: *Oh, that's not how the game is played, right?* By discovering and expressing her superpowers and then assessing the culture of where she worked, she ultimately advocated for her unique talents and a culture shift in her workplace that would recognize and reward these attributes. She soon was promoted to be chief of her practice. She's on track to run the place, and, more important, confident in her own abilities. But it required her to become aware of the external forces at work and to have a language to describe and recognize what she could do versus what the environment dictated.

Women are not immune to having our own biases, especially when we are in positions of power. For example, you may unwittingly promote someone because they remind you of yourself when you were just starting out, not because they are the better employee. Because we understand the adverse impact of bias in our own journeys, we have to be that much more cognizant of our own predilections and expand how we assess skills and leadership.

I am encouraged, though, that the recent #MeToo and #TimesUp movements have put the patriarchy on notice. Women have been systematically fighting "the lesser sex" stigma since Adam and Eve. I don't need to go into the history here, but we do need to remember that systemic change takes time. Borrowing from the adage *it takes two generations to forget*, perhaps it also takes two generations to see next-level progress as each new generation builds on previous ones without being held back by the past. While we will probably be dealing for the present with the persistent income gap, the eye-roll-inducing mansplaining, and being passed over for promotion, we can contribute to changing this systemic bias by following the path forged for us by past suffragists, activists, and other inspiring women. Bias may always exist to some extent, but we can acknowledge it, call it out, and not internalize it or let it stop us from doing what we want to do.

Making the Choice

I fell victim to every one of these forces when it came to writing this book. In my very first writing session with my collaborator, Kathy, we met at one of my favorite sources of inspiration—the Drama Book Shop, where since 1917, countless Broadway shows had been conceived. Rather than feeling excited and eager to get started, I was filled with doubt that I could even write this book. That doubt came from a legitimate place: the previous year had brought a global pandemic that nearly collapsed my business (and many others). Our March 2020 sales were not zero, they were negative. Our customers returned clothing that they no longer needed for the office, a conference, an event, or a party, and we honored our 30-day return policy, refunding more than we sold that month. We had just spent the last 18 months making hospital gowns and face masks to keep our business going. I felt like a failure. I underestimated myself. I felt the cards were stacked against me. I compared myself to other writers and their accolades (Are you there, Brené Brown? It's me, Lisa.). Publishers had turned me down in the book proposal process (I was reminded later by my literary agent, Andy, that a 90 percent rejection rate is common in publishing). Who was I to give anyone advice about how to feel good about themselves?

As we sat, meeting in person for the first time in months, I unleashed my fears to Kathy. She listened quietly, and when I was done, she reminded me that the fact that I had struggled so much and survived was the very reason I could and should write this book (and bonus: systemic bias would not win the day, as I had chosen to work with an editor who is a woman of color). She reminded me of why I embarked on this journey: to empower women to see the best in themselves. And that my unique gift is that I'm the world's best positivity mirror, that I can see the best in another person and make sure they see it and believe it too. That day I had to make the choice to abide by the very principles I spell out later in the book to convince myself that I could do this. She pulled me out of a vicious cycle of deficit thinking.

Bottom line, gravitas is a conscious choice. I had to make the choice to believe in the very principles laid out in this book. Are you ready to make this choice? And how do I know you can do this?

Thanks to Stanford University psychologist Carol Dweck, we know the power of our mindset. In her brilliant book *Mindset*, she shows how success in school, work, and nearly every aspect of our lives can be dramatically influenced by how we think about of our talents and abilities. People with a *fixed mindset*—those who believe that abilities are fixed— are less likely to flourish than those with a *growth mindset*—those who believe that abilities can be developed.

Once we see these forces that hold us back, we have to make an active choice to shift our mindset. Because mindset drives behavior. In Freud's iceberg model of consciousness, our behavior is influenced by our conscious, preconscious, and unconscious. The conscious mind is the visible 10 percent of our psyche—the tip of the iceberg that others can see above the waterline. Below the waterline is a whole host of values and assumptions that drive our mindset and influence our visible behavior, the unconscious and preconscious. If we want to break out of a deficit mindset, we have to make a choice to do the work below the waterline and reset our beliefs toward a self-confident, growth-oriented mindset.

How do we make this choice? And remember, it is a choice, because we're born fully self-confident. We lose it because of those forces working against us. You can get it back if you commit to making this choice. Perhaps you are at a crossroads—here are some indicators that you are indeed motivated to take this leap from self-doubt to self-belief.

Are You Fed Up? Remember Monica? She had the pay she deserved but didn't get the title and so people continued to take credit for her work, speak over her in meetings, and dismiss her contributions. She had all this responsibility, but not the acknowledgment and respect she deserved. She was fed up, feeling like she was always hesitating to speak up and that if she did, it came across as petty in reference to her male colleagues. So I coached her to tell her boss simply and directly that she needed a title change without her needing to gather streams of data to prove her worth. This wasn't a negotiation, but self-advocacy; she and her boss were on the same side because her feeling recognized and valued could only make her an even better colleague. When she went in and talked to her boss, this is what she said: "It is important that my title reflects the accountability I've taken and how others view my role.

This is something that's important to me, something I've earned, and it's commensurate with the value I bring every day."

Her boss immediately called HR, requested the title change, and let her know he saw her potential beyond the title promotion. When we debriefed, her first reaction was "What took me so long? And why was I so worked up before the conversation?" She learned the power of knowing her value and that she had the ability to advocate for it. She realized that in the past, she had worked herself up with anxiety over these types of conversations because she doubted herself and the outcome. I encouraged her to remember this moment the next time she needed to have a difficult conversation, to not waste the precious resource of energy imagining the worst-case scenario, and to believe in her abilities. Being fed up can be a powerful motivator to make the choice toward self-confidence.

Are You Feeling Unappreciated or Unseen? In our focus groups, full-time parent Nicole shared that she always felt like the lead character in the movie *Troop Beverly Hills*, Phyllis Nefler, whose husband questioned what she had to show for her time. Nicole doubted if she was, in her words, "living up to my potential" and "being appreciated for everything I do." She took our quiz to discover her superpowers. When she reviewed her results, she realized how much joy, energy, kindness, and organization she brought to everything she did. She realized how much she contributed to her family and her friends. There was an energy shift in how she saw herself. Making the choice can be about asserting our own inner strength versus focusing on extrinsic motivation.

Are You Experiencing a Life Transition? After 25 years of marriage, Mary's husband asked for a divorce. She wrote to my company asking for help getting ready for her son's graduation (at which her ex-husband would be in attendance), and on top of that she was going back into the workforce for the first time in years. She wanted to find a dress that would work for both. A life upset prompted her to make a choice—to move forward and grow. (I consider her sending a cold e-mail to a company customer service center making a choice!) We found the perfect dress for her, and I'm thrilled to get life updates from her regularly; I am inspired that she chose self-belief over self-doubt and never looked back.

Are You Stepping Out or Up? Healthy self-awareness can easily turn into sabotaging self-doubt, especially in moments when we have a "step out" or "step up" opportunity. Ever feel that you were not deserving of that new job or promotion? Worried that you wouldn't be able to do it, feeling undeserving when you were even given an opportunity? My friend Allison, who had spent most of her career in medical sales, was offered a job at a social media and digital marketing agency. She shared, "I was offered this incredible role, with better pay and in a high-growth sector. But I don't know anything about the industry, and I'm not sure if I should take it. I don't feel worthy of the trust that's been placed in me to do this job well." Together, we took stock of and documented all the reasons why she deserved this opportunity (she builds great relationships, she's a fast learner, she's gutsy and energetic) and how this would stretch her in new ways (she would learn digital marketing analytics, a prized skill in today's world). At the end of the exercise, I asked her if she was still wondering if she was up to the task. Her response: "It's unlikely they made a hiring mistake. I'm going to choose to believe they hired me for a reason. I deserve this, and I'm going to make the most of it!"

Are You Driven to Fulfill a Higher Purpose? Sometimes we get an itch to do more to make an impact on the world, to pursue something that adds meaning to our life and the lives of those around us. This is not about money or status; rather, it is a motivation to do or create something bigger than ourselves. In January 2020, a seasoned pharmaceutical executive, Carol Vu, created the first-ever women's employee resource group at her company, which would prove to be instrumental in navigating the pressures of the pandemic. When I asked her why she did it, she said, "Women at the company were not being seen. We are fragmented in our own little silos peppered throughout the company. It took me twenty years of being in the industry to do it, but I just had to bring us all together. It wasn't about me, it was about all of us at the company who needed this." The choice is akin to an imperative when we're doing it from a place of values and purpose.

Perhaps you have your own reasons to make this choice. Take a moment to reflect on your motivations for taking this leap with me. And making this choice toward gravitas is a *huge* step. It's also not as easy as flipping a switch. It is a lifelong process, one with obstacles, detours and off-ramps along the way.

What is going to help you along the way are reminders. They are a powerful way to make this choice tangible for ourselves every day, and to keep us motivated. It's Dumbo's flying feather. It's best-selling author Mel Robbins's act of high-fiving herself every morning in the mirror. It's my friend Mila who shared with me that this is what putting on her favorite lipstick does for her. It's one of my Gravitas customers, Allison, who wrote to us that before every big meeting, she thinks of the word *gravitas* on the label sewn into her lucky dress to calm her nerves.

I have my own reminder. On my desk, I have a photo of my mother, my younger brother, and me. Growing up in the Southern California desert, my family went on a trip to Big Bear Mountain to see snow for the first time when I was nine. (I am not quite sure where my mother found winter coats for us to wear.) Our smiles are infectious as my mom holds up my little brother so that he won't slip on the snow (she didn't realize snow boots were required for traction since this was her first time navigating snow). Whenever I feel self-doubt creeping in or have a big decision to make, I look at this photo and talk to my nine-year-old self: "Am I being brave enough? Why can't I be the one to do this crazy, bold thing? I'm proud of us for who we've become." This conversation with my inner child emboldens me to make the choice toward self-confidence every time.

Lisa with her mother and brother at Big Bear Mountain.

I am asking you to make this choice. The first step on the journey to having gravitas is believing that you can have it and that you deserve it. It's the first step to creating the foundation of a growth-oriented, self-confident mindset, one that embodies the three Cs (courage, compassion, and connection). This mindset that we are cultivating is the antidote to the forces working against us; it is an authentic and stable center that comes from within, so that we are not defined by life as it swirls around us. Rather, in the face of fear, it emboldens us to take action. I know that if we believe in ourselves, we can go so much further in life, achieve our goals, and find true fulfillment.

Once you've made this choice, we get to the fun part: discovering your unique and authentic version of confidence and using it to communicate, to navigate situations and relationships, and to actualize the things you want in life.

Part II

DISCOVER YOUR SUPERPOWERS

WHAT IS YOUR CONFIDENCE LANGUAGE?

Ready to find your superpower? The survey that follows has been designed to give you a quick and accurate readout on what makes you tick. (You can also take the quiz online at MyConfidenceLanguage.com.)

This quiz was developed based on thousands of interactions with women of all ethnicities, age groups, and life stages, from full-time parents to working professionals, across industries, and at different levels of advancement. These encounters ranged from speaking engagements to focus groups and fitting rooms over the last 10 years, complemented by a prior decade of my work across industries as a consultant. My company's team validated our body of work with a 1,000-person quantitative survey with an unbiased audience. The women surveyed were unaware of the survey's intentions, and they were between the ages of 25 and 75, recruited to be representative across income, age, ethnicity, and employment status (working, not working, not working but worked previously).

This is a self-assessment of where you see your natural talents. There are fundamental traits, emotions, and values that we all encompass to varying degrees. At times, this quiz may also reveal where you fall on a spectrum of demonstrating your innate strengths. The results will show

how you typically track on certain scenarios and provide you with the information you need to understand what powers your success and what you need to move forward in leveling up toward gravitas. We have seen many women deal with triumphs, transitions, grief, regret. With the quiz results, you will better understand your starting-point, or default, confidence language, and from there, we'll give you the tools to put on that cape with your superpower portfolio and continue growing.

Superpower Quiz

Please circle any of the following statements that you feel describe you and how you approach life. There are no right or wrong answers. Please answer as honestly as possible. Select all that apply.

1. I enjoy leading meetings.

2. I've been told that I'm the life of the party.

3. I love setting goals and working to achieve and/or exceed them.

4. I enjoy helping others with no expectation of return.

5. I enjoy gathering and analyzing information before making a decision or forming an opinion.

6. I am really good at coming up with new ideas.

7. I am a calming force in groups.

8. In group settings, I don't feel like I have to prove myself or impress anyone.

9. In group settings, others look to me to take charge.

10. I enjoy meeting new people.

11. I get even more motivated when I am challenged—I love healthy competition.

12. I am a good listener. People often come to me to vent.

13. I live by the motto "knowledge is power."

14. I think often about what the future will look like.

15. I expect good things will come and things will get better, even in the toughest of times.

16. I rarely feel embarrassed.

17. I get energy from giving a speech or presentation.

18. I don't mind being seated next to a stranger at a dinner party—I was born to charm!

19. I believe practice makes perfect.

20. I enjoy putting time and thought into buying the perfect gift.

21. I consider myself a logical and rational person.

22. I enjoy any creative activity.

23. I believe everything happens for a reason; if it doesn't happen, it wasn't meant to be.

24. I do what I want without worrying about what others will think.

25. I've been told that I am a great coach.

26. I care whether or not people like me.

27. I've been known to continue on and/or endure, regardless of setbacks.

28. If a friend is sick, I'm the first to show up to help.

29. I enjoy a good to-do list. I can create a spreadsheet for almost any occasion!

30. I get excited about "firsts"—experiencing or doing something never done before.

31. Even in tough times, I'm very hopeful about the future.

32. I'm comfortable in my own skin.

33. I take charge in planning outings for my friends.

34. I'm great at telling stories; I love being asked to give a toast!

35. I'm always measuring how I'm doing, especially to improve.

36. I've been told that I can be too nice (almost to the point where I feel taken for granted!).

37. I'm not comfortable making decisions without all the available information.

38. I believe in things before I can see them.

39. When I face a setback, I give myself to the universe and/or something greater than me.

40. I don't feel intimidated or threatened by others.

41. I've been told that I like to have things my way too often.

42. I've been told that I can be overwhelming.

43. I can be stubborn and don't know when to let go.

44. I get a lot of satisfaction out of helping others be successful.

45. I enjoy learning new things.

46. I have been told that I am not practical and/or am too much of a dreamer.

47. I practice gratitude (versus worrying about what I can't control).

48. I don't feel the need to explain myself.

49. I'm good at persuading people to participate or contribute to a project or cause.

50. I enjoy being the center of attention.

51. My accomplishments are a big part of who I am.

52. I often feel responsible for the happiness of others.

53. I am a very curious person.

54. I have a really powerful imagination.

55. I usually see the best in every situation and other people.

56. I rarely compare myself to others.

Getting Your Results

Check the boxes next to the numbered statements that you circled. Add up the number of checked boxes in each column. If you have four or more checked boxes for one of the traits, congrats, you've found your superpower(s)! Eighty percent of the women we surveyed score highly in at least one superpower. This is where you feel most comfortable and capable; you already know how to express these forms of confidence naturally. On average, people have two superpowers in which they are strongest. For those where you had two or three checked boxes, you already demonstrate those areas in some form and to some degree. Good for you—you have a base from which to strengthen. Those where you scored one or none: these are areas that you may want to develop, based on relationships and situations you encounter.

LEADING	PERFORMING	ACHIEVING	GIVING	KNOWING	CREATING	BELIEVING	SELF-SUSTAINING
❏ 1	❏ 2	❏ 3	❏ 4	❏ 5	❏ 6	❏ 7	❏ 8
❏ 9	❏ 10	❏ 11	❏ 12	❏ 13	❏ 14	❏ 15	❏ 16
❏ 17	❏ 18	❏ 19	❏ 20	❏ 21	❏ 22	❏ 23	❏ 24
❏ 25	❏ 26	❏ 27	❏ 28	❏ 29	❏ 30	❏ 31	❏ 32
❏ 33	❏ 34	❏ 35	❏ 36	❏ 37	❏ 38	❏ 39	❏ 40
❏ 41	❏ 42	❏ 43	❏ 44	❏ 45	❏ 46	❏ 47	❏ 48
❏ 49	❏ 50	❏ 51	❏ 52	❏ 53	❏ 54	❏ 55	❏ 56

Scores:

Your Confidence Language

Your unique combination of superpowers is your confidence language. *It's your default mode and the source of your self-belief.* Take a moment and summarize your quiz results here.

My superpowers (score of four or higher):

_____

Strengths that I demonstrate sometimes (score of two or three):

_____

My opportunity areas (score of one or none):

_____

In the next chapter, you'll learn more about each strength and how to harness the great power you have within you. No one needs all eight to have gravitas, but being aware of all the forms of confidence can be beneficial because we encounter people who have different confidence languages than we do and face situations that may require us to learn new skills. In our quantitative research, we found that as women age or move into more senior positions at a company, they evolve from having two superpowers on average to expressing three or more!

If you haven't scored a three or four on any of the eight strengths: One, you might not be giving yourself enough credit for your strengths, or you might not be aware of them. Sometimes it takes someone we respect to see how impressive we are. Have a friend, trusted colleague, or family member take the quiz for you. Two—and this goes for all of us—take the quiz a second time aspirationally. Are there statements you wish represented you because you believe they are things you want or need to live the life you want? Now that you know how these questions shake out, what superpower would you like to have? In the Appendix you will find additional quizzes for either retaking it aspirationally or having someone you trust take it for you.

THE 8 STRENGTHS
OF GRAVITAS

Did you find out Giving is your superpower? Believing? Was there anything that surprised you? Whichever quality you are strongest in, you are one step closer to realizing gravitas. This is the language in which you're most fluent—it's where you live comfortably. This is your confidence language, your "go to" baseline superpower, so to speak. Most of us are naturally strongest in one or two of these traits; only 2 percent embody all of them (hello, Mom and probably Oprah!).

Having the power of self-awareness and the firm belief of knowing what makes you distinctive and what gets you up in the morning is a powerful thing. In this chapter, you'll learn about each of the eight strengths. Knowing your specific superpowers and understanding all eight of the qualities will enable you to decode what it means to be confident, how you see yourself, and where you want to grow.

Once you have read about the superpowers that make up your confidence language, you'll read insights from our quantitative survey about the traits, common combinations, and conclusions about us as individuals and collectively as women.

Let's explore each of the eight strengths in greater detail.

LEADING

- ◆ You enjoy leading meetings.
- ◆ In group settings, others look to you to take charge.
- ◆ You get energy from giving a speech or presentation.
- ◆ You've been told that you are a great coach.
- ◆ You take charge in planning outings for your friends.
- ◆ You've been told that you like to have things your way too often.
- ◆ You're good at persuading people to participate or contribute to a project or cause.

People who channel this superpower are strategic thinkers who work toward a long-term goal (versus a moment-to-moment crisis manager). If you are strong in this realm, you have the ability to set direction in an assertive way that inspires followership by outlining a mission that is compelling and concrete, as well as values-driven and measurable in terms of tangible results. You take charge and articulate with certainty a vision, or North Star, for any effort, with clarity in planning the journey to get there.

In addition to being able to set the course, you execute the steps of a broader plan, moving a project forward with determination and always solving problems along the way. You effortlessly navigate being "on the balcony" (seeing and sharing the big picture) while also being "in the dance" (rolling up your sleeves to get into the action when necessary). With the peaks and valleys along the way, you can deftly course-correct, prioritizing what matters, actively mentoring and coaching to get the best out of others, incorporating team members' talents into the overall plan, and taking accountability along the way, from ready and set all the way to go.

You are a clear communicator and an able motivator. You project authority in a way that rallies others to join, or at least to believe in, a shared project or understanding, so much so that those who follow you feel they are in safe hands. These charismatic qualities enable you to inspire others, as your plans can only be completed with the help of others. At the heart of your success is team-building, since no one can do everything alone.

When You Are at Your Best

Because you are decisive and crave momentum, you take initiative and are unafraid to ask for what is needed to accomplish what others think impossible. You advocate for yourself and others in the service of an articulated strategy. In our quantitative survey, women who have Leading as their superpower are the most confident group in navigating every situation across the board: 40 to 50 percent more comfortable than average in asking for a promotion, leading a project, and asking for a raise. Unsurprisingly, you are two times more confident than average in public speaking. You are growth-oriented, and you appreciate thoughtful criticism and seize opportunities for improvement, scoring the highest in terms of being comfortable with and capable of recovering from a loss or disappointment.[1]

Notable Demographics

Nearly two-thirds of women who have this as a superpower are working full-time, and they are twice as likely to be at a senior level. Those with this trait are 59 percent more likely to have their own business, and more than twice as likely to work at a start-up. Women with Leading as a superpower are more likely than the average to come from a position of having been "forced to be a first" as their origin story (first to attend college, first-generation immigrant) or have overcome adversity (financial insecurity, being fired or laid off from a job). In my own experience embodying this trait, I identify with having a chip on my shoulder, feeling like I have something to prove, which is an additional motivation to succeed.

How to Steer Clear of Downsides

BEING INFLEXIBLE

"Follow me" is most powerful as an invitation, not a directive. In its most extreme form, those with Leading as a superpower can sometimes

be labeled stubborn, dominant, and ruthless, working in the service of
an end goal and unsupportive of anything that distracts from pushing
forward a vision. This attitude is otherwise known as "it's my way or
the highway."

After five years at McKinsey, I was promoted to my first leadership
role as a project manager. When the firm conducted a survey of everyone
who had worked for me later that year, I was humbled by the results:
only 2 out of 20 people said they would sign up to work with me again.
When I dug into the feedback, it was clear that while I held the team to
a high standard of excellence and clearly directed the work, I crushed
teammates who I viewed as inefficient and forced everyone to comply
with my way of doing things, leaving little room for differences of opinion. Simply put, I steamrolled my team because of my forceful, larger-
than-life presence.

One of my mentors at the time told me, "Lisa, please remember that
you stand on the very capable shoulders of many." I quickly learned
an essential lesson of leadership: that my stature as a leader could not
come just from my own actions and needed to rely on the actions of
my teammates. My success depended on a servant leadership style that
honored the contributions, talents, and emotional needs of a high-
functioning team, not just to achieve our goals, but also to make me
better. The victories would be much more rewarding when standing
shoulder to shoulder with others versus alone at the top. And empowering my teammates to use their talents and execute at times differently
than I would freed me up to focus on what mattered, and that was getting the job done. Once I got this, the outcome was better *every time*.

HOW TO COURSE-CORRECT

To recognize my team's talents and contributions, I started a weekly
journal to record specific examples of each teammate's strengths and
how they had inspired me or made an impact on our work. Throughout
the course of a project, I took the time to share with each person individually the potential I saw in them and to thank them as a complement
to any coaching I wanted to provide. I also learned that *we* trumps *I* in
sharing credit and that it was important to acknowledge the teamwork
involved in accomplishing the work.

One of my favorite YouTube videos is Derek Siver's "First Follower:
Leadership Lessons from Dancing Guy."[2] In this video, a person stands

up and starts dancing in the park. Soon after, a friend joins in and waves over others to join, and in under three minutes everyone in the park is dancing. The video narrator notes that while the leader has the guts to "stand alone and look ridiculous" so as to be easy to follow, it is the first follower who plays a critical role. The first follower "publicly shows everyone how to follow. Notice the leader embraces him as an equal, so it's not about the leader anymore—it's about them, plural." Over the course of three minutes, each successive follower waves over others to dance, making the proposition of dancing in a park feel less risky since "new followers emulate followers, not the leader." It becomes clear by the end of the video that celebrating followership is a fundamental ingredient for leadership success: "The first follower transforms a lone nut into a leader. If the leader is the flint, the first follower is the spark that makes the fire."

Carving out time to tangibly recognize those who support you creates an environment in which people feel capable and confident. Celebrating the "first followers" creates a beautiful butterfly effect where small changes can yield big results.

BEING SEEN AS "COLD"

Women face a triple standard—having to be highly competent, highly confident, and warm. Because of this third attribute, many female leaders who lack it have been unfairly labeled cold, bossy, or aggressive. Men are not labeled as such in the same role. As author Margarita Mayo shares in her research, "Women must be seen as warm in order to capitalize on their competence and be seen as confident and influential at work; competent men are seen as confident and influential whether they are warm or not." She adds, "To have the influence in their organizations that they would like to have, women must go out of their way to be seen as warm."[3] This might explain why there has been so much controversy over words like *bossy* and *intimidating* being used to describe women who have Leading as a superpower. Because while this trait has so much power, for women there is an expectation that it should be coupled with competence and an expression of warmth.

HOW TO COURSE-CORRECT

Let me start off by acknowledging that this triple standard is unfair. As professor and author Adam Grant shared on Instagram in December

2022, women are "punished for violating gender stereotypes as warm and submissive. . . . Ambitious men and women get promoted. Aggressive women are penalized more than men. End the double standard: if you accept it in men, don't reject it in women." At the same time, how do we win today while we work to change this cultural norm long-term? The Leading trait has built into it an ability to bring out the best in others, and empathy is a powerful component of that. Demonstrating warmth can come in the form of genuine interest in others—their motivations, their goals, what matters to them. It's tapping into the Giving superpower as a source of empathy and care. Taking the time to get to know your teammates—offering time on your calendar to connect, reaching out to catch up over coffee or a meal—brings a human connection to interactions that strengthens followership. There's an opportunity to share a meaningful personal story or company anecdote that provides a window into your life. A personal touch can help: in a 2011 article for the *Harvard Business Review*, former Campbell Soup CEO Doug Conant shared that he often would take time to write a handwritten thank-you note to someone at the company celebrating their contribution to the company.[4] (Apparently, he wrote more than 30,000 during his tenure.)

Being Warm: Not Too Hot, Not Too Cold

Esme was taking on a big role in law enforcement, and she knew she needed to develop a rapport with her team if she was going to succeed. She wanted to get to know them and understand what she could do to make their jobs easier and how to improve the department.

"My first day, I told my team (of mostly men) that my door was always open. They could tell me anything. But I soon realized I had made myself too vulnerable too quickly. I was dealing with men who were used to receiving orders without explanation from male superiors—it was law enforcement, after all—and they didn't quite know what to think of me asking them to come in and talk about their feelings. Next thing I know, I have one of them in my office talking trash about someone else (and surreptitiously recording me, no less) to see if he could get a rise out of me. He wanted to see how far he could push me because I was a woman."

The lesson here? Navigate the right balance within the cultural context in which you're working. Esme needed to inject emotional intelligence into her leadership style and lead with warmth . . . but not too much warmth. Know what you're dealing with. Read the room. Other cultures may lead from the heart. In all scenarios, a commanding presence is valuable, calibrated with the right level of humanity and compassion.

What You Can Do to Channel This Superpower

Whether you are climbing a corporate ladder or heading up a committee for a charity, this is a great trait to be proficient in, especially in moments when you need to ask for and get what you want.

RAISE YOUR HAND

Leading is about taking charge, and the first step in embodying this trait is making it known that you want to lead. Step up, throw your hat in the ring, and be visible, so others know that you're up for the challenge. If you need to be inspired to take that step, prompt it with a source of inspiration. Get fired up, whether that is by listening to a favorite rallying song (just look at what "Running Up that Hill" did for Max in Season 4 of *Stranger Things*) or reading a quote from literature. One of my favorite movie clips of all time is from an adaptation of Shakespeare's *Henry V* where Kenneth Branagh recites the St. Crispin's Day speech. Henry V was never supposed to be the king of England; he was not in the line of succession, and he had grown up in the army and was almost killed by an arrow at the age of 16. In the face of being outmanned five to one on the eve of a battle with France, he tells his story to inspire his troops: he grew up as one of them, and he is in it with them not as their king but as their brother: "We few, we happy few, we band of brothers; for he to-day that sheds his blood with me shall be my brother." In fact, those who were not at that battle "shall think themselves accursed they were not here." I am one of you. I am here on the battlefield with you. Pretty inspiring, right?

TRY THE NORTH STAR EXERCISE

Because Leading starts with clarity in direction, you can channel this trait by stating a long-term goal and giving that destination concrete form. It could range from "In five years, this is where I want to be in life" to "In the next year, I'd like our team to accomplish [x]." It is important to outline why this goal is compelling and how we will know that we have succeeded. Leading is about an intentional mindset, not a reactionary seat-of-the-pants one. Furthermore, the strategies should be clear and easy to follow: outline the steps that will get you there, the resources you might need, the support network on which you will call, the risks you will need to anticipate. The clearer you are in the goal and your control over the path ahead, the easier you will be to follow and the more resolve you will have to take initiative.

CRAFT A CHARISMATIC LEADERSHIP STORY

Channeling this quality is about being a motivating communicator. One way to practice this is to learn how to tell your own story with impact. As former Campbell Soup CEO Doug Conant shares, "A person's life story and leadership story are one and the same. Who you are in work is who you are in life."[5] That is, your leadership is anchored in your beliefs and purpose—and what better way to practice charismatic storytelling than with your own story? It's the type of charisma that connects with others and inspires followership ("I understand that's why you're asking me to do this"; "I feel more connected to you because I know where you're coming from"; "I see points of connection in our life stories"). Distill the qualities of how and why you lead into a few bullet points for yourself, and, if relevant, for others. When I coach women who are interviewing for senior roles, I ask them to write the "Three Pillars" that made them who they are today. In my own leadership story, I share: 1) my second-generation immigrant background and the resilience that has taught me; 2) how my corporate experience has shaped my skills; and 3) that I had the courage to become an entrepreneur and create a way to channel my passion for helping others.

Crafting your life story enables connection and inspires others. For me, it's how I best articulate why I founded my company: the feedback that I didn't have gravitas (many women tell me they've heard the same), the pain points I've experienced in the dressing room (every woman's dilemma), and how I set out to change fashion for them. For my team, these motivations clearly connect their daily work tasks to a deeply personal mission that I've laid out for them. ("It's important we get the sizing right on this dress because when a woman receives it, we want it to fit her like nothing else ever has!")

PERFORMING

- ◆ You've been told that you're the life of the party.
- ◆ You enjoy meeting new people.
- ◆ You don't mind being seated next to a stranger at a dinner party—you were born to charm!
- ◆ You care whether or not people like you.
- ◆ You are great at telling stories; you love being asked to give a toast!
- ◆ You've been told that you can be overwhelming.
- ◆ You enjoy being the center of attention.

This expression of gravitas is public-facing, deriving much of its power (and impact) from an audience, whether literal or implied. If this is your superpower, then you are comfortable in the spotlight, whether performing at Madison Square Garden or selling an idea in a window-less conference room. It's become more mainstream in the last decade, as this form of gravitas foregrounds whenever we post on social media. Entertaining and mood-boosting, this trait is classic extroversion and showmanship.

You engage eagerly and vibrantly, comfortable with attention and craving human contact. You live life in the moment with a fun-loving spirit, looking for excitement in everything and never running out of things to discuss. You are bold and social, deriving your energy from others and encouraging others to partake in shared activities. You give your time and energy generously and enthusiastically because you genuinely enjoy spending time with others. You can easily get caught up in the joy of the moment and want everyone else to feel that way too.

In even the most frustrating situations, you exhibit excellent people skills. Your strong sense of observation includes being able to read a room, befriend nearly anyone, bring people together, persuade others to join in on almost anything, or defuse tension by uplifting the mood. You can be relied upon to pump energy, spontaneity, or fun into any situation.

When You Are at Your Best

If you have this trait as your superpower, you are most confident in public-facing situations and are very persuasive. You can comfortably tell a story in front of an audience (two times more than the average), just as easily as you can sell someone on a plan or idea, start a business, and go to an event where you don't know anyone (35 to 70 percent more than the average). You have an extensive circle of friends whom you can ask for help (you are among the most adept at raising money for a business or charity). You are also observant and attuned to others' emotions, and you often can mollify the intensity of a situation. You have an ability to relate to others that is unparalleled.

Notable Demographics

This trait is most often deployed in public-facing situations. Hence, the highest percentage of people who have this superpower work full-time (more than two-thirds) and are 80 percent more likely to be at a senior level. They are twice as likely as the average to be a business owner and often can be found in more customer-facing or service-oriented professions where there is a sense of excitement, stimulation, and interaction with customers.

How to Steer Clear of Downsides

"IT'S ALL ABOUT ME"

When this trait is at its max, there's little room for anyone or anything else. Manifested at the wrong time, you risk talking past the sale or being perceived as narcissistic or manipulative. Conversation can be lopsided, with two-way dialogue or dissent being suffocated. You thrive on having an audience to validate you, making you feel needed and appreciated. You may, therefore, also struggle when encountering more introverted personalities who do not readily match your energy levels.

If you receive critical feedback, you can spiral downward with a series of negative thoughts, worried about what others think of you, or simply dismiss the feedback and the person giving it altogether. In our quantitative survey, those with this trait are the least likely to admit when they are wrong.

HOW TO COURSE-CORRECT

It may help those with this quality to practice other forms of confidence, such as Giving (genuine interest in and care for others) and Self-Sustaining (which is a true challenge, as it is the polar opposite of Performing in that those with the Self-Sustaining superpower do not feel the need to impress). This will help with learning when their Performing quality should take center stage and when not. If you have this superpower, remember, it is not your job to always be the center of attention or to make everyone like you and it does not need to bother you when someone does not. Giving space and airtime to others will always be a challenge for those with Performing as a superpower, but it is essential so as not to be labeled overwhelming. To balance this potentially overwhelming force of personality, channel your natural gifts of observation into reading the room and being mindful of others. Storytelling is powerful, but so is active listening, asking questions, and being genuinely interested in others' stories. It can be as simple as asking, "What's the latest in your life?" or when listening to a story or feedback, responding with, "Say more about that. I want to know more."

BEING UNFOCUSED

You live in the moment and leap at opportunities, which means any effort that requires repetitive action is torturous. In fact, you score the lowest on feeling capable of getting projects done, and you can be labeled as being unfocused or easily distracted by other people or more enjoyable, higher-energy situations. Worse, tasks that are devoid of human contact and excitement are draining, as there is no audience for whom to perform.

HOW TO COURSE-CORRECT

Because Performing is my top form of confidence, I identify with this downside and have found two ways to address it. First, I look for ways to find day-to-day joy in mundane tasks by thinking about the broader goals and creating fun and rewards so tasks feel less repetitive along the way. Second, I surround myself with people who have Achieving, Knowing, and Giving as their top qualities because their natural talent is to get things done reliably. It helps that my teammates provide the human interaction I crave, but in a way that does not distract.

What You Can Do to Channel This Superpower

Performing can serve you well, especially in meeting new people, building camaraderie with a team, or speaking in front of an audience. Fostering a warm, inviting, and open presence through nonverbal cues and verbal engagement is the hallmark of this quality.

BREATHE

This is the go-to exercise for stage fright, whether it occurs while giving a wedding toast or making a formal presentation in front of others. If Performing is a quality not natural to you, the best thing to do is to trust your own physiology. Breathing techniques have long been proven to help regulate the vagus nerve and thus calm us down. I have a ritual that I follow before I step onto any stage. I listen to a favorite song to set the mood and do a "7-5-7" meditation a few times: I close my eyes, inhale through my nose for seven seconds, hold my breath for five seconds, and exhale slowly through my mouth for seven seconds. This lowers my heart rate, oxygenates my brain, and centers me so I can do what I do best.

PRACTICE STORYTELLING

When it comes to a speech or toast, this is where practice and storytelling preparation come into play. Researchers John Antonakis, Marika Fenley, and Sue Liechti discovered that anyone can be trained in what they call *charismatic leadership tactics* (CLTs).[6] They found that when mapping out a speech or presentation, using nine verbal CLTs (such as metaphors, personal stories, and passion) and three nonverbal CLTs (voice, facial expressions, and body cues) could demonstrably increase "'good' presentation skills—speech structure, clear pronunciation, use of easy-to-understand language, tempo of speech, and speaker comfort." We'll explore this in greater depth in Chapter 6, as we found in our own quantitative research that telling a story in front of an audience is one of the areas in which women are the least comfortable, so all of us need a bit of Performing if we want to be better at it.

ENERGIZE AND ENTHUSE

Remembering names, asking questions, and engaging the other person demonstrate an enthusiasm for the present moment and a desire for personal interaction. If people feel your genuine interest—whether it's expressed in an animated voice, facial expressions, or gestures—they become more receptive to you and your message. Even smiling can be a powerful tool in the Performing arsenal when it is done with authenticity and to solidify connection. It's not about smiling all the time, or hiding your true thoughts by pasting a smile on your face. In fact, leadership expert Janine Driver shares that when meeting someone new, the most powerful people smile after they shake that person's hand and hear their name, not before. What we know about smiling is that seeing another person smile triggers an automatic muscular response that produces a smile in return, lifting the mood and creating a waterfall of positive feelings. Look for times when you sincerely feel this energy on the inside, then make sure to share it on the outside.

The Power of Body Language

Leadership expert and *New York Times* best-selling author of *You Say More Than You Think: Use the New Body Language to Get What You Want* Janine Driver shared with me how she helps clients around the world channel their Leading and Performing superpowers.

"Where the wall meets the ceiling is a confident feeling."

When people think about good posture, they think it's about keeping your shoulders back and head up. That's actually not the best tip because pulling your shoulders back begins to feel uncomfortable after a while, so it is hard to sustain. Instead, think of Iron Man, who has a circle that keeps him alive at the center of his chest. Pretend you have the same circle and, keeping your shoulders relaxed, expand your chest out and up. If you need a visual, direct your chest up to where the wall meets the ceiling. When we expand, we say, "Here I am," and we take up space.

"Stand your ground."

If you're on a phone call and you're feeling pushed around or intimidated, stand up if you are not already. This increases your determination. It's an increase in physical pressure. This works for in-person meetings too. As you begin to speak, find a reason to stand up to deliver your message, such as going to the dry-erase board to make a point and document it. Not only are you standing your ground, you also will begin to feel more powerful. You're also forcing people to look up at you, which is a game changer.

"Move your body, move your mind."

When you feel insecure, get moving—go for a walk around the building or down the hall before the meeting. Even wiggling your body from your arms to your toes for 20 seconds works; after the 20-second mark, the movement activates endorphins and calms your nerves.

"Your hands matter."

When people are nervous, they put their hands in their pockets. Conversely, the more hand gestures you use, the more powerful you seem. Turn your palm up to convey honesty, openness, and confidence. Grabbing your chin is a signal of intelligence. And if you want to make your presence known? Steeple your hands. In fact, I have found this gesture to be useful when people interrupt you in a meeting. Instead of saying, "Excuse me, I'd like to finish what I was saying," push back from the table, lean back, and steeple your fingertips. If you're interrupted again, say nothing, lean back and steeple again. By the third time, someone else at the table will likely step in and say, "Please stop interrupting."

"Use your low voice."

Lower tones are considered powerful. When your tone of voice goes up, it indicates insecurity or doubt. How do you know what your low voice is? It's the voice you wake up with in the morning, before you've had that first cup of coffee.

ACHIEVING

- You love setting goals and working to achieve and/or exceed them.
- You get even more motivated when you are challenged—you love healthy competition.
- You believe practice makes perfect.
- You've been known to continue on and/or endure, regardless of setbacks.
- You're always measuring how you're doing, especially to improve.
- You can be stubborn and not know when to let go.
- Your accomplishments are a big part of who you are.

This form of self-confidence is goal-oriented, consistent, and persistent. You find it natural to adopt a winner's mindset and derive worth from pushing beyond your limits with the highest standards. You are continuously focused on forward progress: you thrive when goals are clear from the start, you put a tremendous amount of effort into attaining them, and you enjoy it when that effort pays off. You appreciate structured paths that have clear markers for success and objective metrics that can be tracked along the way. The more measurable, the better, because you enjoy being recognized for and celebrating reaching milestones.

You're not one to shy away from a challenge; in fact you are even more motivated when you are tested. You believe that performance improvement in service of a goal is possible through hard work. "Practice makes perfect" is a mantra with which you would eagerly agree. When it comes to feedback, you willingly accept it if it betters your chances of crossing the finish line or validates your accomplishments. This form of confidence powers a determination to pursue success of any kind, alongside the dedication to achieve it, come what way. It's a self-improving movie montage made real.

Dedicated, strong-willed and action-oriented, you see things through to completion, viewing shortcuts as irresponsible and setbacks as challenges to be tackled. You pride yourself on diving into projects, getting things done effectively, improving action plans, fairly distributing tasks, and crossing things off your to-do list along the way. As such, you are dependable and you "stick with it/tough it out," with an endurance that pushes through even in the face of setbacks. You have resilience and an ability to endlessly rebound. You may get down, but you are never out: Athletes and comeback stories are powered by this form of confidence. If you lose a match, you learn from the loss, and you move forward and never give up. If anything, you turn your disappointment into fuel to work harder.

When You Are at Your Best

There is a competitive streak to this quality, as you are the most confident in competing for something (e.g., an award, a promotion, a game) because there is a clearly articulated goal in your sights motivating you. You also feel most capable when managing people and telling others what to do, getting tasks and projects done, and working under a very tight deadline and under pressure. In our quantitative survey, those with Achieving as their superpower scored highly on being capable of and comfortable with recovering from a loss or disappointment, a testament to their belief in resilience and pushing through adversity to achieve something.

Notable Demographics

We see this trait among students—who naturally skew toward validation and grades—and those in technical or engineering professions where there are clear facts and metrics. Our data also showed a significant percentage of full-time parents who worked previously. Many of these women may have been on high-achieving career trajectories; they still channel this quality as moms in terms of getting things done effectively but may crave the validation they were used to in their careers. We'll talk about how to manage this a bit later in the book.

How to Steer Clear of Downsides

NOT LETTING GO

People with this superpower may be prone to holding on for too long and find conceding, letting go, or acknowledging failure impossible. In its most extreme form, it can manifest as hard-driving and inflexible, with an inability to walk away even in situations that no longer serve you or others. In our quantitative survey, while women with the Achieving quality score highly on being capable of recovering from a loss, they score the lowest on letting go of a disappointment or failure.

HOW TO COURSE-CORRECT

While having high expectations can be motivating, we also don't want them to become our own worst enemy. If dealing with a disappointment such as a breakup or job loss, is there an opportunity to gain perspective? The superpower that most aids in letting go of a setback is Believing, because if something doesn't work out, it wasn't meant to be and better things are ahead. Take a moment and create a balance sheet of the pros and cons of holding on versus letting go. Reflect on the wisdom you gained, which will help in moving on to the next goal.

BEING TOO HARD ON OTHERS—AND YOURSELF

Achieving can be expressed in an uncompromising and demanding fashion, manifesting as impatience in expecting the highest performance from yourself and others. This quality has the tendency to drive toward a destination at the expense of others' feelings or to miss out on other ways to get things done. In our quantitative work, this quality was shown to not be the one to lean on for emotional support, such as comforting others. You thrive on metrics and recognition of achievement, so you may become trapped in a comparison doom loop, fixated on your status relative to others and concerned about falling short of your own expectations or not living up to external standards. This is the definition of perfectionist peril—never feeling up to par, fearing coming up short—to the point of exasperation and exhaustion.

HOW TO COURSE-CORRECT

Channel empathy and understanding in interactions with others (both hallmarks of the Giving superpower); the goal is best achieved together when others are engaged and committed along the way. At times you may need to release your agenda and enjoy the beauty and the humor of the messy or unscripted; you can appreciate that the detour can be beautiful (to offset the frustration you feel from, say, arriving a half hour late to the party!). There are moments during which you will need to understand that while you are motivated by a goal, the goal does not define you. You should practice a healthy dose of self-compassion when it comes to recognizing your worthiness and strengths (a strong suit of those with Self-Sustaining as a superpower), versus benchmarking against an imposed standard. This means learning from mistakes and embracing teachable moments, which at times means reframing "practice makes perfect" as "perfect is the enemy of the good."

BEING OKAY WITH AMBIGUITY AND SUBJECTIVITY

You may struggle in more ambiguous, subjective situations where there are no tangible metrics. You may also be one of the most vulnerable to systemic bias, because you believe in structures and measurable systems, even when those systems were not designed by you or with you in mind. You feel that if you put your head down and do the work, you will be rewarded. And that is not always the case. Life is not fair—and it may be hard for you to see when metrics are evaluated subjectively by those who have inherent biases.

HOW TO COURSE-CORRECT

Keep your eyes open for situations where there are no metrics, or where the metrics are unfair or being administered with bias. That's the first step—seeing it for what it is, so the burden isn't just on you. If there are no metrics, ask yourself if this is a situation where you need to let go, or bring your superpower into play by creating structure and milestones. If the metrics are unfair, channel the Leading quality in taking charge and advocating for a change to the system (or tap into the Self-Sustaining and Believing superpowers to muster the courage to walk away from the system if change is not possible).

What You Can Do to
Channel This Superpower

SWITCH ON A WINNING MINDSET

The hallmark of this quality is having a performance-oriented focus. You can take inspiration from any competitive arena. Athletes visualize victory or recall a peak performance moment to set themselves up to embody this quality. Relying on visual cues such as a mental picture of the top of the mountain and imagining a sense of accomplishment are critical to activating these motivations so you can hit the deadline on a big project or power through your to-do list.

CREATE TANGIBLE MILESTONES—AND REWARDS

From there, take on a mountain or major goal by breaking the task down into smaller hills. Check them off as you go, and give yourself a reward for ticking them off one by one. I have a friend who wrote tasks of the day on Post-its and stuck them on her computer. That way she couldn't forget them, and as she performed each task, she had the great satisfaction of crumpling them up, throwing them away, and leaving her desk sans Post-its by the end of the day—a visible demonstration of her accomplishments. (To be more environmentally minded, you could make a digital list for yourself—the feeling you get from deleting an errand or task is just as rewarding.) You can also make accountability fun if the goal at hand is a collective one. At my gym, there is a 20-class challenge each month, with a poster board where we put a gold star next to our names after class. I get to pat myself on the back for my hard work, and there is shared, public-facing validation when I high-five others who have also completed the challenge (bonus: there's a prize at the end of each month).

RECOVER WITH RESILIENCE

At the heart of the Achieving superpower is a need for growth and progress toward a goal. When setbacks happen, those with this quality bounce back to keep going. How do they do this? The visual I use is of a trampoline: we keep jumping because each time, we get the chance to go higher and higher. With every challenge, there is something to learn to get stronger; it is a belief that if you haven't given up, you still have a chance to succeed. It is a learning mindset that edits the outlook to learn from mistakes and power through with endurance. The next time you feel like giving up, think through what you've learned from your missteps (like watching game footage), how you can handle things differently next time, and, most important, how to keep moving forward with the finish line in your sights.

GIVING

- You enjoy helping others with no expectation of return.
- You are a good listener. People often come to you to vent.
- You enjoy putting time and thought into buying the perfect gift.
- If a friend is sick, you're the first to show up to help.
- You've been told that you can be too nice (almost to the point where you feel taken for granted!).
- You get a lot of satisfaction in helping others be successful.
- You often feel responsible for the happiness of others.

This superpower is expressed through serving others with generous care and warm support. Empathetic, hardworking, and devoted, those with this quality feel a deep responsibility to others. You remember birthdays and buy great gifts; you are reliable and always determined to finish what you started. You are the rare combination of altruistic and practical, because you don't just hope to help others, you take action in doing whatever is needed to care for friends, family, and colleagues. Moreover, you truly enjoy sharing your know-how and attention with anyone who needs them, striving for win-win situations and choosing teamwork over competition.

You feel most energized and capable when showing up for someone who needs your help. As such, one of your defining characteristics is loyalty. You invest great effort into relationships, maintaining strong connections and dropping everything to lend a hand when someone is going through a hard time. Because you take great care in remembering the details of other people's lives, you have a special knack for making others feel seen and cherished and are always ready to offer advice, help, and reassurance. You demonstrate kindness, with an ability to listen carefully to others' concerns and, more important, to find ways to resolve them. You take pride in knowing that people turn to you in times of need; showing up gives you a sense of purpose.

Your reliable nature stems from an emotional commitment—knowing others or a greater cause are depending on you—and you won't rest until you have done your share, or more than your fair share, to help. Motivated by uplifting others and equipped with humility, you appreciate the value of a supporting role and the power of a collaborative mindset. You are comfortable with allowing others to take the spotlight. You bring clear, consistent resolutions to day-to-day challenges with warmth and humble dedication, applying your gifts to make a real, positive difference in people's lives.

When You Are at Your Best

Those with this quality are the most comfortable when bringing depth to interpersonal situations such as dealing with the illness of a family member or comforting someone who is sad. This quality is also powerful in its responsibility-oriented "can-do" attitude, with its possessors being capable of getting tasks done and working effectively toward a deadline in a patient, thoughtful manner.

Notable Demographics

This is the most prevalent superpower among women; half of all the women we surveyed have this as their top trait. This superpower is often expressed in professions focused on supporting others' growth, healing, and progress. Those with this trait over-index in professions such as teaching, health care, customer service, and sales, which all require them to be attuned to the needs of the people they are serving, to help others excel in practical ways, and to listen to concerns and calmly see things through to a clear resolution. There is a human quality to day-to-day work that never feels tedious. This is also one of the groups whose members are most likely to be a full-time parent and who may be most prone to feeling taken for granted and most frequently frustrated (especially if Achieving is also one of their top traits).

How to Steer Clear of Downsides

TAKING IT ALL UPON YOURSELF

"Don't mistake my kindness for weakness" might be the mantra for the shadow side of this quality. Because of your intense desire to serve, you run the risk of others taking advantage of your helpful nature, leaving you feeling burned out, overworked, and guilty for not doing enough. The paradox of this quality is that it may not be easy for people with this as their primary superpower to show up for themselves in the way that they show up for others. In our quantitative survey, those with Giving as a superpower are the least comfortable in asking for help (such as raising money or asking for a favor). They are most susceptible to a deficit mindset, admitting often when they are wrong (one of their top two characteristics) and working harder to try to compensate for their own perceived gaps. Your loyalty may make you feel guilty about moving on from difficult situations and rocking the boat. Your dedication may lead you to suffer in silence, trying to do everything yourself even when it's simply impossible.

HOW TO COURSE-CORRECT

Give, but don't let it empty you. Setting boundaries and advocating for your own priorities will all be part of your learning journey. Adam Grant, professor and best-selling author of *Give and Take*, talks about people who are naturally givers, as opposed to those who are takers, and how to avoid "the doormat effect." This is the person who everyone turns to when they need help with a project—at 4:50 P.M. on a Friday, expecting you to drop everything (and you do). How to avoid this? By providing boundaries and giving parameters: "I can help, but I have to leave by 5:30," or "That's not something I am able to do, but here's another solution or person who can get that done." Realizing that others enjoy giving too—relationships get stronger when you give *and* ask of them—may help those with Giving as a dominant trait feel permitted to ask for help and avoid burnout.

FEELING UNDERAPPRECIATED

You run the risk of taking things personally, as you are sensitive to others' opinions. And if your efforts go unnoticed? While you underplay your accomplishments, you are appreciative of acknowledgment and recognition, and you wish for validation and respect in return. If you feel taken for granted, you can quietly lose enthusiasm and motivation, becoming resentful toward those who don't seem to appreciate you. You may internalize these negative feelings, which may boil over in uncharacteristic outbursts of frustration. In the workplace, you may place too much trust in your boss seeing your contributions and promoting you, patiently waiting while you are overlooked (even though when those with this quality are promoted, they are often the best suited to building cohesive and productive teams). In our research, women with Giving as their primary superpower scored the lowest in being capable of and comfortable with advocating for themselves (asking for a raise or promotion, taking credit) and being in the spotlight (public speaking, telling a story).

HOW TO COURSE-CORRECT

Instead of waiting to be recognized, you can take a page from the Leading, Performing, Creating, and Self-Sustaining superpowers. By channeling Leading, Performing, or Creating, you can become comfortable with broadcasting your accomplishments, actively advocating for what you want and need and demanding recognition for taking charge of getting things done. The Self-Sustaining quality will remind you to document all the ways in which you make a difference for others, a list you can fall back on when you question your worth.

BEING SEEN AS MEDDLESOME

Having too much of this quality can make you run the risk of being overly intrusive. Those with Giving as a superpower have a propensity to intervene and want to pitch in and help, which at times can exacerbate situations.

HOW TO COURSE-CORRECT

Understand when your intervention is unwelcome or unnecessary. Because this quality is deeply intuitive, channel empathy to sit inside the other person's story and see if they're asking for help. If someone came to talk, are they just wanting to vent and your listening is enough, or are they really looking for help? Create a space where you take direction from the other person by asking questions (versus jumping to problem-solving), so they do not feel that they are being prodded.

What You Can Do to
Channel This Superpower

BE MORE EMPATHETIC

One quick-fire way to practice this is to perform simple acts of empathy and kindness. Take the receptionist at my gym, Aaron, for example. I exercise every day at 7:00 A.M., and most days, I'm still half-asleep when I arrive at the gym. One morning, a perfect storm occurred: I missed the bus, was caught in a rainstorm without an umbrella, the elevator to the gym was stuck so I had to take the stairs, and I was 10 minutes late to my fitness class. As soon as I got to the gym, Aaron smiled and said, "Good morning. It's so nice to see you, Lisa." I explained my morning, and he frowned with empathy and moved into action. "That's awful. Here, let me take your bag, get you a towel, and walk you into class. It's never too late to get your sweat on." In one minute, Aaron turned my emotions from a spiral of frustration and anger to appreciation and happiness. That is the power of Giving—we can make someone feel good with a simple gesture and turn things around for that person. Another example of this? I am that rare New Yorker that you can ask for directions. I'm never too busy to give directions, in almost any language. I know firsthand the distress that comes with not knowing which way is up on this island of Manhattan; I practice this trait nearly every day, even pulling up Google Maps and Google Translate on my phone to aid someone's trek to their destination.

"HOW CAN I HELP?"

You can also ask people "How are you, really?" and listen. Really listen. Be there to help, if they need it. If they do, ask, "How can I help?" This simple question showcases the impulse of Giving and opens up the space for this quality to thrive. Professor Dan Cable describes a situation in which managers at a food-delivery business were trained to ask customer-service employees, "How can I help you deliver excellent service?" Out of this Giving mindset came a whole host of solutions that managers could provide to their employees such as new products and reporting stock shortages. Managers were seen as supportive givers (versus nit-picking evaluators), kicking off a virtuous cycle of openness and ideas that translated into better customer service.[7]

SHOW YOUR VULNERABLE SIDE

This quality is all about leading from the heart. It is by definition personal and requires closing the distance between you and another person. In his book *Lead with Heart*, the former president of Avis Budget Group Tom Gartland noted that he started with himself to create a more "open and connected" culture by realizing business could be "personal—very personal." To do that, he made deep connections that created a committed employee base that drove results. Building that emotional bond starts with us being able to share our own story as a way to build trust and communicate empathy. In opening ourselves up, we are sharing our purpose (this is why I give), values (this is what I care about), acceptance (I respect, value, and care about you), and points of similarity (I've been where you are and that's why I want to help you through it). Those with Giving as a superpower value personal relationships and are often the first ones to open the door to building that close connection.

KNOWING

- You enjoy gathering and analyzing information before making a decision or forming an opinion.
- You live by the motto "knowledge is power."
- You consider yourself a logical and rational person.
- You enjoy a good to-do list. You can create a spreadsheet for almost any occasion!
- You're not comfortable making decisions without all the available information.
- You enjoy learning new things.
- You are a very curious person.

This form of expert confidence is powered by knowledge—briefed and prepped like a lawyer on the first day of a trial, it derives its power from know-how. Always buttoned-up and never caught off-guard, someone with this superpower has a sense of quiet mastery and integrity, with a rational, logical outlook on life. You like to read the whole instruction manual before removing a device from the box rather than troubleshooting one button at a time, because your actions are composed carefully and carried out methodically. You are analytical and objective, often a repository of knowledge with a heavy emphasis on facts. You can analyze everything you come across, spotting patterns and connections and going deep in learning everything you can on a specific topic of interest. And you are a truth seeker, uncomfortable with accepting high-level concepts until you've dug deeply beneath the surface of things. Having done extensive research or thinking on a matter, you convey a convincing intellect and unending curiosity, being well equipped to see all sides to a problem before making a decision and having strong opinions on how things should be done.

You can easily apply data and information to grasp the details of situations and solve problems. Because of this, you can tackle any project with a clear process and seriousness; you can put ideas into practice and are the master of implementation. Responsible, grounded, and practical, you are able to keep calm in the face of hardships with rational decision-making. You are highly productive and adept at creating order from chaos, believing that things get done when there are structures and guidelines and everyone involved knows exactly what is going on and why. At your core, you are honest, direct, and trustworthy, managing the reality of situations with little room for emotional manipulation. You mean what you say and when you commit to doing something, you follow through dependably.

When You Are at Your Best

Your depth of intellectual curiosity makes your commentary and thoughts substantive and worthy of notice. Women with this superpower are the most comfortable when dealing with facts; they score the highest on defending an answer with data. This is the quality most wanted in driving project management and timelines. You are highly confident in driving a process in a rational and logical manner: getting tasks/projects done, working on a very tight deadline or under pressure, and staying calm in bad situations.

Notable Demographics

This is the second-most-prevalent trait among the women we surveyed. This trait is well suited to institutions that value consistency, objectivity, and depth of knowledge. We found many women with Knowing as a superpower were in legal, technical, academic, finance, and consulting roles, where reliability, clear process, and sharp minds are highly valued.

How to Steer Clear of Downsides

HAVING A LOW EQ

This is a see-it-to-believe-it type of quality rooted in facts, and less sensitive to emotions. You can be baffled by the illogical ways in which emotions play into behavior (including your own), judge when others fail to meet the demands of a process, or get caught up in "winning" an argument with facts, being perceived as strict or unempathetic even when your intentions are good. You are one of the least comfortable in comforting others.

HOW TO COURSE-CORRECT

A balance of the Giving superpower is pivotal in helping those with this trait to introduce a relationship-oriented element into their fact-based world. There are moments when being the "smartest person in the room" doesn't serve the process. I learned this early on in my consulting career when I was working with the head of human resources for a public school district. In a meeting, I was hard-driving with facts and figures, keeping to our team's project timeline. It was not until halfway through the meeting that I realized how terrified my client was; the data was overwhelming and indicated that budget cuts would be necessary. I didn't have her buy-in to keep going. The feedback I received after this meeting from my boss? Building and keeping relationships is equal to the intellectual exercise. I learned self-awareness is key, and I had misread the room. I was more interested in being right than in deftly handling the emotional impact of the answer.

An easy way to practice empathy is to place yourself in another person's shoes. By taking on someone else's perspective, you may see a side to the story you hadn't seen before, whether it be a difficult situation or a differing opinion. That insight may change your own preconceived ideas; you will be able to better connect with them and, with practice, be more open and generous. Be as curious about people as you are about facts and data.

Similarly, there's a way to tailor facts to better connect with your audience. Let's go back to Susan, whom we met in Chapter 1. One of the things she noted was that in executive team meetings, she rushed through the financial review because she thought no one was interested in the numbers. We practiced having her channel Leading and Performing storytelling qualities to give life to the numbers, explaining highlights with emphasis, how the numbers affected each of the teams, and teeing up choices to make. This gave her know-how more power and impact as she moved into her CFO role.

OVERTHINKING

"Analysis paralysis" can cause you to overthink even the smallest decisions, leading you to feel ineffective and also uncomfortable declaring yourself "the expert." Because of this, women with this superpower in our quantitative survey scored themselves quite low on being comfortable with "having to be the expert on a topic." You can be thrown off by ambiguity and struggle with spontaneity and working without rules (you are one of the least confident in creating a piece of art or writing a story, and in telling a story in front of an audience). Because you thrive on a clear set of steps and well-defined responsibilities, you may miss out on opportunities outside of the process, be vocal in opposition to new concepts, or feel frustrated when things are shuffled around.

HOW TO COURSE-CORRECT

Step into your expertise with pride. Trust yourself; as much value as you place in facts, you need to embody that same certainty in your command over them. The Leading and Self-Sustaining qualities, which both have a firm sense of self-assurance, may help you to not question, overthink, or second-guess yourself. When it comes to ambiguity, one of the step-out opportunities for those with this trait is to consider when bending the rules or trying new things might be worthwhile, especially when the downside is minimal (those with the Creating superpower are adept at this). When complete information is not to be had, you should trust your gut and experience to take a leap.

BEING OVERWORKED AND OVERLOOKED

You run the risk of feeling that you are the only one who can see a project through reliably, taking on the process, turning away help, and feeling exhausted or discouraged if you're constantly expected to drive an effort. Because you are fact-driven, you may expect others to recognize you for your work and not necessarily take credit along the way. As a result, you may feel frustrated when your objective contributions are overlooked and you are not comfortable with asking for a raise, promotion, or favor. You are one of the most vulnerable to systemic bias, as you value organization and structure, but may struggle when the system is not built to see or value you.

HOW TO COURSE-CORRECT

Feel comfortable in sharing the burden of the process to fairly and effectively delegate tasks. Also helpful is compiling and documenting achievements to better advocate for yourself. As author and journalist Mika Brzezinski shares, "Make a list of everything you do, how much time it takes, and what value it brings to the company. Research what people in your position at other companies make for their accomplishments. How much value do you bring to the table? Do you bring more, and why?"[8] She later goes on to push for using this list as the basis of a conversation about progression, making sure the system sees you or changes to acknowledge you, or to update your resume and move on dispassionately if the system doesn't value your efforts.

What You Can Do to
Channel This Superpower

DIG DEEP

This trait is defined by intellectual rigor and structured thinking. On the first, you can experience this through the lens of curiosity, a desire to fully understand and explore a topic in depth, with patience and commitment. Is there something in the world you've always wanted to explore? This is the moment to choose that subject and go down the Google rabbit hole with zeal, or sign up for that master class.

KEEP THE TRAINS RUNNING ON TIME

Staying organized and on schedule is one of my personal gaps. That's why I surround myself with teammates who amaze me every day with their adherence to the timeline. Take, for example, each morning my company's production team comes to me for 15 minutes with an update on the manufacturing schedule with a list of to-dos. It's a challenge for me, so I channel former president Dwight Eisenhower. When he was a U.S. Army general, he developed a prioritization tool that helped him make many high-stakes decisions (like organizing D-Day). Eventually named the Eisenhower Matrix, it was subsequently popularized by author Stephen Covey. By labeling what was urgent versus not, important versus not, it helps me to rank how we spend our time as a team. If it worked for the landing at Normandy, surely it can work for me, right? Every day I am forced to practice an objective review of which tasks will yield the greatest value in the required timeframe. While I do not naturally have the gift of Knowing, I'm grateful to be surrounded by those who have it ingrained in who they are and how they get things done.

GROUND YOUR DECISION-MAKING

The Knowing quality is powerful in taking balanced and calculated leaps. Before making a decision, think through the three reasons why it's a good (or bad) decision. What data or additional analysis supports the direction you might take? Are there experts or sources of information you might consult before moving forward? This superpower is helpful in putting real information behind a pros and cons list so you'll feel supported and secure in making the call.

CREATING

- You are really good at coming up with new ideas.
- You think often about what the future will look like.
- You enjoy any creative activity.
- You get excited about "firsts"—experiencing or doing something never done before.
- You believe in things before you can see them.
- You have been told that you are not practical and/or are too much of a dreamer.
- You have a really powerful imagination.

The Creating form of gravitas embodies a steadfast belief in how ideas shape the future. Inventive and visionary, you are the boldest of dreamers, one who adopts a pioneering spirit to drive progress and evolution. You are a "believe it to see it" person (versus seeing is believing) who envisions possibilities where others don't. Your vivid imagination and open mind empower you to seek exciting potential in the world; when you are caught up in an idea, you are all-in with passion. Thoroughly original, you can help people around you consider new ways of looking at things.

Comfortable challenging the status quo and conventional wisdom, you are happiest when you can will an idea into existence. An idea is only worthwhile if it works. You can pair imaginative curiosity with ambitious decisiveness to create something from nothing. Grit, resourcefulness, and commitment are inherent in this quality. You see the future, and then can conceive and launch the breakthrough initiatives to get there. These are the writers who, when looking at the blank screen, cursor blinking, can't wait to see what happens. They are entrepreneurs or designers who are responsible for remarkable innovations.

The artists who translate thoughts and emotions into tangible works of beauty. In the service of an idea, you're not afraid to break the rules or risk disapproval; in fact, you enjoy it and are rarely satisfied if the work feels too easy or comfortable.

The nature of creation is iteration; you are comfortable with criticism, as it is part of the creative process. After all, innovation demands embracing change. You don't fear disappointment or failure and recover from both with aplomb (because you do not live in the past; you are a resident of the future!). It all improves the chances of your idea becoming a reality. Think of how many start-ups proudly tout the pivots they had to make along the way to success. As such, you have a high tolerance for risk and experimentation, because you truly believe your actions are shaping a better future. Don't mistake yourself for a behind-the-scenes player: you crave recognition for your hard-earned creativity, and you want to be seen for your "firsts."

When You Are at Your Best

Innovative spirits who are most confident in tasks that require working without a net are self-assured in coming up with an idea, writing a story or creating a piece of art, and telling a story in front of an audience. You are highly comfortable with having to be an expert on a topic because reimagining the future often comes from a high level of domain expertise or insight. You easily let go of the past in the service of the future; those with this superpower score highly on letting go of a disappointment or failure.

Notable Demographics

Business owners (the second-highest group after Leading), artists, writers, and marketers scored high in this trait. They are less likely to be in traditional fields that value structure (consulting, government/public service, legal, health care, academic research). Many of those with this superpower are "firsts," such as first-generation immigrants, who have directly experienced the process of imagining a different future and making something from nothing. This strength skews younger (ages 25 to 34), when life has a longer runway and the future is full of possibilities. We may lose this characteristic as we age because life's demands squelch a sense of possibility; the future is possible in our youth, but life wears us down. But our quantitative work shows that like the inner child, we can return to this state, because this trait reemerges after the age of 55. I believe this is from a need for reinvention and a view toward legacy (plus after the age of 55, this group may have more resources—time, talent, or treasure—to manifest their visions). But you don't have to be a specific age to manifest this; I am proof of that. I became an entrepreneur in my late 30s, and I think that made a huge difference by my being a bit more seasoned and experienced, with a network to tap into. Our culture can tend to celebrate youthful entrepreneurs (just think of those 30 under 30 lists) because they're innately fearless and risk-taking with all the runway they have. However, research has shown that the average age of a founder of the fastest-growing new ventures is 45, and those over the age of 35 have an increased probability of success as entrepreneurs.[9]

How to Steer Clear of Downsides

REALITY BITES

Rules, rigid structures, and traditions are the enemy of the freedom required for Creating to thrive. In our quantitative survey, those with this quality are the least comfortable working on a very tight deadline, completing tedious and repetitive tasks, and reliably addressing responsibilities. A sense of buttoned-down procedures or "that's the way we've always done things" can stifle your creativity because you're constantly inventing a whole new wheel or looking for new ways to approach things.

HOW TO COURSE-CORRECT

This is one of my dominant traits, and there are a few things I do to overcome this. The first is that I remind myself that vision can only become reality when I tackle the tasks in service of that vision or standing in the way of it. Our production manager, Kelly, has a card on her desk from the Whitney Museum of American Art that says, "It always seems impossible until it's done." She purchased this when we decided to launch our brand on HSN and in department stores in the same year, a nearly impossible task for a small company. Kelly said to our team, "Lisa says things out loud and they always happen. Why? Because we remind her of all the boring things that must be done and get them done together." When I have to power through tasks, I start with sitting inside the future I see and being motivated by it. I then work with my team (who have Achieving and Knowing as superpowers) to lay out a concrete, logical path forward with milestones we can track and celebrate along the way—together, with my team's experience and patience, we complete the tasks to realize my vision.

IMPATIENCE

Restlessness and frustration can arise when current realities stand in the way of—or feel far from—your vision. You're living in the future, imagining how things could already be better than today. So the present is dissatisfying. It's even worse when those around you are constantly playing catch-up to meet your lofty goals, meaning at times you can be seen as irrationally opinionated or an impractical dreamer with a strong independent streak. This can create a feeling of isolation when others don't see what you see in your version of the future.

HOW TO COURSE-CORRECT

I often channel my Leading and Performing superpowers to articulate the mission for my team in a clear way, not just as a lofty destination. It's important to take the time to fully explain the vision and find ways to make it concrete, especially for others who might be more see-it-to-believe-it types. Take a step back and invest the time to bring people along on the journey; oftentimes, people can't see what you see because it doesn't feel tangible yet. Plus, sometimes it's good to slow down and enjoy the present.

What You Can Do to Channel This Superpower

The most important element of this quality is freedom, the space to create. It's an imperative to feel free from the pressures and realities of the day-to-day. Research shows that when we're in response mode—answering e-mails, repeatedly working through mundane tasks, feeling stressed—the amplitude of our brain waves shorten. Creative thought requires high amplitude waves with slow frequency to do its best work. The neuroscience is real: when you wake up in the morning, your brain switches from delta waves (deep sleep) to theta waves (a day-dreamy state), and then moves to alpha waves (awake and relaxed). If you grab your phone immediately and start responding to e-mail, your body skips the theta state and goes straight to the alpha stage (awake) and beta state (alert). A *Scientific American* report highlights that "the ideation that can take place during the theta state is often free flow and occurs without censorship or guilt," an ideal time to visualize both what you want and the actions that will be necessary to achieve your vision.[10]

GIVE YOURSELF SPACE

When I founded my company, I didn't force myself to come up with the idea; I gave myself space to dream and imagine. After I learned about Steve Jobs's Stanford commencement speech where he shared his philosophy on connecting the dots of your life, I wrote my own version of the dots of my life on a napkin, which I held on to for months. As I gave myself permission to reflect on it, I considered how my life moments and experiences could add up to create a real solution for women's pain points. I could apply my life's journey to the marketplace. I still practice this every week. Every Sunday, I turn off my phone for two hours and go by myself to an art museum. In those two hours, I don't think about my to-do list or something that is bothering me, and at the end of the visit, I pick one piece of priceless art that inspired me that I'd like to take home. I have curated an impressive gallery of masterpieces in my mind over the years. It's freeing—and it's when I've come up with some of our company's most innovative products (my favorite being a jumpsuit that is bathroom-friendly).

My dear friend the celebrated wellness and fitness entrepreneur Anna Kaiser is known for her progressive approach to dance cardio workouts. To keep the body from plateauing, she choreographs and teaches a new dance routine to her clients every two weeks. It's a lot of pressure to create a new dance routine twice a month for hundreds of thousands of clients. She shared her approach to finding the space and freedom to create within constraints:

> The problem is I never know when inspiration will strike. I've learned how to create a space that inspires me instead of waiting for inspiration to hit. Because unfortunately I don't have that luxury. I'm a former dancer, so I use a technique that dance companies have used for years. I ask another trainer on my team to join me in the studio so I can work off their energy. I am a natural performer, so having someone else in the room forces me to tap into that side of myself and fuels my creativity. It's literally just having their energy in the room, Once I'm on a roll, I ask them to leave so I can work with it and dive deeper. That's where the artist side of me kicks in, getting the time and space alone to connect to the art.

PRACTICE THE WHITE-SPACE EXERCISE

Once you've created this space to create in your life, you will then have the mindset to take on what I call the white-space exercise. This is where you map out opportunities to innovate and create. Before our team starts designing a new collection, we get inside the heads, hearts, and lives of the women we serve. We brainstorm and ponder their needs and pain points. And then we map out whether anyone is solving those problems for her. If not, there's a white-space opportunity that our company could tackle (like a jumpsuit you don't have to fully take off to use the bathroom)! In that white space, we can create and innovate for women. I ask our design team, "If we were interviewing for a job in her life, what's the job description? And how good would we be at it versus every other candidate?" It's a page borrowed from the business consultant and academic who developed the theory of "disruptive innovation," Clayton Christensen, who said, "When we buy a product, we essentially 'hire' something to get a job done. If it does the job well, when we are confronted with the same job, we hire that same product again."[11] I truly believe that no market is too saturated—if you're savvy enough to grasp unmet needs before others do (that is, to see the white space) and you create distinctive products to meet those needs.

EVANGELIZE

Share the passion behind your idea, whether it's crafting an elevator pitch or sharing the inspiration behind what you've created. Be the best cheerleader for your idea: explain the problem you're addressing, why people should care, and offer the solution or call to action. Those with this superpower are comfortable being the expert on a topic and telling a story in front of an audience. You believe so much in your idea that you champion it and advocate for yourself (and what your ideas need) in doing so.

ITERATE AND REFINE

Put yourself out in front with your idea, be open to the reactions, continue to improve upon your idea until it lives up to your vision, and build supporters along the way who feel invested in your success. Every time someone gives you feedback, it's an opportunity to engage them, because only those who care will share. Six months before I launched my company, I invited 200 people to my home (5 to 10 people each night for a month) to give me feedback on my business. I iterated around that feedback: my favorite was a college classmate who thought the original tagline for the company—Be Remembered (because you remember someone who has gravitas!)—felt like "rest in peace" and suggested Own Your Moment, which became the trademarked tagline for my company. It not only made the work better, but also allowed everyone to champion my company because they felt that they had their fingerprints on the process. And people raised their hands to help me, introducing me to magazine editors, being our first customers, and sharing our website with their friends and family when we launched the company.

One of my favorite artists, Henri Matisse, was known for painting over the same piece of art multiple times to abstract the details, and hence extract and strip back the truth. Conservationists found that underneath the swaths of red paint of his well-known piece *The Red*

Studio was a detailed scene of bright colors. Over many months, he kept reworking the art, writing about it in letters to patrons, and painting vermilion over large sections of it until it challenged our notions of illusion and space, making it a seminal, groundbreaking piece in modern-art history.

Transforming Life, Business, and the World

Visionary Mindy Grossman, former CEO of HSNi and WW International, has an abundance of strengths. Her superpowers are Creating, Leading, and Achieving (with strengths in Believing, Giving, and Knowing), which explains her extraordinary track record. She shared with me what she's learned in channeling her confidence language:

"The first thing you need to have is vision, and vision is not what's in front of you."

I'm innately curious, and I will immerse myself in something when it piques my curiosity. Then I close my eyes, block out the noise, see the field of what is happening and the opportunities that are not in the present, and I'm purposeful about what I want to do.

After transforming the Nike global apparel business, I decided it was time for a change. I made a list of what I wanted next that incorporated all of the things I was seeing before anyone else: I had the benefit of seeing what was happening in mobile and digital in countries like Japan in 2005 and saw how people were consuming content in a very different way. I then thought about, with brands consolidating and being captive to their distribution channels, how were entrepreneurs and new brands getting their message out? I like brands that can touch a lot of people and are aspirationally accessible. I knew I wanted to be a CEO and make an impact.

I got a call to run IAC Retail, the parent company of HSN. One night I was watching Food Network, and I switched over to HSN. Wolfgang Puck was connecting cooking with showing product. This light bulb went off: HSN could be Food Network–DIY-HGTV, and you can buy the product. I could bring in the ideas that I had seen abroad and create a place for brands to showcase their stories. I saw a vision that went against the grain and others didn't see yet.

"You can't let other people's judgment hold you back."

What I didn't process when I took the job is that I was the eighth CEO in 10 years, and the business was not doing well. I had come off of six years being one of the number twos at Nike, which meant when you went to a cocktail party, you were the cool kid. When it was announced that I was going to be the CEO of IAC Retail, people thought I had had a midlife crisis. At a cocktail party, someone came up to me and whispered, "I watch HSN." My response was "Why are you whispering? Are you embarrassed?" Fast forward, the company did well, and we took the company public. All of a sudden, you're the cool kid again.

"There's no room for complacency."

The biggest opportunity to rethink what you want is when everything is going well. You have to maximize opportunity, and that means not doing the same thing over and over. Boldness is the essence of transformation, and often not taking a risk can be riskier than taking a risk.

"Take the plunge. What's the worst thing that can happen?"

You have to advocate for yourself. Women have a tendency to think they have to be perfect before they ask for something. We think of all the scenarios in which something could go wrong: "If I do that, what's going to happen?" And then we make a list of the worst things that could happen and nearly talk ourselves out of it. But a man would say, "What's the worst thing that could happen?" I've never been truly qualified for any role I've ever taken, but I knew what I brought to every role and could hire others for what I didn't bring.

Next, put yourself out there; get involved in things beyond your own category early on in your career. When I got to HSN, one of the first things I did was to take a role on the board of the National Retail Federation, which was outside of my network at that time. Ultimately, I became the first woman chair in 100 years.

One more example that I hear all the time is "I'd love to meet that person." My response is, go ask to meet them! I leave time in my schedule every week to meet someone I've never met before or experience something I've never experienced before.

BELIEVING

- You are a calming force in groups.

- You expect good things will come and things will get better, even in the toughest of times.

- You believe everything happens for a reason; if it doesn't happen, it wasn't meant to be.

- Even in tough times, you're very hopeful about the future.

- When you face a setback, you give yourself to the universe and/or something greater than yourself.

- You practice gratitude (versus worrying about what you can't control).

- You usually see the best in every situation and other people.

This form of confidence comes from a hopeful place, one that is optimistic about the future. You believe that this world is the best of all possible worlds, and that good ultimately prevails. This belief powers your ability to live free from fear. Positive intent is the lens through which you see everyone and every situation; you can see the good in anything and that you yourself have the potential to be a force for good. A values orientation, idealism, and a sense of greater purpose underpin your motivations and allow you to never lose sight of what truly matters. Principled, wise, and intuitive, you focus on the best outcome, even when it's not easy or convenient, and seek a meaningful, purpose-filled path that leaves others and the world a better place.

You consult compassion in navigating toward solutions, because you are not judgmental. Tolerant and accepting, you are always willing to hear another person's story in a positive light versus finding fault. As a result, you rarely hold grudges and do not enjoy succeeding at other people's expense. You feel called upon to share the good things in your life, give credit where it's due, and uplift those around you.

Even in the toughest of times, you can remain calm and positive. It would not be unusual to hear these lines from you: "It's okay, we're going to get through this"; "It wasn't meant to be"; or "Life always has a bigger purpose in store for us." Your belief that in the end everything works out allows you to see things through in their own time, as opposed to forcing an outcome. Your optimism and sense of purpose allow you to recover from disappointment or let go of things you view as out of your control. There is a throughline of gratitude in how you view your life, recalling peaks rather than valleys as a way to power through to the next milestone.

When You Are at Your Best

Those with this trait score the highest at staying calm in bad situations and delivering bad news to someone because they have an ability to convey reassurance and optimism in these situations. You are one of the most capable in meeting new people with an open-minded and accepting nature. And when it comes to asking for favors, you do not shy away because you are motivated by a greater purpose. You are also one of the most adept at letting go of a disappointment or failure.

Notable Demographics

We see this trait cut across every age, demographic. and industry segment. What most stands out is that those with this trait are more likely to have experienced some form of loss, to have been fired or laid off from a job, or to have had an experience with addiction (their own or that of a loved one). Perhaps these setbacks—and getting through them—underpin their belief that better days lie ahead.

How to Steer Clear of Downsides

BEING SEEN AS TOO UNREALISTIC

"Those who see the world through rose-colored glasses sometimes miss red flags." While optimism and idealism are beautiful traits, they may overshadow realities. This unrealistic nature may at times frustrate those around you who may be seeking an acknowledgment of hardships versus being inundated with constant positivity. In return, if you have this mindset, you may feel hurt that others don't recognize your good intentions.

HOW TO COURSE-CORRECT

To balance your innate sense of optimism, it may help you to tap into your compassionate and empathetic nature and acknowledge a hardship before offering your positive take on a situation. As Brené Brown shares in *Atlas of the Heart*, "Compassion is fueled by understanding and accepting that we're all made of strength and struggle—no one is immune to pain or suffering. Compassion is not a practice of 'better than' or 'I can fix you'—it's a practice based in the beauty and pain of shared humanity." Sitting inside another's reality or being present to the darker sides of a situation may bring more impact and meaning to your efforts.

BEING TOO PASSIVE

Furthermore, you may have a propensity to see how things play out versus taking action in the face of reality. This is why this quality is so different from Achieving—those with an Achieving superpower keep pushing through with action and never give up, while those with Believing at their core are more inclined to let go.

HOW TO COURSE-CORRECT

So as not to be viewed as a pushover and sensitive, you can think through not only a positive outcome ahead, but also articulate the action steps to get there. You can reflect on and articulate your actions or plans in ensuring that things work out, so there is a sense of agency in the outcome. Executive coach and founder of Speaking Broadly Dana Cowin calls this *practical optimism*, and she shared with me, "I wake up every morning thinking: how can I make this a great day? I have a joy-seeking mindset. Though I definitely experience and acknowledge struggles and difficulties, I am able to hold on to the thought that I can take actions to ensure that things will improve."

What You Can Do to
Channel This Superpower

One of my favorite embodiments of the Believing mindset is from former Pepsico CEO Indra Nooyi, who credits her father with this advice:

Whatever anybody says or does, assume positive intent. You will be amazed at how your whole approach to a person or problem becomes very different. When you assume negative intent, you're angry. If you take away that anger and assume positive intent, you will be amazed. Your emotional quotient goes up because you are no longer random in your response. You don't get defensive. You don't scream. You are trying to understand and listen because at your basic core you are saying, "Maybe they are saying something to me that I'm not hearing."

PRACTICE "POSITIVE INTENT"

Think of someone you might be struggling to relate to, or whose behavior you haven't quite understood. With Believing as a superpower, you are able to ask the question, "What positive qualities do I see in this person? What are their good intentions toward me or the situation we face?" Applying this lens of positive intent empowers you to see the best in others and to work through problems to create solutions together. You can apply this same mindset to replaying setbacks or upsets in your life. When you rewind the tape and think through the good parts and the path those upsets put you on, are you able to see how the setbacks have led you to positive outcomes? After all, we can retrain our brain to remember these instances with strength and learning in mind.

WRITE A GRATITUDE LIST

Another way to practice this superpower is to practice gratitude, because seeing the best in things begins with a thankful appreciation for what you have, tangible and intangible. With gratitude, you can acknowledge the good in your life, and when you see sources of good outside of yourself, you are able to connect to something larger than us as individuals. This can apply to the past (positive memories of childhood), the present (not taking good fortune for granted), and the future (maintaining a hopeful attitude). In a study,[12] psychologists Dr. Robert A. Emmons and Dr. Michael E. McCullough asked participants to write a few sentences each week: one group wrote about things they were grateful for that had occurred during the week; a second group wrote about daily irritations; the third wrote about events that affected them (with no emphasis on

being positive or negative). After 10 weeks, those who wrote about gratitude were more optimistic and reported feeling better about their lives.
I practice this daily: on my commute to work, I reflect on three things
I'm grateful for; at the end of each day, I replay one peak highlight of my
day. I begin and end my days with gratitude.

LETTING GO

This is one of the qualities that can most help when dealing with losses
that have an element of finality—a breakup, a job loss, the death of a
loved one. Take a situation or relationship and reflect on the balance
sheet of holding on versus letting go. See the positives of letting go,
reflect on the wisdom you gained, and look ahead to better days to
come. As Ted Lasso said to a player reeling from a misstep, "You know
what the happiest animal in the world is? It's a goldfish. It's got a ten-
second memory."

Three Tips for Practical Optimism

One of my mentors, Dana Cowin, executive coach and founder of Speaking
Broadly, spent more than two decades at the helm of a major magazine.
Her leadership style is defined by the hallmarks of the Believing superpower
in its best form. Here is her advice on how to embody this quality:

"Suspend judgment."

When you find yourself being critical of someone else, pause and ask: *If I
believe this person has good intentions and is intelligent, how will I react?*
Proceeding with an open mind leads to better outcomes.

"Keep moving."

If something upsets you, instead of reliving and dwelling in the present disappointment, ask yourself what change you can make to the situation or
mindset that would have a positive result, then move toward that.

"Surround yourself with good energy."

Even as a practical optimist, I enhance my good energy by choosing to
spend time with people who are kind and supportive. No room for jerks.

SELF-SUSTAINING

- In group settings, you don't feel like you have to prove yourself or impress anyone.
- You rarely feel embarrassed.
- You do what you want without worrying about what others think.
- You're comfortable in your own skin.
- You don't feel intimidated or threatened by others.
- You don't feel the need to explain yourself.
- You rarely compare yourself to others.

This superpower is free of the need for external validation. You have a composed self-assurance that does not rely on praise; while validation is always welcome, it is not what drives you. You see the seat at the table as yours, without needing to explain and prove why you deserve it. Embodying WYSIWYG (what you see is what you get), you draw on a strong sense of self, and in its best form, an inner smile and swagger without arrogance. You know your worth and hence are not vulnerable to comparison, envy, and status-seeking. Simply put, you like yourself; you draw upon reserves of your own strength (instead of an inner critic, you have an inner cheerleader); and you never ask the question, "Am I good enough?" Because the answer is always "I am enough."

You are deeply self-compassionate, ably navigating your own balance sheet of assets and liabilities. You internally celebrate your fortes and accept your flaws. When you are criticized, you do not take it personally, almost as if you're coated in Teflon. You do not spiral or feel less-than; you acknowledge the feedback and decide how it best serves you. When upsets happen, you are undisturbed and can look inside yourself to replenish your energy and tackle the issue at hand. The dictum, ascribed to Eleanor Roosevelt, that you should do something that scares you every day? That's Self-Sustaining writ large. In fact, Eleanor Roosevelt continued by saying, "Do what you feel in your heart to be right—for you'll be criticized anyway. You'll be damned if you do, and damned if you don't." Self-possessed, you walk calmly into every situation without feeling intimidated; you can ask for what you want without feeling the need to explain, excuse, or defend. Those with this quality look back on their lives without regret or apologies, because they see their accumulated life experiences as the source of their strength and purpose. You take pride in how far you have come.

You are not compelled to be the loudest voice in the room because people pleasing is not your default. Rather than listing your achievements or impressing others with your status, you are deeply engaged in topics outside of yourself. As you live free of judgment, you extend that acceptance to those in your life. Furthermore, you do not expend energy wondering if someone likes you in return.

When You Are at Your Best

You are the most confident in asking for something—a favor, promotion, or raise—and doing it without competing for it or defending yourself with data. You score high in being comfortable with being criticized for something and staying calm in bad situations. Your self-assurance makes you capable and confident in almost every situation we asked about in our quantitative survey.

Notable Demographics

The Ted Lasso quote "You know how they say that youth is wasted on the young? Well, I say don't let the wisdom of age be wasted on you" may best explain why this quality is most expressed in women over the age of 55 (almost half of those with Self-Sustaining as a superpower are ages 55 to 75). She is also 50 percent more likely to be retired; having seen and experienced it all, she has the muscle memory to be comfortable with herself and not feel she has anything left to prove. My own mother is the manifestation of this ("At my age, I've seen and done almost everything. I don't need to impress anyone!").

How to Steer Clear of Downsides

COMING OFF AS ARROGANT OR ALOOF

There's a fine line between self-assured and arrogant, between composed and aloof—and no one risks crossing it more readily than those with this quality. On its own, this superpower has the potential to turn off others; since you don't feel the need to charm, you can come across as disinterested and reserved.

HOW TO COURSE-CORRECT

With this quality, it's important for you to communicate something you care about outside of yourself: what you believe in or stand for, such as a passion for making the world better or making others feel seen. Since you don't feel the need to sell yourself, you can share your values, not your accomplishments, as a way to connect. And when a goal or project lines up with your beliefs, no one is more motivated than you—not by the achievement, but by how it lights you up inside.

STEAMROLLING

In the moments when you assert yourself, you may not feel the need to defend or explain your point of view. While you are comfortable charging ahead without worrying about what others think, this may result in crossing the line from being assertive to being overly demanding.

HOW TO COURSE-CORRECT

You should call on the empathetic qualities of the Giving or Believing superpowers to understand how others might react to your directness. It's important for you to consider how others might feel about the situation and, when necessary, to explain your reasoning—not to defend, but to engage others. What may come most naturally to you is nurturing relationships one-on-one with authenticity, so you do not feel that you are performing for an audience.

What You Can Do to
Channel This Superpower

ACKNOWLEDGE YOUR WORTH

This quality starts with internally owning your worth and placing value in your own opinions. Know who you are and rely on yourself to know what is true about you. If it helps, write a list of everything you like about yourself—whatever comes to mind immediately or perhaps look at your quiz results. How hard was it? Keep adding to this list every day until you feel comfortable with it.

TURN FEEDBACK INTO A GIFT

You can channel this quality by better dealing with feedback or upsets and not giving your power away. Mahatma Gandhi's mantra "Nobody can hurt me without my permission" is a call to action for us to unclutter our minds of worries about what others think of us. When we are less concerned with the personal element of likability, we know who we are, and we can focus on the feedback's constructive elements to improve a situation. This quality is the antidote to spiraling because we can tie ourselves to our own self-worth and not become victims of our perception of someone else's judgment; feedback is no longer a stick of dynamite, but rather a gift.

SHIFT THE ENERGY AWAY FROM PEOPLE-PLEASING

I am personally working on becoming more proficient in Self-Sustaining. I am a people pleaser who cares about what others think, and I tend to fall back on my default mode of Performing when I am at a party where I don't know very many people. I am now practicing what I call the "Dinner Party Challenge." When I have an event to go to, I remind myself that I don't need to prove that I deserve to be at this party; I've already been invited. I don't need to impress anyone, and I am enough. I expend less effort in talking about myself (what I think people will be impressed by, recounting stories so I can be validated and appreciated) and most of the effort engaged in the quality of the conversation and others' interests. In making this shift, I free up the energy that I typically expend on trying to be liked and deploy that energy into being fully present and enjoying every interaction.

USE THE SORRY-COUNTER

The Toastmasters have a practice called the "Ah-Counter" that takes note of any overused words or filler sounds (ah, um, er, you know) used as a crutch by anyone who speaks during a meeting. Inspired by this, I am creating a "Sorry-Counter" because I believe we say sorry too often as a default, and that word should only be used when we've truly done something wrong. Take a day and record how many times you say the word. My hypothesis is that 99 percent of that time we have nothing to be sorry for. As Mika Brzezinski highlighted, "My salary situation at Morning Joe wasn't right. I made five attempts to fix it, then realized I'd made the same mistake every time: I apologized for asking." She says, "I think women have a hard time not apologizing their way into negotiations. We tend to back into these conversations in a self-deprecating and ultimately self-defeating way."[13]

A NEW WAY TO SEE THE WORLD

Now that you have read about your individual strengths, let's see how we fit into the bigger picture. The vocabulary you are learning here can become an empowering tool for not only how we see ourselves, but also how we can understand the power dynamics women face in a broader context. It can explain not only where we are today and where we want to go as individuals, but also how we can collectively change our narrative.

Let's start with the overall view: more than 80 percent of the women we surveyed have at least one superpower. The average number of superpowers is two, and only 2 percent of women have all eight superpowers. The chart below shows us the percentage of women who have each quality as a superpower (we can have more than one superpower, so the total percentage is more than 100 percent—we are greater than the sum of our parts!).

Superpower Frequency
% of Women Surveyed

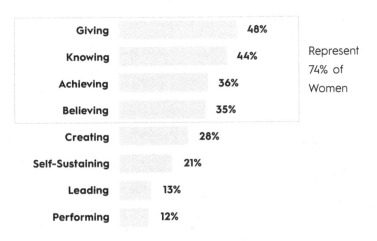

Giving	48%
Knowing	44%
Achieving	36%
Believing	35%
Creating	28%
Self-Sustaining	21%
Leading	13%
Performing	12%

Represent 74% of Women

A majority of women we surveyed—74 percent—self-identified as having Giving, Knowing, Achieving, or Believing as their top qualities. The most frequent combinations among women were ones that featured these four superpowers:

Giving + Knowing
Giving + Achieving
Giving + Believing
Achieving + Knowing

Based on what you now know about these four qualities, I'm sure it will not be surprising that these are the top 10 situations in which women we surveyed feel MOST comfortable and capable:

"I am most capable or comfortable in being able to handle this situation . . ."

1. Getting tasks/projects done

2. Comforting someone who is sad or dealing with loss

3. Admitting when I am wrong

4. Defending an answer with data

5. Explaining or defending my ideas

6. Starting a new project

7. Working on a very tight deadline or under pressure

8. Staying calm in bad situations

9. Coming up with a new idea

10. Dealing with the illness of a family member

Looking at this list, we can see the incredible contributions women make in the world—and how they connect to the inherent strengths we naturally exhibit. As my best friend, Tekla, says, "We are the doers who give out the hugs." If we dig into the reasons why women feel most comfortable getting tasks/projects done and are effective at working on a very tight deadline or under pressure or starting a new project, it's because there is such a high frequency of Giving, Knowing, and Achieving superpowers among women overall. These superpowers drive this outcome, but from different motivations: those with a Giving superpower get things done because others are depending upon them; Knowing, because it's the logical thing to do; and Achieving, because there is satisfaction in a measurable outcome. This is why so many women come up to me and say their superpower is "getting shit done"!

Similarly, because Giving and Believing qualities are highly present in the population of women we surveyed, comforting others and staying calm are hallmarks of what we do for others. It reminds me of one of my favorite paintings, Winslow Homer's *The Gale*. Most of Homer's body of work is landscapes and paintings depicting men struggling against the elements as a metaphor for societal oppression. By contrast, his paintings depicting women always show women persevering against nature. In *The Gale*, he paints a British fisherwoman with a baby strapped to her back, walking on a seashore with her right arm bent and lifted at shoulder height and her left hand cradled around her child. She heads directly into the wind with strength and force. It is the visual embodiment of something my mother always says: "When tsunamis happen, men make speeches. Women clean up the beaches."

While we are focused on getting things done and nurturing those around us, this data also demonstrates how we don't take credit for it. The deficit mindset, which we described in Chapter 2, is well represented here. We readily admit when we are wrong, and we feel the need to defend and explain our answers. These behaviors are the shadow sides of both Giving and Knowing: those with Giving as a superpower underplay their accomplishments and work hard to compensate for their perceived gaps; the Knowing quality drives a defensive mode shielded by knowledge and data. This may explain why "sorry" is a default response for so many of us. It's in our nature to admit our flaws.

In fact, here are the top 10 situations that women overall are LEAST comfortable and capable of addressing:

1. Being criticized for something I did

2. Public speaking/giving a speech

3. Asking for a raise

4. Asking for a promotion

5. Telling a story in front of an audience

6. Starting my own business

7. Letting go of a disappointment or failure

8. Asking for a favor

9. Going to an event where I don't know anyone

10. Selling someone on a plan or idea

Those with Giving, Achieving, or Knowing as their primary super-power struggle with putting themselves out there, from self-advocacy to public-facing activities. Because these qualities represent the largest portion of the population and the most frequent combinations, they reflect many of the issues women struggle with in personal and professional settings. And yet, these are all situations that those with Self-Sustaining, Leading, or Performing superpowers are adept at handling. Translation? The qualities needed to ably navigate these moments represent the smallest portion of our survey population—33% of women have any one of these three qualities as their superpower. To demonstrate this, on the next page you will find a chart that represents the top 10 situations in which women with these three qualities feel MOST capable and comfortable.

In fact, women with Leading, Performing, or Self-Sustaining traits are two to three times more capable and confident than the average woman in every situation across the board. Yet only a third of us spike on one or more of these traits.

With the majority of women having Achieving, Giving, Knowing, or Believing as their dominant quality, it means that we underestimate ourselves in many situations, such as public speaking, leading meetings, or asking for a favor. Yet we are super comfortable in admitting

Self-Sustaining	Leading	Performing
1. Asking for a favor	1. Public speaking/ giving a speech	1. Telling a story in front of an audience
2. Asking for a promotion	2. Telling a story in front of an audience	2. Public speaking/ giving a speech
3. Staying calm in bad situations	3. Asking for a promotion	3. Starting my own business
4. Leading a project	4. Recovering from a loss or disappointment	4. Selling someone on a plan or idea
5. Starting my own business	5. Managing people/telling others what to do	5. Raising money for a business or charity
6. Asking for a raise	6. Raising money for a business or charity	6. Asking for a promotion
7. Selling someone on a plan or idea	7. Asking for a raise	7. Going to an event where I don't know anyone
8. Being criticized for something I did	8. Having to be the expert on a topic	8. Having to be the expert on a topic
9. Meeting new people	9. Writing a story or creating a piece of art	9. Delivering bad news to someone
10. Going to an event where I don't know anyone	10. Going to an event where I don't know anyone	10. Giving advice or coaching others

our flaws and doing all the work. This may explain why only one out of four women we surveyed are highly satisfied in their personal life and professional life (in a current job or the last job they had if they are now a full-time parent).[14]

Those satisfaction levels are meaningfully different for women with different superpowers. The most satisfied women are those with

Leading, Self-Sustaining, or Performing superpowers, especially in being appreciated by their boss, and in being recognized and rewarded for their efforts (awards, promotions, pay, benefits). By contrast, those with Achieving, Giving, or Knowing as their dominant traits—a majority of women—felt much less satisfied on the same dimensions (on many dimensions, almost half the satisfaction rate of those with Leading, Self-Sustaining, or Performing superpowers). Where women felt most satisfied overall, regardless of their superpower, was in being appreciated by people who worked for them and their peers (50 to 75 percent satisfied), in their relationship with their significant other at home (50 percent), and in the actual work they did (40 percent). The true gap, therefore, is the chasm between the groups on overall satisfaction, specifically in being recognized, rewarded, and appreciated by their boss.

This Is an "And" Not an "Or" Story

What does this all say about where we are today, and where we want to go? Two things have to happen simultaneously.

1. Expand the definition of success.

We need to acknowledge the asymmetrical systems of power that have driven the outcomes we read about above. As I shared in Chapters 1 and 2, our society has promoted a singular definition of confidence, and systems have been built around it. Dr. Tomas Chamorro-Premuzic's research highlights the paradox of incompetent but highly confident men becoming leaders over women who have deep emotional intelligence: "Arrogance and confidence are inversely related to leadership talent—the ability to build and maintain high-performing teams and to inspire followers to set aside their selfish agendas in order to work for the common interest of the group." He continues by sharing that the bigger problem is the lack of career obstacles for incompetent, highly confident men because we tend to "equate leadership with the very psychological features that make the average man a more inept leader than the average woman."[15] Maddening, isn't it? There is a triple standard we have to meet: women must be confident, competent, and emotionally intelligent (for which we don't get any credit). Add to this that a majority of women have Knowing or Achieving as their dominant trait, and both of those qualities value and believe in structure and systems. How disheartening, then, is it to realize the demographic or subjective biases at play in the creation and administration of these systems?

We need to expand the narrative and the equation by which we define success, for ourselves and for those who see us. We must open our eyes to the incredible strengths a majority of women have, especially with Giving, Knowing, Achieving, and Believing. Because these qualities deliver a potent double punch: extraordinary competence (Knowing, Achieving) and engaging emotional intelligence (Giving, Believing). In a comprehensive review of studies, social psychologist Alice Eagly and her colleagues at Northwestern University showed that female managers are more likely to elicit respect and pride from their followers, empower and mentor subordinates, approach problem-solving in a more flexible and creative way, and fairly reward direct reports.[16]

It's imperative that those in positions of power recognize and celebrate these attributes. That will come through cultural mindset shifts and concrete levers aligning rewards and recognition with this fuller picture of skills. At the same time, we individually need to believe in our strengths and advocate for them. Because we already have evidence that women drive better outcomes—a 2020 McKinsey study shows how gender diversity drives performance: companies in the top quartile of gender diversity on executive teams were 25 percent more likely to experience above-average profitability than peer companies in the fourth quartile.[17] Looks like our most frequent superpowers carry great value.

I recognize that this broader cultural shift toward an inclusive approach to confidence will take time. As we know, seismic change doesn't happen overnight. My grandfather once told me that he believed social change takes two generations, because the generation today is not held back by the past that they never experienced. The example he used was that Japanese was spoken when he was a child in Taiwan during Japan's occupation of the island, but I didn't speak Japanese because the occupation had ended more than a quarter century before I was born. I believe change is possible: think of how millennials ushered in a wave of activism on behalf of victims of racism and sexual harassment. The recent pandemic highlighted women's natural abilities to nurture and be supportive in the workplace—it was the right strategy at the right time, as it saved many companies during an extraordinary and unprecedented global event. Yet it came with a paradox: women were the ones disproportionately affected,[18] and the pandemic may have regressed the progress toward gender equality.[19] It will take time for us to see all eight of these traits as equal in their power and impact.

2. . . . AND level up to win today.

While all this seismic change is taking place, we need to succeed in the present, within the current systems of how our culture evaluates who is confident and who is not. How do we do this exactly? By channeling new skills to increase our capability level today so we can ace those self-advocating and public-facing moments in which women are least comfortable. And I know we can. A particularly interesting trend we noticed in our data was that the cocktail of strengths changed as women aged. For example, we saw that as working women moved up the career ladder into more senior levels, their average number of superpowers went from two to three or four. In the move from junior to mid-level positions, the superpowers most often added were Leading or Knowing. From mid-level to senior positions, the most often added traits were Leading, Performing, Creating, or Self-Sustaining, with women becoming more self-assured and creative with the wisdom of experience and the desire for reinvention.

The qualities that most level up our comfort across the board are Leading, Performing, Self-Sustaining, and to some extent, Creating. Adding any one of these qualities to your arsenal of skills is cumulative—you will be better equipped for this current world system. Adding Leading, Performing, or Self-Sustaining to any of these combinations amplifies confidence levels in every situation and increases satisfaction levels by two- to three-fold. The work I am advocating is an "and" and not an "or"; we must expand society's definition of confidence and we need to acquire skills that can help us in the present. Most of us do not need to be Leading and Performing all the time, but becoming proficient at these skills for situations we want to master will help us go much further today.

Let me be clear: I am angry about this. You may be too after reading it. You may be sitting there thinking, "After all I read, you are asking us to play the game?!" We've been bringing a tennis racket to a baseball diamond, and until we can change the game we're playing, we've got to swing a bat. Perhaps this is why Sheryl Sandberg, the former COO of Facebook (now Meta), believes we are falling short in giving young girls the tools to lead, and why she is advocating for us to train them on Leading skills sooner. Similarly, this may also explain why many women decide to strike out on their own as entrepreneurs (as we will share later in the book, starting your own business requires channeling Creating, Leading, Performing, and Self-Sustaining superpowers).

One of my mentors, Jennifer Justice, founder and CEO of The Justice Dept., an advisory firm advocating for female talent and executives, has nine-year-old twins, Jack and Nico. She recently relayed to me a story that illustrates this: On the twins' ninth birthday, she offered them both their own individual day to celebrate. When she asked what they each wanted to do, her son, Jack, spoke up immediately: "I want to go to the water park with two friends." When she turned to Nico, her daughter wavered indecisively, which surprised Jennifer as Nico is the more out-going of the pair. When pressed, Nico shared concerns about having an extra friend to invite and how expensive the water park was (even though she also wanted to go there). Jennifer was stunned that her daughter was talking herself out of what she really wanted and responded, "You get zero percent of what you don't ask for. If you want to go to the water park, I will go twice." (Bonus reinforcement for Nico for speaking up: Jennifer took Nico and her friends on a Friday to the water park. The next day, Nico got to go again on Jack's day because of a childcare cov-erage issue.) Jennifer also told me that Jack will brag about a soccer goal for days. But "I have to find out through the school newsletter that Nico gave a speech during school elections about equal rights. She didn't tell me about it until I showed her that the school principal had recognized her great speech."

Adding on these superpowers to the gifts most of us already pos-sess equips us to address the current "triple standard" women face. My dear friend, Ene Riisna, the first woman producer at WCBS New York, recounted a story to me about a trip she took to Italy in the 1990s, where she first encountered the phrase *la donna importante*. That is, in Italian culture, men marginalized most women and only a subset of women—*la donna importante*—were deemed powerful as a triple threat: she was more capable than a man, had the nurturing qualities of motherhood, and led with authority. Ene went on to share with me how condescending and maddening it was that in this construct, men decided who was important, that most women were deemed inconsequential, and the bar was so high for who the men were forced to accept as "importante" in business and socially. The reality is, as Margarita Mayo's work highlights, how unfair it is that we have to lead at a highly competent level, and with warmth.

Let's look at this from the reverse perspective, minus the warmth factor. In our survey population, a portion of women had Leading + Self-Sustaining (5 percent), Leading + Performing (5 percent), or Performing + Self-Sustaining (5 percent) as their only superpower combinations. A former female executive at a Fortune 50 company shared this story: All of the executives were asked to take a leadership self-assessment. Most of the women leaders identified with qualities akin to Giving, Achieving, and Knowing. Only two women leaders had "commanding" qualities as their primary. One was labeled as demanding and cold, one was labeled as all charm and no substance; neither is still with the company despite delivering stellar results.

Where We Go from Here

The work that lies ahead reminds me of the 2015 #LikeAGirl commercial for Always, the hygiene brand. The commercial starts with asking older girls and boys what it means to run, throw, and fight "like a girl," and they express stereotypical reactions that mock and demean what it means to do something "like a girl." The interviewer then asks young girls ages 10 and under to demonstrate how they run, throw, and fight "like a girl," and these girls, not yet old enough to be conditioned to gender stereotypes, respond with powerful determination and vigor. The point? From age 10 to 12, girls' self-esteem plummets, and our culture is dismissive about it ("When did 'like a girl' become an insult?"). When the older girls and boys are shown the video footage of the younger girls, they're taken aback, recognizing their culpability in perpetuating the insult.

Interviewer: *What advice do you have to young girls who are told they run "like a girl," kick "like a girl," hit "like a girl," swim "like a girl?"*

Participant: *Keep doing it 'cause it's working. If somebody else says "running 'like a girl,'" or "kicking 'like a girl,'" or "shooting 'like a girl'" is something that you shouldn't be doing, that is their problem. Because if you're still scoring, and you're still getting to the ball on time, and you're still being first, you're doing it right. It doesn't matter what they say. I mean yes, I kick "like a girl," and I swim "like a girl," and I walk "like a girl," and I wake up in the morning "like a girl," because I am a girl. And that is not something that I should be ashamed of. So I'm gonna do it anyway. That's what they should do.*

At the end of the commercial, the older girls are then asked, "If I asked you to run like a girl, would you do it differently?" The response: "I would run like myself." And the second time around, they run and punch with forceful enthusiasm. The ad's narrative holds society at large—and women as individuals—both accountable for progress.

All eight forms of gravitas are equal, valid, and special. We each have a unique combination of them (256 combinations to be exact), and we deserve to be seen and celebrated for them. I truly hope our society evolves to this more complete and inclusive view of confidence. Because if we do embrace what makes us uniquely special at our core and get credit for it, it will empower us to be courageous, compassionate, and connected—and to overcome the forces that hold us back. This is the work we will delve into in the next chapter: acknowledging, owning, harnessing, and deploying the power of our strengths.

At the same time, I want us to win now. To do that, we have to identify the situations we want to conquer and acknowledge the superpower that's needed today that we might not have (most often Leading, Performing, Self-Sustaining, and Creating). The layering effect of applying new skills where we have gaps today in specific situations we want to master can be powerful. I'm not asking us to be all the same and be all of these eight qualities at once at the highest level, because we all have different aspirations, situations, and relationships we are navigating (although 2 percent of women have all eight superpowers, and this group is the most capable and confident in our entire data set). At the very least, I want to give you the tools to better read others and situations, master the qualities that will get you what you want in the situations that matter to you, and do it in your own way with authenticity and from a rock-solid foundation made up of your existing strengths. This is what we will explore in Chapters 6 and 7.

Part III

LEAD FROM WITHIN

PUTTING YOUR CAPE ON

One of my favorite films is *The Matrix*. The plot centers around Neo, a coder who is told that the world he lives in is a computer-generated construct, and artificial intelligence (the Matrix) has subdued humans as an energy source. But beneath this world is a "real" world in which he is believed to be The One who will free mankind. Early on, he's given a choice to take a blue pill to stay in his current state controlled by the Matrix or a red pill to be awakened to the world as it really is (similar to the choice to embrace self-confidence). After making the choice, he is told by an oracle that he's not The One; he falters in his first attempt to manipulate the Matrix by failing to jump from one building's rooftop to another, and he doubts himself. It's not until the end of the movie, when he stops bullets fired at him by Matrix agents, that he starts to see the world as it really is in a shower of green computer lines, finally believes he's The One, and embraces his powers.

Making the Unconscious Conscious

The Matrix is a nod to Plato's "Allegory of the Cave," an ancient story that speaks to the power of finding out something that changes your perception forever. This is the same concept behind Carl Jung's famous quip about making the unconscious conscious: "The psychological rule says that when an inner situation is not made conscious it happens outside, as fate. That is to say, when the individual remains undivided and does not become conscious of his inner opposite, the world must perforce [necessarily] act out the conflict and be torn into opposing halves."[1]

What does this mean for you? To start, each day affords you many opportunities to put your superpowers to use. Your quiz results helped to make you conscious of which superpowers you have. You can name them, see them, and acknowledge them. Just like Neo when he made the choice to "wake up" and see the world differently and finally believe in his powers, once you see your confidence language, you can't unsee it. You now have a whole new world open for you to explore. Together, we will do three things: one, recognize this strength in you; two, understand what your confidence language's power can mean for you; and three, take credit for it. This is about being vulnerable to our strengths and seeing our own power and agency, not in relationship to others, but to ourselves.

Believe in Your Superpowers

We often have a hard time receiving compliments because we are in a deficit mindset, seeing only our weaknesses or not believing what's being said about us, or we feel the need to be humble. I want you to break this habit. This is the moment to pay yourself a compliment and take pride in its truth. How do we do that? Think about a time when you were at your peak: a moment when you felt you had it all together, you were "in the zone," everything seemed to flow and go right, and you felt your performance was exceptional. Put yourself in the center of this memory and recall as many details as possible. Now, rewind the tape in slow motion and see the connection to your quiz results. Ask yourself, what things about your character led to that positive result? What specific skills did you employ to create this peak moment? How did your superpowers drive that positive outcome?

When I took the quiz, I connected my results to a specific memory from when I was still working at McKinsey & Company. There was a client we were helping launch a new business venture in South America.

The CEO was in his 80s at the time, a high-energy entrepreneur who had started his business 50 years prior from scratch. He was charismatic, idea-driven, and not concerned with practical details because he trusted his team to implement and execute. When we were working on our final presentation, which at that point was 50 pages filled with charts and figures, I told my team, "We can't show Mr. B. this current deck and think he is going to get excited to approve launching this new business. He doesn't care what the financial model says. He wants to see the vision and be excited by it." We instead prepared 10 slides that I presented as if it were a *Shark Tank* pitch, with an energizing narrative about the untapped market opportunity, what this new venture could do, and who it would help. I showed him the dream, not the bottom line (although we had done the work to ensure that there would be an attractive return on investment). After the presentation was finished, he stood up and cheered and approved the deal immediately. In replaying this highlight reel, I could pinpoint with clarity my superpowers in action: Leading (setting the direction for my team), Performing (pitching the idea), and Creating (crafting a bold vision to embark on a new whitespace opportunity).

This peak performance exercise not only is a useful tool for self-reflection, but also can be an empowering one to use with others. I often kick off my speaking engagements by asking the audience to put themselves in the center of a peak moment in their lives. It sets the stage for a cycle of positive thinking that breaks us out of our deficit mindsets.

It's one thing to tell yourself what your strengths are; it's even more powerful to connect those strengths to real life moments. Going backward can help connect the dots between what your talents are and the results that you've achieved, helping you see that your superpowers drive many things in your life. The Pixar film *Inside Out* gives us a glimpse of the inner workings of our minds: Our brain is like a hard drive, with a fixed capacity for what it can remember—memories of our daily activities are typically discarded (for example, I don't remember what I had for lunch yesterday). However, the brain is programmed to remember the highest peaks and lowest valleys; in the film, this is represented by "core memories," glowing orbs that form the basis of what makes us tick. The golden orbs are the positive core memories. These are the ones that will give you insight into the concrete nature of your superpowers and form the basis of your belief in them. This knowledge is vitally important, because now we know that future milestones and accomplishments will hit those same markers and tap into your distinctive capabilities. Once you see how it worked for you in the past and the reserves of power you already have within you, you can believe in it.

Own Your Confidence Language

Emma always thought of herself as a quitter. She felt that way when, at 16, she quit her ill-fitting Filene's department store job where the young woman was placed in the men's custom suit department; she felt that way when she gave up modeling in high school after her father shelled out hard-earned money to build up her portfolio; and she felt that way in college, when she quit the crew team. Her dad, a 30-year Navy vet, was of a generation in which you stayed in a job for your whole career, and his voice would run in a loop in her head every time she thought about quitting. The mere thought of disappointing her father prompted her to stick it out in an entry-level job at an interior design firm for six years—a job she did not enjoy and that had limited opportunities for promotion.

In 2017, married and now in her 40s with school-age kids, Emma pursued a master's degree in special education. She eagerly took a fourth-grade assistant teacher position soon after she graduated, excited that her professional life was finally coming together. "I was putting my classroom together, and I realized all those jobs I'd 'quit' had helped me prepare for where I was today. I knew how to take crud off the floor because I cleaned people's homes. I knew how to handle kids because of all my babysitting gigs and having my own children. From my interior design job, I knew how to put my room together to make it feel cozy and welcoming." She felt everything starting to click into place. But things changed when she was put in a class with a difficult senior teacher who was hard to please. Everything Emma did seemed to be wrong. She soon questioned if she was cut out to be a teacher, but whenever that thought crossed her mind, an uneasy feeling would wash over her. It was the voice of her father telling her, "You're such a quitter." She moved around, teaching different grades to find the right fit, and then the COVID-19 pandemic hit, the workload doubled, and she was working seven days a week answering to angry, frustrated parents and trying her best to motivate children within a 2D virtual format. The stress was so high that she often cried after classes and started having gastrointestinal issues.

"My husband would tell me I was too sensitive, or my sister would tell me that I was taking it too personally," she shared. She persevered as she second-guessed her new career. But then something happened. She was watching the stand-up comedy special *Nanette*, in which Hannah Gadsby recounted a story about an audience member who came up to her after one show to debate her on a topic she covered in her set. Things got heated, but she held her own, she said. He finally quipped back to her, exasperated, "Oh, you're being too sensitive."

Whoa, Emma thought. *That is what everybody tells me all the time.* She continued to watch, and Hannah elaborated on how her sensitivity is part of who she is, and that is exactly what it means to be human.

"Why is insensitivity something to strive for? I happen to know that my sensitivity is my strength. It's helped me navigate through a very difficult path in my life. So, when someone tells me to stop being so sensitive, I feel like a nose being lectured by a fart—not the problem."

Everything clicked for Emma in that moment. She realized Giving is her superpower: "If I weren't this sensitive, I wouldn't have the empathy I need to be a special-ed teacher. That's my superpower." After all the years of being told she was thin-skinned, as if it were a bad thing, she realized it was the best thing about her. She could feel and empathize with others on a level that others couldn't, which is one of the makings of a standout teacher and mentor. She also realized she wasn't a quitter; she had Believing as a unique talent. She was well-attuned to things that were not healthy for her and was able to let go of them. She saw the positive, cumulative effect of her experiences putting her on the best path for her.

Emma reframed her narrative through the lens of her strengths and stepped into her power. She owned it, versus being apologetic or defensive about what made her uniquely her. So much so that she now shares what she learned with others, teaching graduate courses in education at a local college. In her course, she shows that clip from *Nanette* that changed her life, telling her students, "This is what makes me a good teacher."

Wherever or however your superpowers come to light, once you believe in them, you can step into them so that your confidence takes shape. To help you do this, I recommend what I call the "Week of Gravitas" exercise. For a week, reflect each day on how your superpowers played out in your daily life. It's what James Clear has made so clear (pun intended) in his astounding book *Atomic Habits:* every time you do something, it's a vote for the person you want to be. You may say to yourself "I want to be a healthy person." So, you wake up and go to the gym at 8:15. That morning, the very fact that you showed up and did that is a vote for the person you want to be. And the more you cast votes for that person by showing up at the gym versus snoozing your alarm and staying in bed, the more likely you are that person. On the next page is my "Week of Gravitas" grid as an example.

We can see the power in our contributions to everyday moments and the beauty in small details. A strength that I demonstrate to some degree is Giving, and I realized how this was a part of my daily rhythm:

- I helped a tourist with directions, walking her halfway to her destination.

- When my friend asked to be picked up from the doctor, I was glad to help. Because she was still groggy from anesthesia, I fetched her prescription and tussled with the insurance company to make sure her drugs were covered.

- I baked Ted Lasso "Biscuits with the Boss" shortbread cookies for my team.

There's a sense of pride that takes over when you own your superpowers. In many ways, this is the Self-Sustaining quality in action—those with this quality believe that they are enough; they know what they bring to the table and acknowledge it. As Mindy Grossman shared with me, "You have to have ultimate belief in yourself, because why is someone going to believe in you if you can't believe in yourself?"

Deploy Your Superpowers

Let's go back to my equation for courage from Chapter 1: having self-belief that spurs action and then reviewing the results of that action in a

	Leading	Performing	Creating
Monday	Weekly team meeting to review priorities vis-à-vis overall plan; shared the objectives for this quarter		
Tuesday		Presentation to pitch new distribution partner (signed the deal!)	
Wednesday			Blocked out a half day for ideation session with design team to discuss new collection
Thursday	Check-in with team to problem-solve and troubleshoot roadblocks. Fabric delay; called supplier.		
Friday		Happy hour with college friends to debrief on the week	
Saturday	Hosted monthly meeting with college women's alumni group on the topic of "bamboo ceilings"	Hosted monthly meeting with college women's alumni group on the topic of "bamboo ceilings"	
Sunday			Weekly museum visit with digital detox

way that reinforces self-belief to do it all again. Now that we have the foundation of self-belief firmly established, we can act on it.

Let me take you back to March 2020. I run a women's workwear business, and workplaces were closed, with employees sent home. Fears abounded—fear of getting sick, anxiety about the state of the world, the stress of sheltering in place. Gravitas sales were not zero; they were negative. We have a 30-day return policy, so customers who had recently purchased a dress for an upcoming event, conference, meeting, or date night returned their items when they realized they had nowhere to go. Our factories in China had been closed since January; activities in our New York City factory and office ground to a halt.

When upsets happen, our brain defaults to the "amygdala hijack." The amygdala is the most primitive part of our brain—every animal on the planet has an amygdala—and it controls our flight, fight, or freeze impulses, our physiological reactions to perceived danger. In prehistoric times, this would be a reaction to a perceived threat like being chased by a predator. This primordial part of the brain is the first to arrive at the party, whether it's a looming deadline, being criticized for something you did, getting stuck in traffic, or, on a more serious note, being in the throes of a divorce or a victim of emotional abuse. It takes at least 10 seconds for the neocortex, the reasoning part of the brain, to arrive and engage in thoughtful problem-solving (this is why parents tell their children to count to 10 when they're angry). Asking questions in the face of a perceived threat often provides enough time to trigger the appropriate neural response that engages the neocortex.

In the face of our business collapsing, I literally told our team to hit the pause button, to count to 10, and then I asked them a series of questions: "What are our superpowers? What do we have that no one else has right now? Who needs us most in this moment?" When you take stock of your distinctive capabilities and assets, you can deploy them to say, "Here's how I can help" (versus the "Do you need help?" question you get in a store, to which the default answer is: "No, I'm just browsing"). Here were the answers my team gave me:

"We have two thousand yards of Japanese premium quilters' cotton sitting in the New York City warehouse sent to us by one of our partner companies, Tokki, and The New York Times *just said quilters' cotton is good for cloth face masks."*

"Our sewing team is willing to work. Some of them even have machines at home."

"A local hospital needs hospital gowns, and our factory in China is about to reopen. They have capacity because most apparel orders were cancelled for this season."

"A food distribution warehouse in Newark just called to see if we could get them 5,000 cloth face masks for their workers."

"One of our best customers just called and asked if we would be willing to make 50 face masks for her co-workers, who are essential and still going into the office."

So we got to work on April 3, 2020. For 72 days without a break, we manufactured and distributed hospital gowns and cloth face masks to essential workers and our community.

And we did it with a team brimming with superpowers. When the pandemic hit, we took stock of what we were able to do as a company, but what really got us through this time was how our individual superpowers laddered up to what we could do together. First of all, I am the best at Creating, Leading, and Performing. I can make something from nothing. I see possibility. I'm resourceful. I can rally us in a new direction. I can share on social media what we're doing and get people to help us. You need hospital gowns and face masks? We can do that. Second, our head designer, Aruk, is the best at Achieving and Believing. There were many times when I felt like giving up, but he is the master of resilience and optimism. He never gave up on us. He saw the positive in the situation and reinforced that we were doing the right thing ("We are so lucky to be able to work and help others right now!"). Third, our production manager, Kelly, is the best at Knowing and Self-Sustaining. She came in and organized the spreadsheets for production, managed the processes effectively (a challenge when our warehouse was working at partial capacity), and, every day, never doubted that we would make it through. The quality everyone on our team shares to some degree? Giving. Not surprising that we pivoted our company not with profits in minds, but purpose in our hearts.

Entrepreneurs use the word "pivot" a lot. I looked it up in the dictionary, and to my surprise, the word has very little to do with the change in direction you're taking. Rather, it's the central pin on which you turn. And the stronger that central point is, the more capable you are of turning. Strengths give us the fuel to be speedboats and not aircraft carriers, especially in the face of setbacks.

This is how acting on your confidence language can create space for you to do incredible things. If we had not been deeply aware of what we were capable of, and the best at, we would have been out of business. And deploying your superpowers is a muscle that gets stronger over time. I know that we are better off today than we were before the pandemic, more capable of taking on the next challenge ahead. And the combination of our team's superpowers balanced out the downsides of each of our individual confidence languages. Case in point: Kelly's ability to organize processes effectively offsets my inability to complete tedious tasks; my resourcefulness and communication skills provide clear direction for my team in the face of uncertainty.

With our confidence languages, we can more proactively seek out and create opportunities. We can raise our hands rather than waiting to respond. We can align our lives around our superpowers, the qualities that bring out the best in us and give us great joy. The clearest example of this? The full-time parent who used to work. A majority of these women we surveyed had Achieving, Giving, Believing, or Knowing as their dominant traits. Of this group, most were dissatisfied with their lives (less than 20 percent were highly satisfied versus over 33 percent of working parents). They missed many elements of the workplace:

Question: What, if anything, do you miss about working outside the home?

"The satisfaction that comes with accomplishing goals and projects that others in the company depend on being done on time and doing them well. I also miss the socialization. As a stay-at-home mom, it can be lonely sometimes."

"I miss being mentally challenged and having the daily opportunity to be a positive influence on others' lives."

"Feeling accomplished and like what I did mattered."

"Being social with other adults; having a sense of accomplishment. Being identified as someone other than Mom."

"I miss having to do a different task every day, meetings, daily goals, and the people."

Effectively, their Achieving or Knowing superpowers—traits that give them a great sense of self-worth—are not being utilized. Let's go back to Erica from Chapter 1. A former corporate lawyer, one reason she found full-time motherhood challenging was that Achieving is her most dominant quality, along with Knowing and Giving. When she realized this and understood that her Achieving superpower was underutilized and therefore she felt unfulfilled, she took action and created a solution. She teamed up with her friend Shannon (whose superpowers are Leading, Creating, and Self-Sustaining) to start a part-time baking business. She pivoted and created a space where they could deploy their superpowers together.

The Second Shift

When Janet Yellen was chair of the U.S. Federal Reserve, she advocated raising women's participation in the workforce to the same level as men's, which she said a study showed could increase the nation's annual economic output by 5 percent. What is needed, she said, are "reforms such as flexible work arrangements, affordable child care, and paid family leave."

Half of all college-educated women between the ages of 30 and 40 years old will leave the workforce for some time. Gina Hadley and Jenny Galluzzo founded The Second Shift to tap into this talent pool of well-educated, creative, career-driven women. Gina Hadley shares:

> It started from Jenny and me talking. One of the things that we constantly talked about were these extraordinary women that we knew who were not working and were not practicing their craft. We have legions and legions of women who have no reason as to why they are not working. The Second Shift is about trying to figure out alternative ways to work and still practice the craft you have spent your entire career building.
>
> We want to create this ecosystem where women don't ever have to fully step away. You can take a gig a month, or keep your contacts fresh, or do some sort of a sprinkle when you can. We want to be a tool, for businesses and for our members, that makes engaging with this demographic and continuing work for these women seamless.

Women leave the workforce for many reasons—they have a family, a sick parent, exorbitant child care costs, unequal pay, lack of flexibility. But the bottom line is that too many talented women are on the sidelines because, for whatever reason, we can't (or we choose not to) work a traditional full-time job. Owning our individual strengths—and companies valuing those talents while embracing the evolving nature of work—may be part of how we increase satisfaction for women wrestling with personal-professional trade-offs.

Your superpowers enable you to lean into situations with confidence and power, but they can also help you better evaluate if and why you may feel stuck or unfulfilled. Have you ever been to a dinner party where someone asks you, "If you weren't doing what you were doing, what would you want to be doing?" My answer? I'm doing it. There's no Plan B, no greener pasture. For the first time in my life, I can tell you that my superpowers line up perfectly with the life that I've created for myself: everything that my company is and stands for stems from all of my strengths. Writing this book—that is my Creating and Performing superpowers in action. I deploy Giving in being the "dress whisperer" for our customers. My confidence language connects directly to everything that I do. I would not have been able to say the same when I was a management consultant. I owe a lot to McKinsey & Company; I would not be who I am today without that 11-year experience. But the superpowers typically associated with being a great consultant (Achieving and Knowing)—while I am competent at them, they are not what drive me.

You too can line up your life, and choose how you move forward in it, and get what you want out of it. Ask yourself that proverbial dinner party question: What would you want to do, if you could? And then keep going: How does that align with your strengths? Are you like Emma, an optimistic giver who was born to teach? Or like me, a giving entrepreneur who was born to create ways for people to see the best in themselves? When you look at your superpowers, do they spur ideas for opportunities you might not have previously seen?

Lining Up Your Life with Your Strengths

Look at your personal or professional activities and reflect on if and how they line up with your superpowers.

	Superpower	Superpower	Superpower
Personal			
Personal			
Professional			
Professional			

Is there a high overlap with your strengths? If so, does that correlate to your satisfaction with or enjoyment of that activity? If there is not a high overlap, why? Is there a different direction that might better suit your strengths?

Take and Get Credit
for Your Confidence Language

At the start of every project at McKinsey & Company, there is a scheduled meeting called "Team Learning." Teams are put together for three-to six-month stints to serve a client, and in most cases, team members have never worked together. This Team Learning happens in the first week of a project, and it's a jumpstart on understanding each teammate's working style and preferences so that we can be effective during such a short time frame. In my first of these as a new business analyst, I was impressed by how our project manager shared her preferences: "I'm an introvert. What that means is I am a great listener, a sponge. I will take in whatever is going on, and I will step away and process it to come back with my suggestions. If I am quiet or not reacting right away, please know that I am thinking deeply about whatever you are telling me, and it will lead to a better answer." She was unapologetic about her working style and positioned it as a strength, much in the way author Susan Cain celebrates the power of introverts in her book *Quiet*. Our project manager framed her narrative on her own terms so that we could best tap into the best of her. As an extrovert who feeds off the energy of others and is exuberant on most occasions, I was able to see the value in a different way of working and not misinterpret our project manager's actions. To this day, because of her, I work well with introverts because I see their power. I talk a lot in meetings; the introvert in the room will come back to me a few days later having reflected on everything I said, shaped the ideas, and made them even better, because they often think and process best on their own terms and not in the moment.

This type of structured team learning is rare outside of the consulting world, so what can we take away from this? First, we have to know what we're the best at before others can see it too. You've already done this by taking the quiz and learning your superpowers. Second, don't let anything diminish this view of yourself! We know that women apologize too often for anything and everything. We mostly do it out of habit, and it hurts how we are perceived and diminishes our power.[2] When we conducted our survey, we had no idea how much our findings would underscore this trait: nearly two-thirds of us easily admit when we are wrong and the same proportion spiral when criticized (versus holding steadfast in a strengths-based view of ourselves). According to a few studies, people who didn't express remorse showed a greater sense of control and higher self-esteem.[3,4] Third, frame your own narrative. Share your strengths actively in a straightforward way with those who need to hear them: "This is what makes me valuable to this effort"; This is what motivates me"; or "This is how to get the best out of me."

How to Get Credit Without Sweating It

In Mika Brzezinski's book *Know Your Value*, she shares: "Do you need to scream at the top of your lungs like a man and pound on the table? No. Being excited about your work is great. Send an e-mail to your boss about a goal that's been met or a deal that's been struck. You've got to find your own attractive way of communication." What are the best ways for you to be your own best advocate at work? An e-mail, a weekly meeting, a phone conversation?

My friend Monica shared a story with me about an executive joining a task force at her company. The executive had been at the company for 20 years and in introducing herself to the other members of the group, she said, "I'm just joining the team and will make a lot of mistakes, so I hope you'll give me grace as we go through this process. But please know that I'm really smart." Monica cringed inside: why was this colleague giving away all her power from the start? Monica admitted to me that during the debrief with her boss, she expressed concern that she might have to double-check this new teammate's work since she "will make a lot of mistakes." Introductions like this are an opportunity to highlight up front what you bring to the table, so how could Monica's colleague have reframed her narrative from a position of strength? Here's what I would have told her to say if I had a time machine: "I am excited to bring my twenty years of experience to this initiative. I'm known for being dedicated, knowledgeable, and detail-oriented. I'm open to feedback and collaboration when we need to power through problems along the way." In essence, she could have made others aware of her superpowers, taken credit for them, and made sure errors were collectively owned, not automatically assuming the fault always lay with her.

No Time for Apologies

Next time you write an e-mail or text message, scan it for deficit language. Did you slip in a sorry? Take it out, now. This is one of my pet peeves. When I help a woman, she will often say, "I'm sorry I took up so much of your time." My response? "You did nothing wrong, why are you apologizing? What you can do is thank me for my time." *Thank you* can often be a suitable replacement for *sorry*.

The next time you have the opportunity to introduce yourself, frame your narrative with your confidence language in mind. Your peers will respect you for owning who you are and taking control of your narrative. This kind of thinking can play out similarly in how we accept compliments. We default to humbly denying the compliment or being embarrassed by it. See if this resonates with you:

Friend: "You were great tonight during book club. I loved what you had to say."

You: "Really? I barely finished the book, and I didn't really know what to say."

How do we respond when we believe in and own our superpowers? Well, let's take the above scenario. Instead of falling over ourselves with denial or embarrassment, we could express gratitude: *"Thank you, that means a lot. I really got a lot out of this book because I appreciate the author's optimism."* A compliment is someone seeing you for your strengths. There is not enough positive validation in this world; what a gift it is when someone takes the time to recognize and acknowledge your contributions.

Manage the Inner Critic

Let's go back to Emma's father—the voice in her head calling her a quitter. We all have this inner critic, the one developed in our adolescence that is intent on keeping us in our comfort zones. It's the voice that says, when you're handed a stretch assignment: "I'm not ready yet."

As women's leadership expert Tara Sophia Mohr shares, the mistake managers often make is to "think their job is to encourage, compliment, or cheerlead when their people are struggling with self-doubt. They say things like 'You really *can* do this!' or 'I have complete confidence in you. I wouldn't have given you this role if I didn't think you had the capability to do it.'" She goes on to suggest that it is a waste of energy to assuage the inner critic with performative platitudes because it is rarely convincing, and it doesn't provide the tools to navigate self-doubt effectively. Rather, we can deflate the inner critic's tires by identifying it for what it is, understanding why it shows up, and moderating the impact it has on us. We manage the inner critic and take away its power because it never goes away for good.[5]

How do we do this? We embrace the inner critic. We acknowledge its existence, we name it, and we recognize that it reflects unrealistic thinking. It is irrational and harsh. The inner critic sounds anxious, pessimistic, repetitive, backward-looking, and focused on problems. So call it out for what it is. And contrast it with realistic thinking that is grounded in your superpowers: that voice is conscious, calm, and forward-moving, and it seeks solutions. Next, you make a choice to not take direction from it and to take direction from your strengths instead. It allows us to consider the worst-case scenario (the inner critic) versus the best-case and most-likely scenarios (our superpowers). One woman in a workshop I led shared in a follow-up e-mail afterward, "An insight I found about myself is that I will take one of my negative thoughts about myself and turn it into a fact in my brain, even though it's not true. I've found that positive self-talk can go a long way, and changing my internal dialogue in my head is challenging, but worth it in the long run. The more I think about the superpowers I have, the better I feel every day." The most effective way to silence the inner critic is to drown out its voice with the megaphone of your superpowers.

How to Handle Outside Critics

While you manage the inner critic, you may have to fend off systemic bias, microaggressions, or negativity from naysayers out in the real world, too. Be ready to keep your narrative your own and not fall back into the default mode of overexplaining and letting a detractor win the day.

Here's an example: My friend Hannah has a job in operations at an online retail company. She is responsible for vendors getting products shipped out and delivered on time. One day when we were having lunch, she told me about an awkward conversation she had with one of her colleagues. It happened after a vendor meeting. It was a tough conversation because the vendor wasn't meeting deadlines, so she told them she would hold them accountable if they failed in stepping up. When they were done and walking out of the meeting, one of her male peers, with whom she is fairly close, turned to her, shook his head, and said, "You were intimidating in there." In shock, she stumbled to explain herself, "I'm sorry. I was just walking them through the timeline. Because if they don't deliver it on time, it is our necks, I need to hold this person accountable."

I stopped Hannah right there and said to her, "I cannot believe you were explaining yourself. If you were a man, he probably would have high-fived you and said, 'You rocked that meeting. Way to hold their feet to the fire.'" We then discussed other ways she could have responded, from owning it (*"Yes, I was intimidating. That was exactly what I wanted to project."*) to asking him about his intent (*"Is that a criticism or a compliment? If the former, that's inappropriate. If the latter, thank you."*). Why do we default to explaining ourselves? And why did Hannah think being intimidating was automatically a negative? There was nothing she would have changed about how she handled that meeting—and she should have called out her male colleague if he was inferring the opposite.

This is one of the benefits of anchoring ourselves in our strengths: you own who you are and do not let others diminish your power. You protect it, just like a mama bear protecting her cub—and it helps when we are supported in pushing back. After graduating from law school, Esme started working at a small law firm and was taking her first-ever deposition. The opposing counsel threw her off by addressing her with "Listen, little lady. . . ." Esme doesn't remember what else was said because her mind stopped short at what he had called her.

"Wait, what did you say?" she replied. Taken aback, Esme asked for a five-minute break. She got her mentor on the phone for advice. After she told him what happened, he replied, "You know what you need to do? You need to put everything on the record. And threaten to show it to the judge." When she came back to the conference room, she made it clear to the opposing counsel that the record would reflect how he spoke to her: "Everything that is going to be said in this room is going to be on the record, no matter what." He was on his best behavior after that.

At the time, Esme needed that mentor. She needed someone to tell her how to handle the situation. Now, cut to 20 years later, Esme didn't need to call her lifeline. As a top legal counsel, she was in a meeting with one of her staff members when he called her "honey." It was degrading. She stopped the conversation, "What did you just say to me?" He didn't repeat it. Instead he replied, "I'm sorry." She ended the meeting right then and there, because her impulse was to fire him on the spot and she knew she needed to cool her head. He later apologized via e-mail, but Esme had already stopped the bias in its tracks.

Grow with Your Confidence Language

During the writing of this book, I often went to museums to clear my head. On one trip to the Museum of Modern Art, I came upon the sculptor Richard Serra's large-scale piece, *Equal*. It is an installation of eight forged-steel rectangular cubes stacked in twos—four pairs in total. Each cube is the same size: five by five and half by six feet (weighing 40 tons!), but each pair has a slightly different orientation in the way the blocks are stacked. While the individual units are the same and every stack is exactly 11 feet tall, each stack looks different. As I walked around the towering pieces, I couldn't help but think how they reminded me of the eight superpowers combined into confidence language stacks. Whatever combinations we embody, they are unique but equally as valid.

By acknowledging that each of our unique combinations are powerful (like Serra's distinct, but equal stacks), we build the mindset that allows us to be authentically confident. This mindset *drives* the behaviors you want in your life. If you want to take action in your life, it starts with believing in your strengths. "Fake it until you make it" might help in the short term for a presentation, but it doesn't change your underlying beliefs about yourself. We tamp down the inner critic and silence outside critics with the mastery of what we know to be true about the best part of ourselves. This mindset focuses on abundance (what we have versus worrying we are not enough); if you operate from an abundant viewpoint, you are able to create good things in your life to your fullest potential.

The growth mindset, according to Carol Dweck, is based on the belief that our qualities can be cultivated, nourished. "Although people may differ in every which way—in their initial talents and aptitudes, interests, or temperaments—everyone can change and grow through application and experience." When we start to put this in practice, and again, borrowing from James Clear, the act of owning, deploying, and taking credit for our strengths becomes a habit. You achieve mastery to the extent that they become unconscious again—you can perform them so effortlessly that you are not even aware you are doing them. That's your authentic basis for confidence.

When do we most need this growth-oriented mindset? When do women most need to own their power? During times of major transition, when self-doubt is at its peak: starting a new job, being fired or laid off, leaving the workplace to be a full-time parent, reentering the workplace after being a full-time parent, going through a divorce, experiencing the death of a loved one, becoming an empty nester. In each of these transitions, believing in our strengths is powerful and necessary. Here are some examples.

Reentry: After 20 years of raising three children as a full-time parent, Helen had decided it was time to focus on her needs again. A former lawyer, she questioned if she had anything to bring to the workplace after having been away for more than two decades. Her top traits were Giving, Achieving, and Knowing. "My superpowers reassured me that I actually had something to contribute to a potential employer. Giving made sense. That's 90 percent of what I did every day for the last twenty years. Achieving also feels right—that's why I took up long-distance running and marathons. I have the endurance to take on tough things. Knowing meant that I kept everything organized, made sure academics were a priority for my kids, and would be buttoned up in a work environment." Helen is now a top recruiter for placing executive women in C-suite positions, a role that taps into all of her superpowers.

Reinvention: Carla had risen to a senior executive position at a major industrials sector company as one of the few women at the top. She had created her own family by adopting two children as a single mother. In discovering her strengths, she shared, "Self-Sustaining is my top superpower, which makes sense why I've gotten so far in this company. You have to hold your own around here. Being a woman in a male-dominated industry, and in management, I have to tell myself 'I've got this' when there's not a big network to utilize, especially in difficult times. But what I didn't expect was scoring so high on Creating as a superpower. It resonates in the sense that I created my own family by adopting my children and created a new beginning after divorce. I also created a voice within the company and opportunities for myself and others. I've been thinking about life, what my next step is going to be. I've worked in the same job for almost three decades. Once my kids graduate from high school, what do I have? I'm excited that I have Creating as a superpower, because maybe I'm on the cusp of reinventing my life!"

Recovery: Kathleen had just been fired from the company she founded. She loved her role at the helm for more than a decade and had built the organization into an admired industry leader. She had not seen it coming, and she felt concurrent waves of anger, shame, and despair. Anger in being asked to leave the company she had created, embarrassment in having to share the news of her departure, and despair in sorting out what was next. Her top quiz result? Believing. It was the superpower she credits with building her business, but also getting her through this time.

Are you going through a life transition? How can your superpowers guide you through this time? Reaffirm your value? Give you insight into replaying your highlight reel of life events with compassion and looking ahead?

The good news: your superpowers have gotten you this far and will power you through everyday challenges. That's most of the work. But there might be something you really want to master, like giving that wedding toast or getting that raise. To accomplish it, you may need to call upon one of the other superpowers in which you are not currently strong. Or perhaps you want to expand your universe—create a new outer concentric circle of your life, such as starting that business? The next chapters are going to help you do just that.

LEVELING UP
WITH GRAVITAS

Remember that quote I mentioned in Chapter 2 from my good friend Jane Park, "Life doesn't get easier, we just get stronger"? In this chapter, I am going to show you how to do exactly that by making the most out of the opportunities in front of you and tackling setbacks and losses from a position of strength. We've learned how to see, deploy, and own our confidence language. Your confidence language is based on your primary strengths, and it is your default that you go to most often. Now, let's explore how to add supplementary superpowers beyond your primary ones to your tool kit. You have a full menu of superpowers from which to draw; leveling up with new strengths will make you even stronger, more self-assured, and more resilient in navigating both the opportunities and the challenges that lie ahead.

In reflecting on my own journey, I have felt the cumulative power of adding superpowers—some to the point of proficiency and others to mastery—to increase my ability to do more and to expand the outermost circles of my life. I started my life in the company of immigrants who owned a small business (so I inherited the Creating superpower from my parents) and ran it with extraordinary compassion. My family's all-you-can eat Mongolian BBQ restaurant was the hub of our tiny desert town, and my mother was its unofficial mayor, welcoming everyone who came through the restaurant's doors (you can see where I get my Giving trait). She was also a self-proclaimed tiger mom, and so she raised me to take my academics seriously (Achieving, Knowing). My father discovered a local chapter of Toastmasters whose members sponsored student speech competitions for which the prizes were $5,000 to $10,000 college scholarships. We went to their meetings and learned how to deliver presentations, improving my father's English skills while I honed my skills (my Performing superpower) to fund my college education. After I graduated, I worked my way up through McKinsey & Company, where I was called upon to set direction, mentor teammates, and develop strategic plans (Leading). I can look back now and see why I was able to start my own business with an abundance of strengths. This layering effect of capabilities expanded the possibilities in my life.

Our quantitative research confirms that this layering effect works for many of us. As women gain more life experiences, including rising to more senior levels at work, their average number of superpowers goes from two to three or more. We also saw that as women age, their dominant superpowers may evolve over time. For example, Creating is a top trait among women ages 25 to 34, for whom possibility and new ideas are energizing and feel attainable. Among women ages 35 to 54, this trait decreases significantly, but interestingly, it comes back in full force after the age of 55 and among retired women. There could be a number of reasons for this bump: she was a full-time parent who is now an empty nester and reflecting on the next chapter brimming with possibility; she's been with the same company for decades and is looking to reinvent; or she's reflecting on her legacy and how she can make an even bigger difference.

We can evolve and progress, and superpowers are a powerful tool in helping us each step of the way. Our confidence language is the authentic foundation of our self-belief (the work we've already done together). The next part of the journey is becoming proficient in or fully mastering the ones outside of our default confidence language to enable us to get stronger and stretch the limits of what's possible.

Where You Want to Grow

To figure out which new superpowers we want to explore, we need to first step back and think through the outcomes we want to see in our lives. We asked women how comfortable or capable they felt across a range of situations, and we focused on five areas of outcomes: effective execution, emotional support, resilience, persuasion, and leveling up.

We learned that women are the most confident in areas related to effective execution (three out of four women felt highly capable) and emotional support (more than two out of three felt comfortable in handling these situations). On the other side of the spectrum, where women feel the least confident is in persuasion and leveling up: leading a project; asking for a favor, promotion, or raise; starting a business; public speaking. In these two areas, women feel comfortable only when it comes to defending their answers, giving advice, and managing people. For resilience, women overall are comfortable with admitting errors and staying calm, but not as comfortable with bouncing back from disappointments and criticisms. On the next page you will see the results from our quantitative research.

As you review this summary, I invite you to consider how comfortable you are in each of the situations described. Put a star next to the ones where you feel highly capable. These are likely to be the ones that most closely tie to the superpowers you have today. Then, put a check mark next to the scenarios in which you feel fairly capable. These probably reflect strengths that you demonstrate to some degree. Lastly, circle the ones where you do not feel capable today, but you would like to be. These are the areas where you want to acquire new strengths and skills. This is the focus of our work in this chapter.

	MOST Comfortable	SOMEWHAT Comfortable	LEAST Comfortable
Effective Execution	Getting tasks/projects done	Working on a very tight deadline	
Emotional Support	Comforting someone who is sad	Dealing with the illness of a family member	Delivering bad news to someone
Self-Recovery and Resilience	Admitting when you are wrong	Staying calm in bad situations	Recovering from a loss or disappointment Letting go of a failure Being criticized for something you did
Persuasion	Defending an answer with data Explaining or defending your ideas	Giving advice or coaching others Managing people	Raising money for a business or charity Having to be the expert Selling a plan or idea Telling a story in front of an audience Public speaking
Leveling Up		Starting a new project Coming up with a new idea Meeting new people	Leading a project Competing for something Writing a story or creating a piece of art Going to an event where you don't know anyone Asking for a favor Starting a business Asking for a promotion Asking for a raise

The Superpowers
That Will Get You There

Now that you know where you want to go, which superpowers can help to get you there? We looked at the women who were most comfortable and capable in taking on a particular situation and identified their dominant strengths to determine which superpowers drove those outcomes. Along with the detailed descriptions in Chapter 4 in the "What You Can Do to Channel This Superpower" sections, this will be your road map to claiming the superpowers that you want to layer into your life. While your default confidence language can power you through the everyday, what follows are situations where you may benefit from upskilling. Although these situations—we cover 30—are not exhaustive, they can be used as a guide for similar situations and determining which superpowers will be most effective in taking them on.

This exercise allows us to focus on a quality we want to develop for a specific purpose. Take for instance, Amelia, a busy lawyer and mother of three. She knew she was great at her job and a good mom—she scored highest in Achieving, Knowing, and Leading. After looking at her quiz results, her first reaction was "I want more Believing in my life." If you identify with Amelia, the next step is to get curious about the following: Why do you want more of that trait? What will it do for you? What situations do you want to be better equipped to handle? Amelia came to realize that she wanted to stay calm and be more positive with her husband. Because they were both busy managing their careers and three children, she tended to be negative and judgmental in their interactions. She also wanted to be a better role model for her three daughters in seeing the best in others and life in general. Once she knew what her "why" was, she could channel the Believing mindset and test-drive new behaviors. Similarly, a workshop participant who had taken the superpowers quiz shared with me, "I found it insightful that my lowest form of confidence is Believing. I had always thought of myself as a positive person, but I have had comments in the past that I could be a little more hopeful things will go right. It gave me pause, and I decided I wanted to be more positive during the day. I've had happier days and better interactions with people at work and outside!"

After you've determined your "why," here's a primer for the most common situations and which superpowers will be most effective in helping you navigate them. A visual quick-guide of this follows on the next two pages.

EFFECTIVE EXECUTION

The ability to carry out a plan through concrete steps, in which responsibility and dependability are highly valued

♦ **Getting tasks/projects done**
♦ **Working on a very tight deadline/under pressure**
   Superpowers required: **Achieving, Giving, Knowing**

Need to get it done and on time? This is where Achieving, Giving, and Knowing will be your greatest allies in following up and following through. Achieving will ensure that you set a measurable goal, track metrics along the way, power through with endurance, and celebrate when you have crossed the finish line. Giving creates a sense of responsibility to others or a cause that gives implementation a satisfying sense of purpose. Knowing will empower you to map out the logical steps needed to complete a task, along with a detailed to-do list to hold you accountable. Any one of these qualities will give you the boost you need to drive a project to completion.

EMOTIONAL SUPPORT

The emotional intelligence that it takes to speak from and to the heart and to demonstrate a depth of understanding, empathy, or warmth in interactions with others

		Giving	Knowing
Effective Execution	Getting tasks/projects done	✓	✓
	Working on a very tight deadline/under pressure	✓	✓
Emotional Support	Comforting someone who is sad or dealing with loss	✓	
	Dealing with the illness of a family member	✓	✓
	Delivering bad news to someone		
Self-Recovery and Resilience	Admitting when you are wrong	✓	✓
	Staying calm in bad situations		✓
	Recovering from a loss or disappointment		
	Letting go of a loss or disappointment		
	Being criticized for something you did		
Persuasion	Defending an answer with data		✓
	Explaining or defending your ideas		
	Giving advice or coaching others		
	Managing people/telling others what to do		
	Raising money for a business or charity		
	Having to be the expert on a topic		
	Selling someone on a plan or idea		
	Telling a story in front of an audience		
	Public speaking/giving a speech		
Leveling Up	Starting a new project	✓	✓
	Coming up with a new idea		
	Meeting new people		
	Leading a project		✓
	Competing for something (e.g., an award, promotion, game)		
	Writing a story or creating a piece of art		
	Going to an event where you don't know anyone		
	Asking for a favor		
	Asking for a promotion		
	Asking for a raise		
	Starting your own business		

Achieving	Believing	Creating	Self-Sustaining	Leading	Performing
✓					
✓					
	✓				
	✓			✓	✓
	✓				
	✓		✓		
✓				✓	
	✓	✓			
		✓	✓		
✓					
	✓	✓			
		✓		✓	✓
✓				✓	
✓				✓	✓
		✓		✓	✓
			✓		✓
		✓		✓	✓
		✓		✓	✓
✓		✓			
	✓		✓		✓
				✓	✓
✓				✓	✓
		✓		✓	
			✓	✓	✓
	✓		✓		
✓		✓		✓	✓
			✓	✓	
		✓	✓	✓	✓

◆ **Comforting someone who is sad or dealing with loss**
 Superpowers required: **Giving, Believing**

In tough times, people want to feel seen and not necessarily cheered up. Comforting someone is about cultivating the space to share, including acknowledging unpleasant and painful emotions ("I'm on your side. In fact, I'm here for all the sides, not just the bright side."). Giving is the quality that most empowers us to show up for others. In moments of distress, this is the quality that will drop everything to lend a hand or simply be an empathetic ear. The Believing superpower boosts that emotional commitment further by bearing witness and paving the way for the loss to be accepted as a step in the direction of finding greater meaning.

◆ **Dealing with the illness of a family member**
 Superpowers required: **Giving, Knowing**

In addition to the generous care and warm support of the Giving quality, the Knowing superpower is one that brings order to what can be an emotional and turbulent time. When we have so little control over the outcome when a family member is ill, Knowing is a balancing quality that allows us to feel useful. These qualities can bring warmth and a sense of control to emotionally charged moments.

◆ **Delivering bad news to someone**
 Superpowers required: **Leading, Performing, Believing**

Most women struggle with delivering bad news. Less than one-third of women feel comfortable doing this, probably because our inner critic plays out all the stories in our mind about how that person will respond, or we put ourselves in that person's place and imagine how we would take the news. This is where the extroverted storytelling qualities of Leading and Performing will give you the tools to craft and deliver the message with the audience in mind. Add in the Believing quality, which can provide the reassurance that the person is strong enough to make it through this dark time and highlight the optimistic component of the bad-news-good-news equation. These are qualities I tapped into when I had to deliver a tough message to a client in my consulting days, or when I've had to let someone go on my team.

SELF-RECOVERY AND RESILIENCE

The ability to ably navigate and address setbacks, including how we react, self-soothe, recover, and bounce back

* **Admitting when you are wrong**
  Superpowers required: **Giving, Knowing, Believing**

Made a mistake? The Giving quality relies on a deep sense of responsibility to others that will allow you to take your fair share of the burden. Knowing is powered by knowledge and data, so finding an error maintains the trustworthiness of that information and expertise. And the Believing quality sees the bigger picture: if a mistake is made, own up to it and its implication because then there's a chance to fix it. This quality assumes positive intent and that the misstep creates space for solutions—"I made this mistake, but I didn't mean to. I am hopeful we can get to a better outcome going forward." Admitting when we are wrong can push us into a deficit mindset, but not if we employ the Believing quality. It allows us to not be held back by our flaws; it turns those flaws into learning moments that make us stronger.

* **Staying calm in bad situations**
  Superpowers required: **Knowing, Believing, Self-Sustaining**

The Knowing superpower can bring a sense of control to chaotic environments, so it is a worthy trait that brings order to mollify a situation. The Believing quality can help you see the positive in a challenging situation and provide a forward-looking perspective that says, "This is a bump in the road to better times. No need to be anxious or waste energy on getting worked up. There's a reason for all of this." Those with a Self-Sustaining quality are self-possessed, with full knowledge of what they're capable of; they have deep reserves of energy within themselves to power through tough times.

◆ **Recovering from a loss or disappointment**
Superpowers required: **Achieving, Leading**

Need to bounce back? Both of these qualities are forward-moving and motivated by progress. Setbacks don't faze them; in fact, they relish the recovery. Those with the Achieving quality are masters of the comeback story; powered by endurance and an endless desire for self-improvement, this is the superpower that thrives on being challenged. Because with resilience, you can push through adversity to reach the goal. The Leading quality adds the ability to course-correct in the right direction and, in more team-oriented environments, to bring people along with you with inspiration and motivation. The mission at hand is always clear and communicated, so setbacks—and resolving them—are viewed with that in mind.

◆ **Letting go of a loss or disappointment**
Superpowers required: **Believing, Creating**

It's one thing to recover from a setback; it's another to let go of the emotional baggage. Two superpowers—Believing and Creating—can work together to support letting go of failure. The first, Believing, is forward-looking and understands that something positive will come from the disappointment. Creating allows you to envision that better future and to have the ability to generate ideas to let go of the past. Entrepreneurs are empowered by the Believing quality in that they search for the positive lessons in the failure and pivot with the Creating superpower to generate the next iteration of their idea. I have employed both of these traits in overcoming bad breakups in my personal life (especially when I've been dumped). It's not uncommon to feel like you've failed in a relationship (as in "What did I do wrong?"), but we can channel the Believing superpower ("I learned a lot in that relationship about myself and what I want. This wasn't meant to be.") and Creating qualities ("I can envision finding love again!"). When I was fired for the first time, I had to believe that there was something better out there for me and that this experience meant something in terms of my development—and then channel Creating to envision what my next role would look like and turn those ideas into my next job. Social scientist and therapist Dr. Pauline

Boss offers similar guidelines for dealing with grief and ambiguous loss: "making meaning out of loss; relinquishing one's desire to control an uncontrollable situation; recreating identity after loss; becoming accustomed to ambivalent feelings; redefining one's relationship with whatever or whomever they've lost; and finding new hope."[1]

♦ **Being criticized for something you did**
Superpowers required: **Creating, Self-Sustaining**

Meet the antidote to spiraling. Less than one-third of the women we surveyed feel they are capable of handling criticism. Many of us fall back on letting it confirm the inner critic's worst fears about ourselves or prompt concerns about what the other person thinks (dreading disappointing them, fearing that they don't like you, worrying that they're judging you). The Creating trait is useful in that it views feedback as a helpful tool to improve the success of an idea. The Self-Sustaining quality is like Teflon armor that deflects any energy devoted to taking criticism personally. Self-Sustaining is rooted in the fundamental belief that "I am enough" and so criticism is benign; it can be fairly evaluated on its merits and not seen as judgment.

PERSUASION

Elements of influence that can be used to convince and sway others, or to enlist the aid and support of others in the accomplishment of a common task

♦ **Defending an answer with data**
Superpowers required: **Knowing, Achieving**

When you need to make sure your insights are rock solid—whether for trying to get more money for the PTA or finalizing a presentation— channel the Knowing superpower to ensure that you have done the homework and depth of research required to confirm that your conclusions are supported with the best information possible. The Achieving mindset values the integrity of metrics and applies a desire to meet or exceed the highest standards in backing up an answer.

◆ **Explaining or defending your ideas**
  Superpowers required: **Creating, Believing**

The Creating superpower is fueled by the power of ideas and being able to articulate a vision of the future with clarity. If you need to explain your idea, this is the quality most able to help others see what you're seeing. In terms of defending your idea, the Believing trait can power your ability to see the best in the path forward, including viewing feedback as a positive. Your ideas have the best chance of succeeding when you have a forward-looking mindset.

◆ **Giving advice or coaching others**
  Superpowers required: **Leading, Performing, Creating**

Those with Leading as their top superpower can see how team members' talents fit into the overall plan and are adept at mentoring to get the best out of others. The Performing quality boosts the power of perception and storytelling so you're able to provide feedback that is specific and has an emotional connection. Those with the Creating quality can lend their expertise, are able to help others navigate setbacks because they're comfortable with iteration and handling criticism with grit, and can help imagine a path forward because they thrive on envisioning the future.

◆ **Managing people/telling others what to do**
  Superpowers required: **Achieving, Leading**

Teamwork is essential in leading others to obtain a result. Those with the Achieving and Leading qualities understand the power of working together to accomplish a goal or moving in the same direction to reach a destination. Those who channel the Achieving superpower are often strong-willed and action-oriented, which allows for a fair distribution of tasks and clearly understood metrics for their completion. Women with the Leading quality can communicate, rally, and motivate others around a North Star, which creates followership.

◆ **Raising money for a business or charity**
   Superpowers required: **Achieving, Leading, Performing**

When there is a purpose-driven goal, those with the Achieving super-power are motivated by hitting or exceeding a goal (think of visible markers such as a fundraising thermometer and the satisfaction of see-ing the temperature rise with your efforts). These efforts are amplified if we add in the Leading and Performing qualities, which can help you cre-ate compelling storytelling behind the efforts and rally people around the cause. These qualities are often seen in *Shark Tank* pitches, where all three are necessary to convey the strength of a potential investment.

◆ **Having to be the expert on a topic**
   Superpowers required: **Leading, Performing, Creating**

Women at times doubt their own expertise. "Do men doubt themselves sometimes? Of course. But not with such exacting and repetitive zeal, and they don't let their doubts stop them as often as women do," Claire Shipman and Katty Kay wrote in their 2014 essay "The Confidence Gap" for *The Atlantic* (which later became a best-selling book, *The Confidence Code*). Women may question whether they really are the most qualified on a topic, or perhaps perfectionism keeps them thinking there is still more to research or do. To step into the role of being the expert con-fidently, channeling Leading and Performing superpowers can help. These two traits will give you a leg up in terms of storytelling and com-municating authority. The Creating superpower helps by adding some innovation to the mix—after all, reimagining the future often means you are at the top of your field!

◆ **Selling someone on a plan or idea**
   Superpowers required: **Performing, Self-Sustaining**

Performing is the quality most often associated with selling, because it is an extroverted superpower that can engage an audience (e.g., get-ting to know the person on the receiving end of the sales pitch) and share an idea in a compelling way. But when you need to close the sale? That's when the Self-Sustaining superpower can help in not talking past the sale. It's a quality that truly believes in the strength of the plan or idea; that self-assurance can power even being willing to walk away from the table.

- **Telling a story in front of an audience**
- **Public speaking/giving a speech**
  Superpowers required: **Leading, Performing, Creating**

Only one-third of women are comfortable standing in front of an audience. This explains why everything from bridesmaid toasts to traditional meetings can induce sweaty palms, butterflies in the stomach, and dry mouth. These three superpowers can help you effectively channel charisma for your moment: Leading helps you focus on where the speech is going ("I have three things to share with you today"), Performing helps you engage an audience (with an animated and authoritative voice, facial expressions, gestures), and Creating taps into imaginative impulses that form the basis of great stories (personal, impassioned, idea-driven).

LEVELING UP

Tackling new opportunities that take us outside of our comfort zone and may expose us to varying degrees of risk, such as rejection, disappointment, or criticism

- **Starting a new project**
  Superpowers required: **Knowing, Giving**

The Knowing superpower is inherent in the self-starter, the one who ignites a clearly defined process and takes initiative in kicking it off. Those with the Knowing quality outline the tasks to be completed, and say, "Let's get going!" with authority because the road ahead is logical and well thought out. Layer on Giving to inspire reliability and dependability, the best foundations for any initiative.

- **Coming up with a new idea**
  Superpowers required: **Creating, Achieving**

Need to ideate? The Creating superpower will create a sense of freedom and space to brainstorm, from seeing new white-space opportunities to how to go after them. Achieving is a quality that is comfortable with "practice makes perfect"; if something doesn't work, those with this quality will try again . . . and again. It creates endurance to search for the next idea that may lead to success. I see the combination of these superpowers in sports: coaches and players will watch endless hours of game tape to see strengths and weaknesses in their own team and their opponents and to develop tweaks and breakthrough strategies.

♦ **Meeting new people**
Superpowers required: **Performing, Self-Sustaining, Believing**

When meeting strangers—from first dates to new colleagues—any one of these three qualities can level up your confidence. The Performing superpower can bring sociable energy and the enthusiasm to engage with new people, from asking great questions to sharing an entertaining story. Self-Sustaining is a quality that frees you from feeling intimidated; those with this quality have a strong sense of self and don't expend energy worrying whether others will like them. Those with the Believing quality see the best in others and situations; they may believe new people come into their life for a reason.

♦ **Leading a project**
Superpowers required: **Leading, Performing, Knowing**

When it comes to heading up a project, Leading will be the primary superpower that ensures that you feel your best. Success can be amplified when the Performing quality is employed, because it engages others throughout the process on an emotional level. Knowing helps with setting up a structure and keeps things moving, which can offset the shadow sides of Leading and Performing (those with these qualities struggle with effective task completion).

♦ **Competing for something (e.g., an award, promotion, game)**
Superpowers required: **Achieving, Leading, Performing**

Reaching a milestone—and being recognized and validated for it—is at the heart of competition. Not surprising, then, that these three qualities can all drive effectiveness in competing for something: Achieving focuses on a measurable finish line and the desire to win come what may; Leading leads a group to a compelling destination; and Performing enjoys the validation of an audience. The qualities of each of these superpowers can push you to throw your hat into the ring.

- **Writing a story or creating a piece of art**
  Superpowers required: **Creating, Leading**

Staring at a blank page or canvas can be daunting. Channel the Creating quality for the freedom and space to ideate. Those with this superpower are comfortable tapping into their imaginations and letting their minds wander to new and exciting places. The Leading quality will bring mission and direction to putting pen to paper; natural storytellers, those with this quality step out and see the *why* behind the story or art. One of my friends once had to explain contemporary art to her husband; he was staring at a piece and asserted that he could have made it. She replied, "But you didn't. This artist had the idea first and then took that vision and had the guts to put it out into the world. You didn't have that initiative. The idea has value, and the courage to put it out there has value."

- **Going to an event where you don't know anyone**
  Superpowers required: **Performing, Leading, Self-Sustaining**

Showing up to a group gathering alone (at a party, a workout class) requires us to deploy more extroverted skills. The Performing quality asks us to see the value in the energy of others and to ask questions, share stories, and be genuinely interested in those interactions. The Leading superpower is a people motivator and clear communicator, which helps when we're advocating for ourselves among a group of strangers. The Self-Sustaining quality gives us a sense that we belong there—after all, we've already been invited!

- **Asking for a favor**
  Superpowers required: **Believing, Self-Sustaining**

When we ask for a favor, our inner critic can create stories about the potential response (rejection, no response at all), and we make ourselves vulnerable to judgment by the person we're asking (perceptions of shame or guilt in admitting that we need help). The Believing and Self-Sustaining qualities overcome the inner critic's objections: Believing suggests that everything happens for a reason, so there's no harm in asking because it all works out in the end ("What's the worst response? No? Then it wasn't meant to be. On to the next!"). The Self-Sustaining quality shatters fear of judgment, because the ask comes from a place of self-assurance ("Even if the answer is no, it doesn't change what I believe about myself").

⬥ **Asking for a promotion**
Superpowers required: **Achieving, Leading, Performing, Creating**

Many self-advocacy tactics can be employed in achieving a promotion. In the best case, asking for a promotion should not feel like a negotiation between two parties; it should create a sense that we're on the same side of the table working toward the best outcome for all. By employing Achieving, you will gather all the wins and successes as a case for the promotion; with the Leading quality in play, you can make a case for how this promotion is in line with the overall strategy and your contributions to it; Performing will sell the merits of the promotion with compelling storytelling; leveraging Creating will make you comfortable with asking in light of a vision for the future ("leap without the net"). Figuring out which superpower to channel will depend on who the decision-maker is and the relationship you have with them (we will explore this in greater depth in the next chapter when it comes to reading others' confidence languages).

⬥ **Asking for a raise**
Superpowers required: **Leading, Self-Sustaining**

When money comes into the equation, a commanding quality is required. Both the Leading and the Self-Sustaining superpowers help you show up unafraid to ask for fairness in the effort-reward equation— without apology ("This is my market value, and my salary should reflect that value"). Channeling the Self-Sustaining quality helps to ground you in the mindset that you are worthy and deserving of that raise; the Leading quality gives you the tools to communicate the ask with authority. Perhaps this is why those with these superpowers are among the most satisfied on the dimensions of recognition and rewards (awards, promotions, pay, benefits). As author Barbara Huson shares, "If you're going to command more—whether it's a higher fee, more flexible hours, or a corner office—you have to truly believe you're worth it." She continues, "Asking for more is an act of self-love. Saying no is a show of self-respect. Refusing to settle is a statement of self-worth. And walking away is a sign of self-trust."

- ◆ **Starting your own business**
  Superpowers required: **Self-Sustaining, Leading, Performing, Creating**

I am often asked about the steps I took to start my own business. The advice I give? First, you have to solve for three variables to feel truly ready to do it: industry know-how, resources (money, time, talent), and a network (people you can call on to help you). If you have at least two of these and a clear path on the third (for example, I have worked in the industry and know it deeply, I have mentors who can help, and I have savings or can fundraise), then you are ready. That is Self-Sustaining, affirming you have what you need to start and not questioning your capability in taking this on. Because you will question yourself often in the face of setbacks and will have to self-soothe (one of my teammates once said to me, "Lisa, we've been here before, and we've gotten through. So this is no different. I believe in you, and so should you!"). Next, you're on your own now, and you can set the direction, put your plan in motion, and rally others to join you with the Leading superpower. When you've got to sell your concept to customers, vendors, or investors, call upon the Performing quality. And of course, Creating is at the heart of making something from nothing.

The Benefits of Adding Leading, Performing, Self-Sustaining, and Creating

As we move from the areas of effective execution to leveling up, women feel less capable and must increasingly step outside their comfort zones. Women are often most comfortable with situations involving effective execution and emotional support, completing tasks and comforting others. When it comes to the areas of resilience and persuasion, many women ranked their comfort levels as low to medium, with women feeling capable of admitting flaws, staying calm, managing others, and defensive tactics, but not of recovering from loss, being criticized, and performing public-facing activities. The greatest gap for women? Leveling up. Less than one-third of women felt comfortable advocating for themselves or being recognized for their accomplishments and potential, defaulting to activities with a defined scope or with others' comfort in mind.

Why do we see these patterns? Getting out of our comfort zones can bring out the inner critic, who might warn us of failure. We have to put ourselves out there in front of an audience or a boss, so we must be vulnerable to emotions such as shame, judgment, embarrassment, guilt. For example, we found that women overall were highly capable of coming up with an idea, but struggled when it came to being rewarded for that idea or getting credit for it (although I believe some of this struggle should be attributed to systemic bias). The greatest correlation to success in these higher-risk, higher-reward situations is channeling the Leading, Performing, Creating, or Self-Sustaining superpowers. Where women are the least comfortable correlates to the superpowers the fewest number of women have. See the chart on the next two pages for a visual representation of this.

Situations in which you feel most capable/confident

	Effective execution	Emotional support	Self-Recovery and Resilience
Giving 48%	Getting tasks/ projects done Working on a very tight deadline	Comforting someone who is sad or dealing with loss Dealing with the illness of a family member	Admitting when you are wrong
Knowing 44%	Getting tasks/ projects done Working on a very tight deadline	Dealing with the illness of a family member	Admitting when you are wrong Staying calm in bad situations
Achieving 36%	Getting tasks/ projects done Working on a very tight deadline		Recovering from a loss or disappointment
Believing 35%		Comforting someone who is sad or dealing with loss Delivering bad news to someone	Admitting when you are wrong Letting go of failure Staying calm in bad situations
Creating 28%			Being criticized for something you did Letting go of failure
Self-Sustaining 21%			Being criticized for something you did Staying calm in bad situations
Leading 13%		Delivering bad news to someone	Recovering from a loss or disappointment
Performing 12%		Delivering bad news to someone	Asking for a promotion Competing for something Going to an event where you don't know anyone Leading a project Meeting new people Starting your own business

	Persuasion	Leveling Up
Giving 48%		Starting a new project
Knowing 44%	Defending an answer with data	Leading a project Starting a new project
Achieving 36%	Defending an answer with data Managing people Raising money for a business or charity	Asking for a promotion Coming up with a new idea Competing for something
Believing 35%	Explaining or defending your ideas	Asking for a favor Meeting new people
Creating 28%	Explaining or defending your ideas Giving advice or coaching others Having to be the expert on a topic Public speaking Telling a story in front of an audience	Asking for a promotion Coming up with a new idea Starting your own business Writing a story or creating a piece of art
Self-Sustaining 21%	Selling someone on a plan or idea	Asking for a favor Asking for a raise Going to an event where you don't know anyone Meeting new people Starting your own business
Leading 13%	Giving advice or coaching others Having to be the expert on a topic Managing people Public speaking Raising money for a business or charity Telling a story in front of an audience	Asking for a promotion Asking for a raise Competing for something Going to an event where you don't know anyone Leading a project Starting your own business Writing a story or creating a piece of art
Performing 12%	Giving advice or coaching others Having to be the expert on a topic Public speaking/giving a speech Raising money for a business or charity Selling someone on a plan or idea Telling a story in front of an audience	Asking for a promotion Competing for something (e.g., an award, promotion, game) Going to an event where you don't know anyone Leading a project Meeting new people Starting your own business

Simply put, adding any one of these qualities to your arsenal of skills will double or triple your capability levels in every situation and increase your satisfaction in your work and personal life by up to two times. For example, if we compare women who have only Giving as their top superpower to women who have Giving plus Leading, the latter's comfort level on every dimension increases, and it doubles or triples for higher-stakes situations. See the charts on the next page for a visual representation of this.

Satisfaction levels increase with the introduction of a new super-power: women who have Giving plus Leading are two times more satis-fied overall than those with Giving alone, and they feel more capable in advocating for themselves. Having Giving plus Leading make for some of the most powerful people in the world, because they are thoughtful about their leading and they don't run the risk of being doormats. And the cumulative effect of adding superpowers is powerful: if we take the most frequent combinations of superpowers among women and add in Self-Sustaining as a third quality, satisfaction levels nearly double across the board.

These are the qualities most required as working women climb the corporate ladder in its current construct. One of the toughest transi-tions is getting past middle management into positions of senior lead-ership. This is often referred to as the "messy middle" because it is a period in which many women may face systemic barriers or biases that hold them back, or when they gain more responsibilities at home just as they are gaining more responsibilities at work. We found that from midlevel to senior positions, the traits most needed to drive success are Leading, Performing, Creating, or Self-Sustaining. And among the most senior women, especially those over the age of 55, Self-Sustaining and Creating were the most dominant traits; this group was the most self-assured and open-minded given the wisdom of their experience. These four superpowers are also most correlated with starting a busi-ness, which may explain why we see women strike out on their own as a route to pursue their passion or as a salve to dissatisfaction with their current environment.

Leading, Performing, Self-Sustaining, and Creating qualities are necessary to win in the present. In her book *Know Your Value*, Mika Brzezinski suggests that women practice speaking publicly so they can handle the discomfort of asking for a raise; build rapport with a boss so

Comfort/Capability across situations for those with Giving only as a superpower vs. those with Giving + Leading superpowers*

	Giving	Giving + Leading	
Public speaking/ giving a speech	24%	71%	**Three times more capable**
Telling a story in front of an audience	28%	76%	
Asking for a raise	28%	65%	
Asking for a promotion	29%	65%	
Being criticized for something you did	30%	52%	
Asking for a favor	30%	61%	
Starting your own business	35%	70%	**Two times more capable**
Going to an event where you don't know anyone	36%	70%	
Having to be the expert on a topic	38%	79%	
Competing for something	39%	86%	
Selling someone on a plan or idea	40%	79%	
Raising money for a business or charity	41%	76%	
Leading a project	47%	92%	

*Comfort/Capability defined as percent of women who scored Top 2 Box (4 or 5) overall on this question: *Please rate on a scale from 1 to 5 how capable or comfortable you feel about being able to handle this situation (1 = Not at all comfortable or capable and 5 = I feel extremely capable or comfortable).*

there's trust at the negotiating table; never apologize; and be comfortable with being told no. All four qualities most correlate to success. To complement the exercises in this chapter and Chapter 4, here are ways to practice these qualities tomorrow:

1. **The "No-Edit" Story:** High-impact self-advocacy starts with sharp, clear storytelling that articulates who you are, what you stand for, and what you want. Without any editing or overthinking, what are your strengths (this should be quick if you've taken the quiz and gone through the exercises in Chapter 5)? Next, what's your life story in three bullets? Who are you to the world, and what makes you tick? Lastly, what is it that you want? The answers to these questions should become second nature to you. Because the Leading, Performing, and Creating superpowers are grounded in setting direction and storytelling; what better way to start than with your own narrative. If you're going to ask for a promotion or get in front of an audience, you've got to feel comfortable in your own skin (and story) first.

2. **Practice with Support:** In his book *Outliers*, Malcolm Gladwell popularized the 10,000-hour rule, the level of intensive practice required to achieve mastery of skills.[2] Mastery requires time . . . and practice. Take the time to prepare for an important conversation; I rehearse a speech three to five times in front of a mirror the day before I deliver it. There is another component to practicing: the importance of a teacher. One of the researchers from the 10,000-hour rule study, K. Anders Ericsson, shared that practice is important, but "deliberate" practice under the guidance of a teacher is the most effective. A teacher can provide expertise and help target specific areas for improvement. Find someone with whom you can practice. The first time I had to do a television interview, I called two friends, Heather and Mark, both of whom are television journalists, to enlist their help. They gave me tips and rehearsed with me; Heather even filmed video of me in a practice studio and gave me detailed pointers as we watched the footage together.

3. **Transfer Between the Parts of Your Life:** As you get more comfortable with adopting one of these qualities in one part of your life, reflect on how that same quality could cross over into another part of your life. When I help women prepare to negotiate their salary, if they have children, I will often say to them, "What if someone was bullying your child at school— would you walk into the principal's office as a cub or a mama bear? Well, you need to advocate for what you're worth and what you deserve in the same way that you would fight for your child." Sometimes, we already have these qualities, but we haven't deployed them for ourselves. My friend Cecilia told me that she realized she had been practicing Leading and Performing qualities as the head of her homeowner's association. It was a low-risk venue for her to try out a more assertive style, and she felt that she could take those skills into negotiating a raise. Plus, it takes a lot of energy to be two different versions of yourself! Isn't it more efficient to be only one version with your full suite of superpowers ready for all parts of your life?

4. **The Power of "One Thing":** When I was at McKinsey, I carried a "one thing" notebook. I found that the open-ended question "Do you have any feedback for me?" always elicited an ambiguous response such as "You're doing great, just keep doing it" or "Not at the moment, but I will let you know." Instead, I started to ask a simple question: "What's one thing you think I can do better and how?" Everyone had one thing they thought I could improve upon and a way they would handle the situation. I collected these "one things" in a notebook and as I mastered the skills, I would cross them off. I still have this notebook from my business analyst days as a reminder of how to continue building skills. Go to people in your life who embody Leading, Performing, Self-Sustaining, or Creating and ask for advice on one thing they think you could do better, one thing they do that makes them successful. If you ask your boss or a colleague, it will also send the signal that this is something you're actively working to improve. They'll take notice, feel involved in your

learning journey, and give you credit as you demonstrate these skills.

5. **What Would [insert name] Do?:** We all have people in our circle, personal or professional, who embody at least one of these three qualities. My friend Monica, who is introverted, tells me that she often thinks, "What would Lisa do?" when she has to give a presentation. She recently had to give toasts at an event. She thought about how I would do this with my Leading, Performing, and Creating superpowers, after having watched me give countless birthday toasts for our circle of friends. Tap into the power of those around you. (I discuss this exercise a bit more in the next chapter.)

Feeling Appreciated and Useful

In our quantitative work, we found that full-time parents were the least satisfied group overall (19 percent of full-time parents reported feeling satisfied versus 26 percent overall). The largest drivers of dissatisfaction were "being appreciated by others" and "being able to use my talents." The most frequent superpower combinations for this group were Giving plus Achieving (33 percent), Giving plus Believing (33 percent), and Giving plus Knowing (31 percent), which explains their gaps around feeling valued (those with Giving may feel taken for granted) and being useful (Achieving and Knowing traits are centered around accomplishments and metrics). Here are some tools for boosting this group:

Awareness: In Chapter 5, we saw the power of being aware of our superpowers. This awareness can provide direction on what activities to take on. For example, my friend Camila had Achieving as her dominant quality, and she channeled that into leading fundraising efforts for Ukrainian refugees.

Assuredness: Once you know your superpowers, you can channel Self-Sustaining to validate yourself first. Let's go back to Nicole, whom we met in Chapter 2. Her quiz results? Performing, Knowing, and Giving were her top attributes. In every aspect of her life, she realized that others relied on her for energy, kindness, and support. Seeing her superpowers gave her a chance to see how much she contributed to her family and friends.

Advocacy: Leading, Performing, and Creating can come in many forms. Take a step outside of your comfort zone and practice self-advocacy. It could be as simple as raising your hand to give the presentation at a school meeting or to start and lead a project in your community. Adding the Leading quality to the Giving superpower doubles or triples confidence and satisfaction levels across the board.

While Leading, Performing, Self-Sustaining, and Creating most drive up capability and satisfaction levels, it is important to note that because they involve interacting with others, implementing them will require understanding the confidence language of the other party. These cannot be practiced in a vacuum to be effective, so understanding what drives the person you're making the ask from will be critical. This is the focus of the next chapter, understanding the confidence language of your audience.

We also have to take into account cultural norms and additional hurdles we face in expressing these qualities, from gender to racial biases. This is especially true for women of color, for whom the starting points are different. On satisfaction, capability, and competence, women of color are not statistically different, according to our survey, and a few studies show they actually score higher in self-confidence. But there is another layer of cultural barriers for them to overcome. As I recommend these solutions, I recognize that we each might have a different starting point.

For example, being an Asian woman, on top of having to demonstrate Leading and Performing qualities to get what I want, I've had to address the fact that my physiology makes me look 10 years younger than I actually am. In my consulting days, I was tapped to be the lead on a project for a major luxury department store chain client. In the introductory meeting, as I entered the room, the CEO made the assumption that I was the most junior member of the team (not the lead partner) and asked me for a cup of coffee. I channeled Performing and Self-Sustaining qualities and used humor to call out his unconscious bias in our introductions as follows: "I'm the lead partner for this study, Lisa Sun. I've been at McKinsey for over a decade. I know what you're thinking: those are some amazing Asian genetics because

I don't look like I've been a consultant for that long." In this instance, I owned my ethnicity as part of my story and stood in my own power and narrative. Deepa Purushothaman, leadership expert and author of *The First, The Few, The Only: How Women of Color Can Redefine Power in Corporate America*, calls this "shedding messages that harm us." She shares, "Once you shed what doesn't serve you, you'll make space for your own truth, be able to write your own narratives, and decide what you want to carry forward." That's the reality of cultural context—we shouldn't have to overcome this additional layer, but we must acknowledge and address it, until the system and those in positions of power evolve to include us.

My Continuing Journey

I'd like to come full circle to where I started this chapter by sharing that I am a work in progress when it comes to my own gravitas. I have taken our quiz multiple times over the last few years, and I've assessed my own stars, check marks, and circles on the situations grid. Where am I today? The qualities I am working on are Believing and Self-Sustaining. I've seen that these qualities can balance out the shadow sides of my most dominant traits: I'm a people pleaser, I care what others think, I am really hard on myself. Channeling Believing and Self-Sustaining qualities has helped me power through three setbacks during the pandemic: the near collapse of our business in March 2020, being the victim of an Asian hate crime in March 2021, and the ending of a five-year romantic relationship in February 2021.

The first setback occurred when our company's sales were in the negative at the start of the pandemic. I showed myself little compassion as I took on all the blame. My parents gave me the tools to achieve early on in my life, but that gift also has a hard edge to it: it equates accolades and perfection with self-esteem, which means I beat myself up for not measuring up to self-imposed and external markers of success. The pandemic was the perfect trigger for that. I focused on how much further we had to climb rather than appreciating how far we had come and was pessimistic about outcomes. Our designer, Aruk, exemplified the power of Believing because he felt we would figure out how to rebound as well as find the opportunities to keep the lights on. Something good did come out of this—we made face masks and hospital gowns for first responders. And people raised their hands to help us, just as Aruk said they would. My former McKinsey client, Bonni, who was stuck on Long Island with her children home from college, saw our story on LinkedIn. She offered us the use of her car so we could pick up fabric for face masks and drop off finished face masks at warehouses for workers who needed them. All the stores in New York's Garment District found ways to get us the supplies we needed, oftentimes leaving them outside their stores on the deserted street so I could pick them up on my walk to work. There was also a specific moment when, under stress, I thought our New York City seamstresses had not finished a 2,500-unit mask order for a warehouse in New Jersey. Our designer paused and said to me, "They wouldn't short the order. No one wants to be bad at their job. Let's trust they're in it with us. Let's count again." And we did count again, and of course every mask was there, as they had said it was. Believing the best in others, the best in situations—this is one of my go-forward goals.

Second, in March 2021, I was harassed on the streets of New York City: I had a beer thrown at me, and I was shoved on the street in broad daylight. In the wake of this (and another verbal attack on one of my teammates) and the increasing anti-Asian American sentiment in the country, I've had to channel Self-Sustaining and speak up without worrying about what others would think. I continue to reconcile what it means to be a Taiwanese American woman, and practicing a new form of gravitas is helping me on my journey. As a minority, I have always lived with an inherent tension between "fitting in" and "standing out," as well as the tension of being sandwiched between two very different generations. My parents' generation is firmly in the fitting-in camp—focus on achievement, ignore suffering, be grateful for what you have, and assimilate. My younger brother's generation is speaking up to call out injustice. Me? I'm stuck between these generations and becoming a reluctant activist. I had never filed a police report before, let alone one documenting a hate crime, but I did. When I was dismissed by law enforcement, I didn't give up and worked with the Asian Hate Crimes Task Force to get all the video footage that showed what had happened to me. I joined the dialogue publicly and privately. I participated in protests. I raised money for Stop AAPI Hate. I supported friends in reporting what they experienced. I let go of shame and feeling weak, and unapologetically embraced my upbringing and culture. Self-Sustaining has given me the courage to stand out and stand up for my community.

Lastly, I am going to share something incredibly personal (not that I haven't been open before this!). In 2021, I had a breakup with my boyfriend of five years. While I have been through breakups before, this one was the hardest thus far because it came at a time when my sense of self had already been shattered by the pressures of pivoting my company during a pandemic. When we broke up, I beat myself up—I asked myself what was wrong with me, what I could have done differently. One night while I was still licking my wounds, I went to dinner with a group of women mentors, all of them a bit older than me. We usually talked about professional issues at these gatherings, but this time, they each opened up about their love lives; half of the group was divorced and had remarried, some had found their husbands in their mid-40s. One of the women, Vivian, shared, "After my first marriage ended and I had to raise two young girls on my own as a single working parent, I thought about what I wanted in the future. I had this memory of my parents. Each night after dinner, my father would wrap his arms around my mother in the kitchen and tell her how much he loved her. Every night until he passed away. I thought, *That's what I want and deserve,* and that's who I found in my second marriage. Lisa, you will find love again." It was important for me to hear that and believe it. They kindled the Believing superpower in me that night, and I reflected on what I had learned in the last relationship and what I wanted in the next one. But in the meantime, I conjured up some Self-Sustaining qualities to help me reassert my own self-worth and also brave the online dating world for the first time. (I've learned this quality helps a lot because you can't take anything too personally on a dating app, especially when you are ghosted or unmatched!).

This is proof that we grow from experience. Tapping into these other superpowers helped me cope with isolation and uncertainty. What I say to all of you is that through all of this, I got stronger. And it proves that with any sort of loss or grief, you can show your mettle and resilience. On my Spotify breakup playlist, I had on repeat Kelly Clarkson's song "Stronger," which includes the Nietzsche-inspired line "What doesn't kill you makes you stronger, stronger." Science would support Kelly and me: the "Whatever Does Not Kill Us: Cumulative Lifetime Adversity,

Vulnerability, and Resilience" study of 2,398 subjects over the course of three years found that those who experienced "adverse events" tested stronger in mental health and well-being than people who didn't.[3] And who doesn't have adverse events in their life?

With the skill set you are learning here, you will be better equipped to handle anything that comes your way. In the next chapter, we'll see how this skill set will help build out the pivotal relationships we have throughout our lives.

BUILDING BETTER
CONNECTIONS

A majority of this book thus far has been focused on self-examination, reflecting on what makes you tick, believing in your strengths, stretching yourself in new ways, and, ultimately, developing a strong and nurturing relationship with yourself. That's real work—learning to be authentically confident, to show up and advocate for yourself, and to feel appreciated. Now let's turn to how we see others and create meaningful connections, or as Brené Brown describes it in her book *The Gifts of Imperfection*, "the energy that exists between people when they feel seen, heard, and valued; when they can give and receive without judgment; and when they derive sustenance and strength from the relationship."

Applying the confidence language lens to others helps us to better connect with the important people in our lives, personally and professionally. All of us have different confidence languages, and being able to see others' strengths creates a stronger foundation for those relationships. Once we understand and appreciate other people's superpowers—and they understand and appreciate ours—we can strengthen each relationship to better communicate, find common ground, and resolve conflict. When people feel appreciated and receive gratitude, it improves stress responses and boosts resilience and performance.[1] And it's a self-reinforcing cycle! When we can identify the unique forms of gravitas in others, we are able to deepen our connections, which further fuels our own confidence. Strengthening our connections to others is also essential for mental health,[2] and in an era of endless e-mails, texting, social media, and DMs, effective communication is more important than ever.

Let's start by exploring two foundational elements of strong relationships—trust and empathy—and see how applying the confidence language framework can enable both.

It Starts with Trust

Business management expert Patrick Lencioni created a theory to describe the most effective teams, which fulfill the requirements of the Lencioni Trust Pyramid. The pyramid has five layers, and the bottom layer, the foundational and largest building block of the pyramid, is trust. Trust is the foundation upon which the other layers are built: conflict, commitment, accountability, and results. All together, these form the basis of strong relationships and teams. His model was intended for the boardroom, but this can work outside the office as well, as every relationship starts with trust.

When trust is present, everything else falls into line. You can engage in a productive debate of ideas, commit to decisions and plans of action, hold each other accountable, and focus on achieving results. Everyone wins. Yet if one or more members of the team (or couple or family) lacks trust, the team falls apart. They don't feel they can be open, nor do they feel compelled to deliver on all the other markers that make for success in a team.

While most people think of trust as what we can see (reliability—I do what I commit to; congruence—what I say and what I do match), two other components are essential: acceptance (I respect you and value you) and openness (I am open to feedback and freely give it in return).[3] Seeing the unique confidence languages of others can help us to create the acceptance and openness that enables trust. In other words, if I see your strengths and respect you for them, and I feel confident in my own strengths, we can enjoy a stronger connection and achieve more together.

The Answer Is Always Empathy

American novelist David Foster Wallace, in his commencement speech at Kenyon College in 2005, begins with an allegory that takes place in a fishbowl. An older goldfish meets two young fry and says, "Good morning, boys, how's the water this morning?" The two little goldfish look at each other quizzically and ask, "What's water?"—a metaphor for how we humans go around in our little bubbles, oblivious to what is going on around us. Later in the speech, he recounts the daily grind of going to a packed grocery store after a long day of work: a super long line, the woman in front of you is on her phone, the lady behind the cash register is frantically trying to keep up, you're angry at all of it. But if you take a moment to "see the water," and be "aware enough to give yourself a choice, you can choose to look differently" at the woman in front of you:

> Maybe she's not usually like this. Maybe she's been up three straight nights holding the hand of a husband who is dying of bone cancer. . . . It just depends [on] what you want to consider. If you're automatically sure that you know what reality is, and you are operating on your default setting, then you, like me, probably won't consider possibilities that aren't annoying and miserable. But if you really learn how to pay attention, then you will know there are other options.[4]

When we sit inside another person's story, we create the basis for connection; from there, we can make every action—and reaction—more meaningful and impactful.

Being able to understand another person's superpowers is empathy in action. It gives us a language through which we can pay attention, get out of our own heads, and see the world through another's eyes. If we go back to Freud's iceberg model of consciousness, which asks us to dive below the 10 percent of our psyche that is visible (the tip of the iceberg) to truly examine underlying values and beliefs, understanding another person's confidence language allows us to see below the surface and understand the 90 percent of the iceberg that is not readily visible. We not only "see the water," we see below the waterline.

Getting to Know the Other Person

We can use the vocabulary of superpowers to see others with empathy and be more open and accepting to build trust, leading to more meaningful relationships. While we can't have every person in our life take our quiz (although wouldn't that make things so much easier?), we can use Chapter 4 as a tool to ask questions of, and observe behaviors in, the people who matter most to us. Here's a shorthand list of questions to consider for developing an understanding of someone in your life and what their strengths are:

LEADING	PERFORMING	ACHIEVING	GIVING
In group settings, does this person take charge?	Do you hang on their every word when they're telling a story?	Does this person take game night the most seriously?	Is this the first person you call when things get tough?
Is this the person who makes and drives plans?	Is everything more fun when they're around?	Does this person share stories about not giving up?	Does this person seem to always give you the perfect gift?

KNOWING	CREATING	BELIEVING	SELF-SUSTAINING
Does this person always have a fun fact to contribute to the conversation?	Is this a person with a powerful imagination?	Is this person an optimist who always looks for the best in others and situations?	Is this person comfortable in their own skin or who always seems to "have it together"?
Does this person research a topic thoroughly before making a decision?	Does this person talk about the future, ideas for improving it, and "firsts"?	When things go wrong, is this the person who tells you not to worry?	Does this person not worry about what others think of them?

Once we understand another's superpowers, we can do for them what we did for ourselves: we can validate them. We can make sure they feel seen and valued for what makes them tick. A sibling whose dominant trait is Performing? You'll see that they need an audience and perhaps you let them have the floor a little bit longer. This is the acceptance component of trust: each respects and values the strengths the other person brings to the table.

Next, we need to figure out how our confidence language interacts with theirs. When we understand how we overlap and diverge, we can create space for openness, transparency, and engagement.

Look for Common Ground: When we share the same superpower, does this explain the basis for our relationship or why things work? Are there times when our shared quality conflicts?

Recognize Your Differences: Do our superpowers complement each other and form the basis of a great partnership? Or do they explain why we don't agree, or why we see things differently? Does it explain why I feel your behavior falls short of my expectations, or vice versa? Or does your superpower dominate mine, so I feel underappreciated?

When we see each other's strengths, we create a larger set of choices for how we can act and react. On the next page, you'll see an example of this.

Some strengths can be complementary, but differences in superpowers can also lead to misunderstandings when they go unrecognized. When this happens, it's easy to spot: it can be like locking horns. For instance, Barbara, whom I met at an event in Nashville, came up to me in tears after my speech. Her aging father was physically declining, but he had rejected all of her suggestions for his care. She shared, "We've been fighting, especially since my mom died. We've chosen a nice retirement home and created a plan with his doctor, but all he says is 'If it's my time to go, then it's my time to go. I don't want you telling me what to do.' This quiz has helped me realize that my main superpower is Achieving, and my dad's are Believing and Self-Sustaining. THIS is why we aren't getting along. I'm trying to control everything and manage him, and he just wants to be left alone. If I could let go and be more optimistic— and if he could acknowledge that I'm getting all the things done that Mom used to do for him—we could make the most out of the time we have left together." Barbara was able to see this relationship with more

How Do Our Superpowers Overlap?

Our Superpowers Overlap 100%

Common Ground: We understand each other's Giving nature.

Conflict & Adapt: Are there times when we might conflict? If we both have Leading as a superpower, are there times when we might need to let the other one be in charge?

Stretch & Support: Are there new superpowers we might need to help each other cultivate? Do we want to help each other add a new strength? If neither of us have Believing or Self-Sustaining qualities, but we have experienced loss, how do we help each other recover?

Our Superpowers Overlap Partially

SAME SUPER-POWER

Common Ground: We both have Achieving as a superpower. We value metrics and winning as part of the way we work together.

Conflict & Adapt: Since we both have Achieving as top strengths, are there times when we might get too competitive with each other?

DIFFERENT SUPER-POWER

Complement: Do the qualities on which we differ complement each other? Your top superpower is Knowing, and my top one is Performing. Together, we can get things done and communicate effectively.

Learn: Can we learn from each other? Can you please help me stay organized and on track? Can I help you craft a story and share it?

Conflict & Adapt: Do the qualities on which we differ conflict? There are times when your Knowing quality is too linear, and I know my Performing trait can overwhelm.

Our Superpowers Are Completely Different

Complement: Do the qualities on which we differ complement each other? You have Achieving as a superpower, and I have Giving as my top strength. You can bring goals and I can bring nurturing to our work. Together, we get things done!

Conflict & Adapt: Do the qualities on which we differ conflict? Your dominant quality is Leading. There are times when I feel you are inflexible, and I do not feel heard.

Learn: Can we learn from each other? I'd like to learn how to have more commanding qualities. I can help you with Giving attributes.

empathy and compassion, and she chose to change her dynamic with her father in a way that reinforced their love for each other.

Making Our Differences Work

Each superpower has the potential to clash with others: for example, let's revisit the sibling whose superpower is Performing. What if this strength is not in your confidence language? If, in fact, you're an introvert. This may explain why she's always seeking validation and frustrated that she doesn't get enough praise from you. Can you adapt, especially when you know she might need that extra word of affirmation? While it's outside of your natural tendencies, is that a place to stretch yourself to strengthen your bond? And vice versa—can she know when to tone down her extroversion to better meet your need for quiet?

Too much of a good thing can also lead to conflict. Put two people with Leading qualities together, and watch for disagreement over who will take charge; two people with the Performing superpower equals a lot of attention-seeking and very little getting done.

Here's how to get the most out of these clashing forms of confidence:

- Recognize and understand each other's strengths (and the potential downsides of those strengths). Together, discuss observations about each other's dominant traits and preferred working styles.

- Decide how the strengths of each can complement the other. When necessary, adapt your style to get the most out of the relationship. And vice versa.

Key Relationships

Now that you understand your superpowers and know how to acknowledge the superpowers of others, let's navigate through five important relationships you might have so you can gain a fresh perspective on each. This is by no means a substantive course on every relationship and combination of superpowers, but it is a primer on how we can approach the relationships that matter.

FRIENDSHIPS

Psychological research identifies female relationships as the strongest we can have. A landmark UCLA study demonstrated how being with female friends can counteract stress by releasing oxytocin, buffering fight-or-flight responses and producing a calming effect.[5] Physician Kristen Fuller reinforces how friendships between women are special: "Women feel they can count on their friends to pull through for them no matter what they are struggling with in their lives. Women are each other's emotional support system."[6]

While writing this book, I hosted a focus group with a book club of seven women. The group formed several years ago; all are mothers, some are full-time parents, some work. All of them took the quiz, and they wanted to share their results with each other. Why? Because they were friends, they were curious about each other's strengths, and they wanted to support each other's growth. They discovered that they all had Giving and Knowing in their top superpowers, which, when you think about it, makes sense: They came together monthly to read and discuss a book (Knowing). They all noted that this group was the only place where they felt comfortable being completely vulnerable, and that it was a judgment-free and supportive outlet for each of them during the COVID-19 pandemic (Giving). Then the discussion turned to what the results meant for them individually. For example:

The oldest member of the group scored high on all eight of the superpowers (she's in the 2 percent of women who have all eight), and it explained why everyone always went to her for advice.

Those who had Achieving and were full-time parents who used to work shared how much they missed working, which prompted them to create ways to channel their energies in new ways that could activate their superpowers.

One woman who did not have Achieving as her top trait realized that might be why she was so unhappy in her high-pressure job.

One woman shared the story of the loss of a child and how that grief has stayed with her, and how the Believing and Creating qualities could be helpful.

Another woman who had immigrated to the United States more than a decade ago shared why Creating was her top form of confidence in that she had created a new life for herself, but had always felt like an outsider. She felt this group had truly accepted her.

Seeing each other's confidence languages opened up a new dialogue and levels of support for this friend group.

There are also times, though, when female friendships may be a source of conflict, because we're coming at life from different strengths. Sandra, an attendee at one of my workshops in Dallas, confided, "I'm really struggling with my friends. I took your quiz, and I'm all Leading and Self-Sustaining. At work, I can see how that's helped me and hurt me; I take charge even when my colleagues see me as sharp-elbowed. But what really bothers me is what it means in my personal life. People think I'm cold and have to have things my way. Just recently, I was disinvited from a bachelorette party because they thought I'd bring the group down." I told her first and foremost that she should be proud that she recognized the strengths that she had (in fact, these two superpowers are highly correlated with being capable in most situations!) and also for acknowledging that they may be hindering her relationships. She was initially resistant, but I reinforced to her, "You have to be open and let someone in your friend group know this hurt you and ask that person for feedback. Being vulnerable elicits compassion." We then role-played Giving and Believing techniques: we changed up her body language to convey warmth (her default stance was with crossed arms and a stern face); we practiced an open body stance and softening her facial expressions; and we also practiced asking questions to see the best in others ("How did that work event go? I'm sure you did well." "I remember you said you were taking up yoga. How's that going? What are you enjoying about it? I'd love to join the next time you go."). There are times when you need to practice another form of confidence to connect with others.

Take my friends: I affectionately refer to the group as "*The Golden Girls* meets *Sex and the City*" in part because some of us have lived together at one point, and we've navigated the struggles and victories of living in New York City together. We all have different strengths that we bring to the group, and I find power in those friends who have the traits that I don't have. In any given situation, I will often think of one of my friends who has a superpower that I don't naturally have, and I will try to think of how they would handle it. It goes both ways: one friend who is the most introverted of the group often thinks, "What would Lisa do?" when going into presentations at major meetings. When I had to build a large IKEA wardrobe that had been sitting in my apartment in boxes for weeks, I called up my Achieving and Knowing friend, who showed up ready to read the entire instruction manual and navigate what she calls "two-person moments," the parts of the process that require two people, like flipping over the wardrobe. And there's the Giving and Believing friend who we all call first when we have been fired or dumped; she's the first person to show up with takeout and tissues. In our friendships, we can ask these questions to get the most out of every interaction:

1. What are the strengths of my friend(s)? What can I learn from her? When can I lean on her?

2. What are my contributions to the friendship?

3. Where have we butted heads in the past? What was the reason for that? Were we too similar, or too different? Or were the shadow sides of our strengths coming out?

FAMILY

Some of us grew up in nurturing environments, while others may have had tough childhoods. Some have close relationships with members of their family; others haven't spoken for years. Needless to say, these relationships are formative, in part because they are usually given to us by birth and not by choice. As we more deeply understand grandparents, parents, siblings, children, and other relatives, we gain insight into how we might strengthen these bonds.

I've only recently come to fully understand my own family through the language of confidence. Taiwanese culture is not known for open communication—in fact, we don't talk about our feelings. At all. So a lot of the work I have done on myself has been trying to understand my family members on a deeper level. I know now that my younger brother cannot stand it when I don't see things through to completion (Achieving and Knowing are two of his top superpowers); my feathers are ruffled when he doesn't match my extroverted energy levels in our interactions (my Performing and Leading superpowers are at odds with one of his top ones, which is Self-Sustaining). But there are also moments when his strengths have truly supported me. After a speech, an audience member came up to me and criticized my delivery. I was very upset by this because I invest a lot of myself into every event; giving speeches is one of the things I'm best at in the world. When I told my brother about the criticism, his response was, "Why do you care what that person thinks? Do you think you crushed it? If so, that should be enough!" In that moment, his Self-Sustaining superpower helped me overcome the people-pleasing tendencies of my Performing trait.

As you've read in previous chapters, my parents have an abundance of superpowers: Creating, Achieving, Knowing, Giving. And my mother is among the 2 percent that has them all, especially Leading, Believing, Self-Sustaining, and Performing (she is not one to shy away from a karaoke mic). What I've realized now is that we have had our darkest moments when our Leading qualities were in conflict: we both wanted to take charge, or we both thought we knew the best way to get something done. And in our best moments, she taught me how to channel Believing and Self-Sustaining, the two qualities I most want to develop. Every month, as an entrepreneur, I go through a soul-destroying process called "closing the books." That is, I have to make sure everyone gets paid or if we can't do that, work with vendors to sort out payment plans. It's disheartening when you realize that you're always indebted to someone. My mother is one of my first calls on the last week of the month. Here's what that conversation sounds like (verbatim, including how my mother actually sounds; please remember English is not her first language):

Lisa: *Mom, I don't think we're going to make it this month.*

Mom: *You know, I your age once too. I build business. It happen.*

Lisa: *I can't make the math work. I'm going to let everyone down.*

Mom: *It's okay. I believe. I know you can do it. You get this far. You are my beautiful daughter. Mom believe. And I not dumb. I very smart. So you believe in you. You will success. I know it.*

Lisa (tears streaming down face): *I needed to hear that. Okay, I'm going to go to the office and show up and face everyone.*

Mom: *Yes, you show up! You can't run away or hide, it does not solve problem. Everything can be solved.*

A few months before we launched our company, I asked her to take a look at the website before it went live. This was her e-mail response:

From: **Mom >**   Hide

To: **Lisa Sun >**

Re: Mom-- do you like the web site? (eom)
June 11, 2013, 6:59 PM

yes, you will success.
mom

Never tell a tiger mom what Google Analytics is because to this day, I still wake up every morning and when I check my company's analytics, I notice we have dozens of clicks from Taiwan. I know those clicks are from my mom. Her response when I bring it up? "I go on website, click everything, and make sure nothing broken." (It is clear that all of my best qualities come from her, and I still want to be just like her when I grow up.)

With your family members, think through the following on your own, and also together with them:

1. What are the qualities that bind us together, the traits that we share? (One of my best friends, Sofia, had her husband and two daughters write a family mission statement and values, which read like a list of their family's superpowers— Giving, Knowing, Achieving, Believing—and it is posted on their refrigerator door.)

2. When we get along, why is that? Are we sharing the same qualities or complementing each other's strengths?

3. When we are there for each other, what are we each bringing to that interaction?

4. When was the last time we fought? Were we coming at the situation from different points of view?

5. How could we have handled it differently? Should I have adapted my style to suit yours, or vice versa?

SPOUSE/SIGNIFICANT OTHER/PARTNER

People usually pick partners because of their attributes ("He is so smart!" "They are so passionate!"), but as time goes by those attributes may be less endearing and more annoying ("They are a know-it-all!" "She is always on me with her to-do lists!"). The tedium of a relationship over time may cloud our perceptions. But if love is still there, it is worth understanding your partner's superpowers so you can better communicate and resolve differences, whether it is about who takes out the trash or more serious issues like parenting.

My married friends Camila and Brian took the quiz together and when they read their results, their immediate reaction was, "This makes so much sense. This is why we work."

Camila
- Knowing
- Creating

- Giving
- Achieving

Brian
- Leading
- Believing
- Performing

They both share Giving and Achieving as superpowers, so they are on the same page in how they parent their three children and what they want out of life. Their family motto is: "We never quit!" They each recognized immediately how their individual strengths complemented the other's. Camila is the organized one who keeps the entire family on a schedule and structures their lives (her Knowing superpower in action); Brian is extroverted and brings joy and fun to that structure (he scored high on Leading and Performing). For Camila, Brian's Believing superpower has brought optimism to their relationship, especially in helping her to navigate upsets. But their differences also explained why they at times talk past each other, Brian from a more emotional lens and Camila from a more logical one.

When relationships are at their best, each person is being seen and valued for their strengths, and when upsets happen, each person's strengths can support the other in seeing them through that tough time. At their worst, our dominant traits may create conflicting points of view or compete with each other, losing sight of common ground. On a daily level, it can be as simple as decoding household decisions. My friend Maggie recently moved in with her boyfriend, Jack. She took the quiz and one of her frustrations made sense: "It has been so hot in the apartment, and we needed a new air conditioner. It took Jack days to research the best one; I would have looked for the first five-star review and added it to the cart immediately. He is all about Knowing and has to analyze everything thoroughly; I'm Creating and Achieving and just want to get it done. I was so mad, but now I see that I make snap decisions, and he's more methodical. In the long run, I should have trusted him on this one. The air conditioner he chose ended up being super quiet and will last us a long time. We just have different strengths."

This confidence-language approach enables us to see our partner for their strengths. Renowned relationship expert Esther Perel says we are most drawn to our partner when:

> I see them in their element. This is the category of radiance and confidence—and it's probably the biggest turn-on across the board. "I am most drawn to my partner when I see him in the studio, when she is on stage, when they are doing something about which they're really passionate."
>
> When we see our partner in their flow state, it's as if this person who is so known to us, is momentarily once again somewhat elusive. And in this space between "me" and "the other" lies the erotic élan—that movement *toward the other*. Because, sometimes, as Marcel Proust said, "mystery is not about traveling to new places but about looking with new eyes. . . ." There's something inherently sexy about that. We're allowed to let go of our caretaking impulse and bask in their shine.[7]

I love the phrase, "bask in their shine," because that is what it means to see someone for their superpowers. Have you and your significant other been together for so long that it feels like you are more like roommates than lovers? And your household is more like running a small business as you coordinate a hectic schedule between your kids' activities and your work commitments?

If you are in a new relationship, you may still be in that phase of everything they do being just adorable. But it is never too early to ask yourself if you think you have what it takes for the long haul. Perhaps ask your partner to take the quiz as a shared activity. Here are some questions to ask yourself about your relationship with your significant other, whether the relationship is three months old or 30 years strong:

1. What are my partner's strengths? Do I recognize them for those strengths? Which ones do I lean on most often?

2. Does my partner see me for my strengths and the contributions I make?

3. Am I communicating what I need from them? Am I sharing where I want to grow?

4. When I think of when we're at our best, how are our strengths working together? Are we using the same ones or different ones? What can we learn from past experiences to help us get through future ones?

5. At our worst, what traits are coming into play? Is it the downsides of each other's strengths, or are we coming at something with very different points of view? Are there other superpowers we want to build together?

YOUR BOSS

The relationship with your boss is pivotal to your career. While having a good connection with your superior can improve your performance, increase your confidence, and boost your career, people often take a back seat in forming that relationship. They let their superior take the initiative, but studies show that the opposite—being proactive—can be helpful in meeting your career goals, as most superiors favor those employees who show initiative in building that rapport.[8] This is especially important given the increasing prevalence of virtual and hybrid work environments in which in-person face time is no longer a given. And research shows that our relationship with our boss factors heavily in job satisfaction—unfortunately, it mostly results in dissatisfaction. Research shows that most people find that relationship lacking,[9] and another study shows that 75 percent of the participants found that their relationship with their boss was the most stressful part of their job.[10]

So how do you change this relationship if you are among that 75 percent? First take a moment and understand your boss's leadership traits. What superpowers do they bring to the table? Susan from Chapter 1, the financial head at a major health care company who was told she didn't have gravitas, could describe her boss's confidence language as Leading and Performing, while Susan was an intellectual to the core who took care of her team with a more introverted style (Achieving, Knowing, Giving). Her boss had a commanding, take-charge personality, having come up through the sales division. They had two seemingly opposing confidence languages, but as I talked Susan through the points of overlap and common ground, she could see how she could better communicate with him.

This is what I told her: Take a moment and reflect on your boss. What are their strengths? Which do you share? Which are different? You can use our questions from earlier in this chapter ("Getting to Know the Other Person") to identify their strengths and refer to the "How Do Our Superpowers Overlap?" chart to understand which actions to take based on common ground and differences (complement, learn, adapt).

One of my favorite sayings is "You don't choose the mentor. The mentor chooses you, so make yourself mentorable." Susan's awareness that her strengths were different from her boss's allowed her to channel the Self-Sustaining quality. She knew she added value in so many ways, so she did not have to spiral from the feedback. Rather, she could interpret it from his point of view and understand his desire to help her improve. If you find yourself in a similar circumstance, enlist the help of your boss in getting stronger. How do we make ourselves mentorable? We can say to our boss, for example, "I hear you and am grateful for the feedback. What's one thing I could do more of tomorrow to be more Leading in our interactions?" If you assume your boss is always "too busy" to help you grow, then you need to advocate for the time. When you get that time, you can do a few things: make sure your boss knows your strengths, be transparent about your goals to improve, and ask for their help in learning new skills. You have the opportunity to build trust with your boss by sharing how they can get the best out of you ("I value Achieving. When there is a clear process and metrics, I thrive.") and expressing your desire to learn ("I'd like to be more commanding in meetings. Can you share one way in which you do that?") and set the agenda for your journey with your boss. The more we are open to this back and forth, the stronger that relationship can be.

This all sounds straightforward in theory, but I know firsthand the twists and turns these interactions can take. However, Susan did execute the action plan we came up with in the dressing room together. She rooted her self-belief in her superpowers as a starting point and chose to level up by evolving her confidence language. She set up a standing time with her boss to share her team's accomplishments and how she had made a difference, to get acknowledgement for the unique ways in which she was contributing. She practiced demonstrating new Performing traits, including leveling up her presentations in a way that would have her audience as fascinated by the data and numbers as she was. She was open with her boss about wanting to practice Leading and Performing skills and asked him to give her feedback after every meeting. She was eventually promoted to CFO. And in the long term, her efforts helped the organization see her in a new light, both in terms of appreciating her contributions and supporting her in new skills.

When we build up the strength of this relationship, we can feel more comfortable and confident in advocating for our needs. Let me revisit Monica from Chapter 2. She had built up significant goodwill with her boss; she had already demonstrated her strengths to him and advocated for herself as they built their relationship. So much so that when she felt the need for a promotion, she didn't default to her Achieving and Knowing qualities to have to prove that she needed it. She matched her boss's Leading and Self-Sustaining superpowers in conveying that the title change simply made sense because it was in line with how she saw herself and how she needed the organization to see her. His response? He called HR immediately to put in the promotion request, and then communicated to her how much he valued her and saw her potential beyond this title.

In my time at McKinsey & Company, my favorite boss of all time was a British man named Andrew. We had no demographic points of connection. At one of our first lunches, he asked me, "So, tell me something you're really proud of, from your childhood. Give me an accomplishment that you really loved, or something about your childhood." He was looking for something he could connect with on a personal level. While he was seeking to learn more about me, our relationship became a values-based mentorship rather than a demographic one. When I reflect on why we worked so well together, it made sense. His superpowers are Self-Sustaining, Knowing, Achieving, Giving, and Believing. He was never the loudest voice in the room; he felt confident enough in his own value that he let others shine—he certainly let me Lead, Perform, and Create to my heart's content. At the same time, he pushed me to be better: I typically delivered my team's work at the last minute because Performing is one of my top superpowers, and those of us with this trait are not the most capable at getting tasks done! However, he was adamant about process and clear metrics (Knowing, Achieving) and coached me on how to be better at both. He taught me how to be a servant leader and to bring Giving into my coaching and the development of my teams. He saw me for my strengths, but he also understood where his strengths would bring value to my leadership style. To this day, I'm a better person and leader because of him. He was the first person to invest in my company, and he's one of the first phone calls I make when I need advice on how to navigate a challenging business situation.

I recognize that some of us have difficult bosses, but decoding your boss has the potential to make your day-to-day more enjoyable. You'll have a better understanding of their strengths (and the drawbacks of their strengths). If there are points of common ground from which to build, that makes things easier. If your confidence languages are different, you can navigate that relationship with self-awareness and better read the situation. Ask yourself:

1. What are my boss's strengths? If our confidence languages are different, how can this person be a mentor to me? Will I learn new ways of working and thinking by adding to my style?

2. Do I need to advocate for the strengths I bring to the table that my boss might not naturally acknowledge, or take for granted? Can I advocate for how my boss can get the best out of me? Are there moments when I can give upward feedback to build trust without fearing retribution?

3. How can I take initiative in this relationship and demonstrate my commitment to growing and developing?

COLLEAGUES—PEERS AND SUBORDINATES

Some of us spend more time with our colleagues than we do with our family, even if it's in a virtual format. The best working environments are created when you are aware of your team's strengths. The language you are learning here is powerful because it can help you see your colleagues more fully, especially if they have strengths that are not the same as yours, which can form the foundation of a much more inclusive and diverse workplace. We as humans seek out people like us, and we tend to promote people who look like us or have similar backgrounds. But when you look beyond demography and you make connections based on values, you start to promote people who are different from you racially, culturally, or socioeconomically. You can build trust and create a supportive environment when you know and understand your team. And it fosters a virtuous cycle around mentorship, which we will explore in the next chapter.

Since I have developed my own sense of gravitas and learned to see others' confidence languages, I now know that I love working with more introverted personalities. My Leading, Performing, and Creating qualities mean I like to be in a group brainstorming, talking out my thinking, coming up with big ideas. But I lack execution capabilities and follow-through at times. It's the people on my team with Achieving and Knowing superpowers who take the time to plan, schedule, and actually get the job done. They are very different from me, but then, if I had a whole team of people just like me, we'd have a problem. I always celebrate teammates with complementary skill sets, and I also let them know my strengths—both the upsides and the downsides. I'm incredibly open about this, so they know what they're getting into!

I am clear about each role on our team and what superpowers are best deployed in that role, so as we are hiring, we look for certain qualities. For example, production roles require detailed planning, execution, and metrics. So we look for people with Achieving and Knowing as their superpowers in those roles. Overall, we screen every candidate for Giving and Creating qualities, because we want to work with emotionally supportive teammates who get excited about the company we are building together. And when someone is ready for a promotion, I take an active role in coaching them through my Leading and Performing qualities. For example, when Eliza on our team transitioned from the customer experience manager to marketing director, we practiced her presentation skills—including rehearsing meetings together—so that she felt confident pitching our retail partners on marketing plans.

There are moments when our superpowers can conflict to the point where a relationship can become toxic. I've seen this play out with co-founders who have disbanded. In one situation, one co-founder's spikes were Leading and Performing; the other's were Achieving, Knowing, and Giving. The former wanted to give speeches and post on social media all the time and never pitched in to do any of the work; the latter did all the work and felt like she was in it alone while the other was taking all the credit. They did not find balance in their working relationship and never valued each other's contributions. They eventually closed their business. In another instance, two friends, both spiking on Performing, co-founded a company. They both wanted the spotlight and could never agree on who would be featured in the press; they didn't know how to take turns and neither wanted to be seen as the supporting teammate. All that fighting for attention took away from the work that needed to be done to make the company successful. Sadly, they disbanded less than two years into their partnership.

Our confidence languages have the potential to help us rebuild teams as well. I worked with the passionate founder of a young company who was dealing with some issues with her team. She found out a few managers were keeping things from her because they feared retribution and were anxious about meeting her high standards. This created a vicious cycle of hiding mistakes and poor performance. I helped introduce Giving and Believing in their team—the assumption of positive intent, mutual support, and seeing the best in others—and the founder communicated to her managers that it was okay to be up-front about mistakes, which would give them a chance to learn and improve together. They also started to use facts (versus emotions) as a way to review situations, bringing the Knowing quality into the team dynamic. Over time, trust was rebuilt, and they exceeded their sales targets.

Celebrating the strengths of your team (both peers and subordinates) and having the words to articulate appreciation of their strengths is the goal here. This vocabulary can also give specificity and actionability to feedback, so that "I need you to be more confident" can become "I would like you to practice or become more comfortable with [insert one of the eight superpowers]." We can build relationships and mentor people who have our same or different confidence languages, and that's where the power is both personally and for the organization as a whole. Here's a confidence-building exercise you can do with your team:

1. Reflect on the people you interact with the most. What are their superpowers?

2. Carve out time in every month to acknowledge a specific moment where you saw their superpowers in action. Make the example as specific as possible so they feel valued and seen.

3. Offer feedback regularly, not just at scheduled times, but in the moment, whether to reinforce a strength or suggest an idea for improvement or a new strength to develop.

While this chapter covers a lot of ground when it comes to relationships, it is by no means a substantive psychological dive into how people interrelate. What our confidence language approach can do is provide another tool to help you better understand the people who matter. With the vocabulary you've developed to understand what makes others tick, you'll be able to strive for deeper, more meaningful, and more rewarding relationships in all areas of your life.

THE SISTERHOOD
OF GRAVITAS

When I told you my friend Monica's story in Chapter 5 about her witnessing an executive undercutting herself in her introduction at a company taskforce meeting, I didn't tell you the whole story. I saved one part for this chapter because it perfectly illustrates what we need to do as women for the sake of our collective future.

After Monica recounted the story to me, I asked her a question. "Are you going to give her any feedback about how she came across in the meeting?"

"Why would I do that? I don't know her at all, and I don't feel comfortable giving someone who's been here longer than I have that kind of feedback," Monica responded.

"But your silence is complicity. You just told me that your boss asked you about her, and you expressed your concern to him. Don't you want women at your company to succeed?"

She looked back at my quizzically. "Of course. There aren't many of us."

"Okay, so if you say nothing to this woman, you are confirming your boss's opinion. By not helping her, you're part of the problem."

"Lisa, I never thought about it that way. . . ."

"So . . . what are you going to do about it?"

We discussed her options and decided that the next time they were together in person (they both worked remotely from different states), she would ask her out for coffee. Monica would take the opportunity to be encouraging and supportive, saying something like: "We're both women at this company. There aren't many of us. While we are siloed in our own departments and don't see each other very much, there's more power in us being together than apart. I want us all to succeed, and I want to share something because I see it in myself. In our first meeting, I noticed you were self-deprecating when you didn't need to be. I have had to overcome being self-deprecating too, and I think we could help each other." A few months later, Monica shared with me that she was wrong about her first impression of this colleague; in fact, this person was incredibly capable. Monica not only corrected her initial impression of this executive with her boss, but also scheduled that coffee date with her colleague to strengthen their relationship.

What happens when fully actualized women who are aware of their superpowers band together? It becomes a sisterhood of friends, family members, and colleagues in which we lift each other up and do even more together (yes, I'm envisioning the gravitas version of an all-female Avengers crew). I know from personal experience that the feeling of belonging, of knowing that people have your back in any situation, is life-affirming. I have many times avoided a mental and emotional breakdown because of a fiercely loyal group of fellow entrepreneurs. We keep in steady touch via text messages; one of my favorite messages ever was "Let them have the old boys' club. The sisterhood is so much stronger."

It's true. The brave who have come before us have cleared a narrow path, and it is up to us to continue to machete our way forward on that path, leaving it clearer and wider for the next generation. In 2013, Sheryl Sandberg helped create a seismic shift in how we talk about women in the workplace with her blockbuster book *Lean In*. Its publication and the dialogue it inspired encouraged women to be more willing to take risks. But in 2016, she teamed up with McKinsey & Company to conduct a series of co-branded "Women in the Workplace" studies to see how women were faring. The insight? While *Lean In* gave women permission to ask for more raises and credit, they were faced with being labeled as aggressive or pushy, didn't have the skills to make the ask, or faced systemic and cultural biases: "They leaned in, and the world pushed back."[1] *Harvard Business Review* recently surmised:

> The problem with these leaders' approaches is that they don't address the often-fragile process of coming to see oneself, and to be seen by others, as a leader. Becoming a leader involves much more than being put in a leadership role, acquiring new skills, and adapting one's style to the requirements of that role. It involves a fundamental identity shift. Organizations inadvertently undermine this process when they advise women to proactively seek leadership roles without also addressing policies and practices that communicate a mismatch between how women are seen and the qualities and experiences people tend to associate with leaders.[2]

How do we use gravitas to reshape the cultures within which we operate to make them more inclusive and empowering? In the words of Gloria Steinem, "We need to be long-distance runners to make a real social revolution. And you can't be a long-distance runner unless you have some inner strength." We can show up for ourselves, reframe the narrative around our distinctive strengths, and take credit for them. In doing so, we are ambassadors for this complete vocabulary of what it means to be confident. The more we show up for ourselves, the more able we will be to set the precedent for those around us and those who come behind us—and the more we will recognize strengths in others. It will take time for us to eradicate systemic bias, but we can still be part of the path to reversing it. This means leveling up on Leading, Performing, Creating, and Self-Sustaining skills in the near term so we can be competitive, while also expanding our society's definitions of what it takes to be viewed as successful.

We have to do this work individually and then support each other in doing this work collectively. Embodying every fundamental lesson in this book so far is one thing. But we've got to be a part of the larger cultural change required for us to succeed together. One of my favorite *New Yorker* cartoons is of an anthropomorphized squid working behind a sushi bar, and the head chef tells a customer that "He wants to change the system from within." There are four ways I believe we can do this together: calling out bias, amplifying the power of the pack, embracing role modeling, and embodying allyship.

Calling Out Bias

When I am working with a client for a speaking engagement or workshop on confidence, I will sometimes get the question, "Lisa, do your topics work for men? It's a mixed audience, and we want to make sure they feel included." My graceful response is "Absolutely; my lessons are universal and speak to women, men, nonbinary people, everyone." But my inner monologue is seething and what I really wish I could say is what Abby Wambach shared in her book *Wolfpack* when she was asked the same question by a company hiring her to teach about leadership: "Good question! But only if you've asked every male speaker you've hired if his message is applicable to women, too." When I read this in her book, it was so empowering to know that she had the self-assurance to call out the person who had asked her the same question.

How many times have you witnessed or been the target of this type of asymmetrical perspective? In writing this book, I've been confronted with my own experiences or complicity in circumstances that I have observed. I have been writing them down as I go—the times when I've stayed silent, the times when I've complained to a friend about an unfair situation, the times when I've accommodated because it's easier than changing the system. But there are instances when I was able to step out and be brave. One example? In one of my speeches, I describe the dressing room as an analogy for how we take on the day (most women walk in with their own set of insecurities) and share a story of a woman bouncing back after divorce. Before I do, I say, "Men in the audience, I'm about to give you the gift of seeing the world through the eyes of every woman you know. You're welcome. It will make you a better person." Because it's true. For too long, we've seen the world through the patriarchy, and I can be a part of the solution in calling it out and sharing our points of view.

We do not have to be alone in calling out bias. My friend the veteran television journalist Hadley Gamble told me about being the last Western journalist to interview Russian president Vladimir Putin in the fall of 2021 before his invasion of Ukraine. She had asked the question, "Are you using energy as a weapon?" and Putin accused her of being too beautiful to understand him. In response, she laughed in his face. "I had just turned forty and this man was telling me I looked beautiful instead of answering the question." She then responded with intensity and full force by putting him on the hot seat, pressing him to answer her question. "I laughed in his face and said, 'No, Mr. President. I heard what you said.' The subtext being, 'I don't believe you and I'm not letting you off the hook.' There's this element of no fear. I don't see anyone as more powerful than I am. Once they are in the seat, I have them. Unless they run off the stage, they're mine." That day, one of her colleagues, David Sheppard, energy editor at the *Financial Times*, posted on Twitter in support of Hadley: "It's patronising, it's sexist. . . . Would he have said the same to a male journalist? No."[3]

Surprisingly, we are not immune to this behavior even among ourselves. Growing up in our culture, it's impossible not to participate in some form of toxic femininity, or what may be better phrased as "internal misogyny."[4] Patriarchal perceptions of women have been around for so long that some women accept the submissive feminine traits like passivity and empathy to sustain those around them, specifically men.[5] Ever have a woman (passive-aggressively) knock you down for the way you looked? Shame you if you are not married or you don't have kids? That is toxic femininity. Whenever I find myself going down this road, I try to understand why I'm finding myself in this unsupportive position. When we learn to recognize this in our behavior and that of others, we can see and treat each other with full agency.

We also have to watch out for the queen bee syndrome. Named in 1973 by University of Michigan psychologists, this trait has been described as "a woman in a position of authority who treats female subordinates more critically and often refuses to help other women rise up the ranks as a form of self-preservation."[6] Theories about its development differ, but one was put forth by Marianne Cooper, a sociologist at the VMware Women's Leadership Innovation Lab at Stanford University, in 2016: They are "women with low levels of gender identification—who think their gender should be irrelevant at work and for whom connecting with other women is not important."[7] For example, I attended a dinner party with a group of accomplished women executives who proudly shared

how they had fought so hard to have a seat at the table at their respec-
tive companies. As the night progressed, the discussion turned to how
they had not yet pulled up additional seats for other women. No matter
what sort of bad behavior we have seen from our own kind, we have to
watch out for each other and hold each other accountable.

When I think about all the times when I've been silent, the roots of
this complicity are complex. Sometimes I ignore the microaggression—
that subtly sexist or racist comment (sometimes cloaked as a joke)
—because I am tired, busy, or just used to it. I try to watch out for
moments when listening to the injustice in a woman's story makes me
furious, just like Monica, who felt angry that her colleague was so def-
erential in that first meeting. If we feel self-assured in our own power,
what can we do about it together? I will openly say to you that I don't
have the full answer, but calling it out for ourselves and enlisting the
help of others are the first steps.

Amplifying the Power of the Pack

Before we can amplify the power of the pack, first, the pack must be
visible. Shelley Zalis, the founder and CEO of The Female Quotient,
a thought leadership platform for women, uses "power of the pack" to
describe the vibrant community she founded. In 2013, when she wanted
to go to her first Consumer Electronics Show, she heard that the event
was notorious for its lack of female representation. She felt alone in
going, so she decided to invite a few other women executives to join her.
Those executives invited others, and suddenly there were more than
50 women who showed up that first day. As they walked the show floor
together, they were visible and noticeable. (With 50 women striding
together down the aisles, men had to move out of the way.) What began
as a small group turned into the Girls' Lounge (as opposed to the boys'
club) and later evolved into the Equality Lounge, a go-to destination
for over one million women across 100 countries supporting each other
at corporate events and conferences such as SXSW and the World Economic Forum.[8] Abby Wambach also echoes this idea in the title of her
previously mentioned book, *Wolfpack*. From the academic perspective,
a *Harvard Business Review* article concluded that women who thrive in
the workplace are fueled by female relationships: "Women benefited in

terms of post-MBA job placement from being central in the network too; but to achieve the executive positions with the highest levels of authority and pay they also had to have an inner circle of close female contacts, despite having similar qualifications to men, including education and work experience."[9] When women support each other unconditionally and without judgment, we can flourish. The power of the pack is extraordinary; a critical mass of confident women reinforces that we are not alone on this journey.

Marcia Davies, the COO of the Mortgage Bankers Association (MBA), is another example of a successful executive who worked hard to create a community of women colleagues. Marcia rose through the ranks of the mortgage banking industry during a time when single women could not have a bank account without a husband listed on the account. She learned this fact the hard way when she went through her divorce from her first husband and had to save enough cash on her own to pay the deposit on an apartment. Later, when she was contemplating the offer of a promotion at work, she talked to her boss and advocated for the salary it would take for her to accept the new role. He agreed. In 2015, as she was planning the MBA's annual meeting in San Diego, she decided to host a luncheon with a handful of women: "The more I traveled, the more I met women who didn't know other women in our field. So I decided to do something to bring women together. I sent out invitations to seventy-five women and imagine my surprise when I showed up to lunch and found a hundred and fifty women." That was the catalyst for Marcia to create a network for women. She called it mPower (MBA Promoting Opportunities for Women to Extend their Reach). Fast forward to 2023: the online community has more than 9,000 members from across the country and is so in demand that Marcia created a full-day add-on to the annual MBA convention just for women to network, learn, and be inspired. Women in the network help each other find jobs, share advice, work on business deals together, even support each other in times of personal crisis. As Marcia shares, "Early in my career, I worked with an amazing, dynamic woman who became a champion of my work and coached me on how to lead others. She taught me leadership lessons that I still practice today. I want every woman in the industry to have that too."

The power in the pack can start from anywhere. Remember what Violet, Judy, and Doralee did to their tyrannical, sexist boss in the movie

9 to 5? After abducting him and running the business themselves, they implemented several programs like equal pay, on-site day care, and flexible hours. (How was this film made more than 40 years ago and we are still fighting for these same benefits?) It takes just one of us to build it, and then they will come. It may be as simple as the book club we spent time with in our focus groups. I have a group of women I exercise with every Monday morning at 7:15 A.M., Amber, Amy T., Amy Z., Chelsey, and Jeannette, all five of whom are executives and business owners. While we are foam rolling, our conversations range from the state of the economy to what's going on at home. I also have two entrepreneurs in my life, Anna Kaiser and Jane Park, who I lean on because they never judge and often will share that they're going through the same struggles (we have an end-of-the-month message we send to each other: "Congratulations, we survived another month running our businesses. I see you and know how hard it was to close the books. You are so strong."). In fact, when my company was making face masks for the frontline workers during the pandemic, we partnered with Jane Park's company, Tokki. Her team had access to quilters' cotton that was ideal for making high-quality face masks and also created all of the marketing assets; my team handled the design and manufacturing. We co-branded the effort and kept the lights on for both of our companies. During this uncertain time, we ended each day with a phone call: "We're doing something. It's greater than zero, and it's better together."

These are women who sit inside my journey with me, celebrating not just the results, but the process and how hard I'm fighting. I'm not alone in the tough moments. When we lock arms, it's much harder to push us over.

Embracing Role Modeling

This confidence work is not just for ourselves. When we engage more deeply with our own superpowers and recognize them in others, we also create an example that opens up space for others. When we are inspired, we are also inspiring. When we step into our own light, we end up shining that light on others. Because in addition to all the forces we're working against, we also have to defeat queen bee syndrome—the age-old notion of women pitted against each other—once and for all. I hope to be a part of reversing the norm: as we move up, we need to seize the opportunity to bring other women with us.

So much of our gender identity is learned from watching others, so doing the work for ourselves also results in role-modeling the possibilities for others. We mirror—consciously or not—our mothers, sisters, classmates, colleagues. A photograph by artist Carrie Mae Weems from her *Kitchen Table Series* shows herself at the head of a table, applying makeup with a small vanity mirror. Next to her is a young girl with her own small mirror, putting on lipstick with the same posture, stance, and studiousness. It's a reminder that so much of what we accept as the norm is learned from and performed based on others. This is why we need to step into our power as role models, in even simple ways such as purchasing from women-owned businesses. To put this act in perspective, women make up more than half of the U.S. population and control or influence 85 percent of consumer spending; worldwide, women control over $31.8 trillion in spending.[10] When we deploy the spend we control to support other women, we amplify and boost their chances of success, and it creates a connective tissue that has an even greater impact. In bigger ways, we can offer our time and expertise to mentor others, being a sounding board in moments of crisis and publicly cheerleading for one another. We can create around us a circle of influence in which we become practitioners and evangelists for gravitas.

Let me start with the concept of the Batphone, Commissioner Gordon's secure line (a red phone) that he used to call Batman in times of crisis as depicted in the 1960s TV show. I have a few Batphone numbers for women I call in times of distress. One is for my friend Jane Park, because she's the one person who I can be completely vulnerable with; she can immediately calm me and help me when I face a setback. More than that, she draws potential options out of me so I can stop spiraling. We role-play a few scenarios, which is always very empowering; she helps me sort through what needs to be said or done. And what is said out loud, especially to a nonjudgmental friend, immediately quashes any feelings of shame. The possibilities feel more possible when I can hear them coming out of my mouth instead of just floating around in my head.

This relationship is reciprocal. I am a Batphone for Jane, and for other women too. For example, I was on the receiving end of a Batphone call when my former colleague Laura made the decision to leave McKinsey after being there for almost eight years. She was considering taking on her next role with a start-up but felt intimidated by the founder. We rehearsed channeling a Self-Sustaining mindset (critical for negotiating a salary), with me playing the role of the founder. We played out the possible scenarios so that she felt prepared and strong going into her meeting. Guess what? She got exactly what she asked for.

What a joy and a privilege it is to be able to support another woman in achieving greater success. As Mindy Grossman shared with me, "I've made my focus making others successful, because it makes everyone more successful. It sets up the next generation of leadership." To reshape the cultures in which we operate, we have to be in it with each other first and foremost. We can be agents of change and lend our strengths to other women. Take a moment and write down who is on your Batphone list—and whose list you are on.

Embodying Allyship

I was in Plano, Texas, for a speaking engagement when an Asian woman in midlevel management came up to me and said, "It's amazing to see someone like you on stage. I feel like everyone assumes I am young and inexperienced simply because I'm an Asian woman. I'm doing the best work of my career, but I feel invisible to the powers that be." Listening to her, I felt so frustrated and angry. I was frustrated that she didn't have the tools to advocate for herself, and even if she had had them, I was angry at the system that didn't see her and left her without any allies in the wings to support her. I was angry for her that she felt held back by her demography, over which she had no control. I thought about how much stronger she would feel if she had even one advocate who saw her true talents.

Each of our starting points are different in building connections, and some of us face an additional layer of demographic barriers (socio-economic, racial) on top of systemic gender dynamics. I grew up as an outsider with very few birth-based privileges. When I entered the workplace, I couldn't find anyone in a position of power who looked like me. Being of Asian descent worked against me because I look 10 years younger than I am, and to this day, I am constantly underestimated when people meet me for the first time. So the burden is solely on my shoulders to be seen, and I recognize this as unfair. On my best days, I'm able to make meaning out of my resentment by using it to fuel my passion to do everything I can to make sure no one in my network experiences the loneliness and powerlessness of going unseen.

Putting allyship into action is even more critical as we achieve positions of power. The McKinsey *Women in the Workplace* 2021 study found that "although more than three quarters of white employees consider themselves allies to women of color at work, far fewer are consistently taking key allyship actions."[11] A year later, in the 2022 study, McKinsey found that 77 percent of white employees consider themselves allies to women of color. However, when surveyed on specific allyship actions, that number fell dramatically: mentoring or sponsoring women of color (10 percent), advocating for new opportunities (21 percent), actively confronting discrimination (39 percent), publicly acknowledging ideas (43 percent), and educating oneself about their experiences (45 percent). This disconnect showed up even among women. When women of color were asked to rank what top three allyship actions they most wanted, their ranking was: 1. advocate for new opportunities; 2. actively confront discrimination; 3. publicly acknowledge their ideas. However, white women ranked the top three most important allyship actions differently: 1. actively confront discrimination; 2. publicly acknowledge their ideas; 3. advocate for new opportunities. Perhaps this is why author Jodi-Ann Burey in her riveting TED Talk concludes, "So no, this Black disabled immigrant woman will not be bringing her full, authentic self to work. But she is asking you, those of you with the power of your positions and the protection of your whiteness and other societal privileges you did not earn, to take on that risk instead."

Yes, there is risk involved with allyship. We all are certain to say the wrong thing, to stumble through our good intentions, to cause discomfort, but as Maya Angelou taught us, "Do the best you can until you know better. Then when you know better, do better." Active allyship requires empathy, creativity, and courage.

Sit Inside the Story: Get as close as you can to being inside another's story, embodying passionate curiosity—a true desire to understand underlying beliefs, values, and experiences. Be courageous enough to dig into the points of pain. One of my favorite campaigns is from

Ascend, and it highlights barriers Asian women face, specifically that they are "most likely to be hired and least likely to be promoted." Getting inside this conundrum, getting granular about how the trap is constructed and how it impacts women of color, is the first step in being a part of dismantling it. As P&G's commercial "The Name" highlights, it can also be as straightforward as saying someone's name properly; the video shares the journey of a Korean American girl named Yeong Joo [yUHng-ju] and how the the impact of learning and respecting AAPI names can be a powerful act of allyship and belonging.[12]

Share the Stage: Taking a nod from "Pass the Mic" in which those with privilege give their platforms to voices that need to be heard, I am inspired to seek opportunities to share the stage, from platforms to my Rolodex. I had coffee with inclusion expert Ruchika Tulshyan, and her first question was "How can I help? How can I amplify your work?" That was her greeting, the first thing she said to me. She then continued on to offer up her resources and network to me. It's not a zero-sum game. I committed to doing the same for her.

Look for Good, See the Good: Looking actively for the good work being done by women of color to shine light on these contributions is an important and joyful way to move toward progress. We can go a step further and create opportunities, open doors, and invest in systems that reward these behaviors. Allyship is a personal mindset that builds a habit of turning on the light to see what historically oppressive systems won't allow us to see. Then we can call others over to see the same.

Choose Compassion: Compassion is empathy combined with tangible action. Making allyship tangible can start with small achievable steps, like underscoring a helpful comment made in a meeting to build new norms. I spent a week with a group of Asian female entrepreneurs learning about the microaggressions and discrimination they have faced and sitting inside each other's stories. We've followed and reposted one another on social media and showed up to support one another's businesses. This small start will grow into a longtime partnership of women who have each other's backs.

The Joy I Feel for All of Us

In 2023, actor Michelle Yeoh was nominated and won her first Golden Globe Award for Best Actress—Motion Picture—Musical/Comedy for

Everything Everywhere All At Once. What was notable about this moment was her co-star Jamie Lee Curtis's ecstatic reaction seated next to her as the win was announced: Jamie was photographed with her arms stretched out overhead and cheering for her, as Michelle covered her face with emotion. In Jamie's words, "I'm still stunned that a moment of natural exuberance and joy, became some sort of symbol for women supporting other women." The photo went viral when Erin Gallagher, CEO and founder of gender equity company Ella, shared the photo on social media with a call to action to "unlearn what you've been wired to think: that women are your competition" and to instead "Find your Jamie. Hype their Jamie. Be her Jamie." It was a reminder that another woman's triumph doesn't take away from our own wins; her victory amplifies our collective success.

This is the joy I feel for all of you on this journey, and it's the joy I hope you pass on to others, as you fully realize the power of gravitas. Journalist Juli Fraga described this feeling in a piece for *The New York Times,* "Finding pleasure in another person's good fortune is what social scientists call 'freudenfreude,' a term (inspired by the German word for 'joy') that describes the bliss we feel when someone else succeeds, even if it doesn't directly involve us." She goes on to share the positive effects of freudenfreude, including improved life satisfaction, boosted resilience, and increased cooperation during a conflict.[13] When we end the cycle of zero-sum thinking, which relishes delight in other's defeats, we can celebrate each other's successes in a way that becomes a "social glue" that helps all of us triumph together.

While I was finishing this book, I was on a speaking tour and an executive in Houston sent me this email message after I had spoken with her women's leadership group: "It was a joy to discover my own superpowers with you. You are the ultimate cheerleader and I left that room ready to conquer the world." When I dig into why I can unabashedly cheerlead for others, I realize that this is the power of gravitas in my own life. I have such a secure sense of self, free from comparison and envy, so much so that I can fully and genuinely celebrate others. Perhaps that's the ultimate expression of gravitas, knowing ourselves in a way that gives us strength and then being able to do that for others.

I've always loved the notion of sisterhood, "a community of women linked by a common interest." What could we accomplish if the basis for that sisterhood was gravitas?

AFTERWORD
This Is You Beyond Doubt

If you've gotten to this point, thank you for going on this journey with me. Thank you for choosing self-confidence, for owning your strengths, for being brave in exploring and expanding the concentric circles of your life. Thank you for embracing courage, compassion, and connection as the antidotes to the forces working against us. Thank you for taking on the call to action to enable those around you—family, friends, colleagues—to see their best selves too. Thank you for trusting me. I see you. I value you. I believe in you.

Take a moment and look at how far you've come. Sometimes we're so focused on looking at the summit that we don't turn around to look back to measure the ground we've covered. Seeing the progress in and of itself is confidence-building. And this is not a snapshot in time, it's a lifetime of real, ongoing work, work that I'm still doing for myself every day, especially in letting go of what others think of me and loving myself the way I love others. Writing this book has been a way to give myself the advice I most needed. Because the inner critic never goes away for good, we drown out its voice with the megaphone of our superpowers. We move to a place that is beyond doubt.

Living beyond doubt is not the same thing as living without doubt. Moving past doubt means moving from a fixed deficit mindset to living every day with a growth-oriented mindset that is courageous, compassionate, and connected—fueled by a vocabulary of superpowers. This language empowers us to see things as they really are and to ably navigate whatever opportunities and challenges lie ahead. It helps us to live beyond fear, shame, and guilt. We can stand rooted in our confidence language and our strengths, and choose self-assurance, resolve, and boldness. Whether you want to be a better friend, co-worker, mom, partner, sibling, or daughter, or you want to make that dream a reality, your believing in and living your superpowers to their full potential will make all of that possible.

What do I wish for as you the reader—and all women—going forward? In the near term, I hope to see an increase in Leading, Performing, Creating, and Self-Sustaining attributes in us all, because these superpowers can double or triple our confidence in almost any situation. Long-term, my dream is a world where we are able to embrace all eight superpowers as equally valuable. If in 20 years we conducted the same quantitative survey, I would love to make the prediction that we'd have more people satisfied in their lives, and more women feeling highly capable in navigating the most challenging situations.

One woman at a time. That's what it will take. The mantra going forward: We are proud, confident, beautiful, supportive, and unstoppable at every turn. We are moms, entrepreneurs, creative souls, partners, thinkers, makers, and doers. We live in the moment. We embrace the bumps in the road and the curves of our lives. We wear our confidence on our sleeves. We own it. We love it. We wouldn't have it any other way. Watch out world, we are Gravitas.

APPENDIX

The Superpower Quiz

Below are additional copies of the Superpower Quiz found in Chapter 3. You can retake the quiz to measure progress, aspirationally as the person you would like to be, or you can have someone you trust take it on your behalf. You can also take the quiz online at MyConfidenceLanguage.com.

Superpower Quiz

Please circle any of the following statements that you feel describe you and how you approach life. There are no right or wrong answers. Please answer as honestly as possible. Select all that apply.

1. I enjoy leading meetings.

2. I've been told that I'm the life of the party.

3. I love setting goals and working to achieve and/or exceed them.

4. I enjoy helping others with no expectation of return.

5. I enjoy gathering and analyzing information before making a decision or forming an opinion.

6. I am really good at coming up with new ideas.

7. I am a calming force in groups.

8. In group settings, I don't feel like I have to prove myself or impress anyone.

9. In group settings, others look to me to take charge.

10. I enjoy meeting new people.

11. I get even more motivated when I am challenged—I love healthy competition.

12. I am a good listener. People often come to me to vent.

13. I live by the motto "knowledge is power."

14. I think often about what the future will look like.

15. I expect good things will come and things will get better, even in the toughest of times.

16. I rarely feel embarrassed.

17. I get energy from giving a speech or presentation.

18. I don't mind being seated next to a stranger at a dinner party—I was born to charm!

19. I believe practice makes perfect.

20. I enjoy putting time and thought into buying the perfect gift.

21. I consider myself a logical and rational person.

22. I enjoy any creative activity.

23. I believe everything happens for a reason; if it doesn't happen, it wasn't meant to be.

24. I do what I want without worrying about what others will think.

25. I've been told that I am a great coach.

26. I care whether or not people like me.

27. I've been known to continue on and/or endure, regardless of setbacks.

28. If a friend is sick, I'm the first to show up to help.

29. I enjoy a good to-do list. I can create a spreadsheet for almost any occasion!

30. I get excited about "firsts"—experiencing or doing something never done before.

31. Even in tough times, I'm very hopeful about the future.

32. I'm comfortable in my own skin.

33. I take charge in planning outings for my friends.

34. I'm great at telling stories; I love being asked to give a toast!

35. I'm always measuring how I'm doing, especially to improve.

36. I've been told that I can be too nice (almost to the point where I feel taken for granted!).

37. I'm not comfortable making decisions without all the available information.

38. I believe in things before I can see them.

39. When I face a setback, I give myself to the universe and/or something greater than me.

40. I don't feel intimidated or threatened by others.

41. I've been told that I like to have things my way too often.

42. I've been told that I can be overwhelming.

43. I can be stubborn and don't know when to let go.

44. I get a lot of satisfaction out of helping others be successful.

45. I enjoy learning new things.

46. I have been told that I am not practical and/or am too much of a dreamer.

47. I practice gratitude (versus worrying about what I can't control).

48. I don't feel the need to explain myself.

49. I'm good at persuading people to participate or contribute to a project or cause.

50. I enjoy being the center of attention.

51. My accomplishments are a big part of who I am.

52. I often feel responsible for the happiness of others.

53. I am a very curious person.

54. I have a really powerful imagination.

55. I usually see the best in every situation and other people.

56. I rarely compare myself to others.

Getting Your Results

Check the boxes next to the numbered questions that you circled. Add up the number of checked boxes in each column. If you have four or more checked boxes for one of the traits, congrats, you've found your superpower(s)! Eighty percent of the women we surveyed score highly in at least one superpower. This is where you feel most comfortable and capable; you already know how to express these forms of confidence naturally. On average, people have two superpowers in which they are strongest. For those of you who had two or three checked boxes, you already demonstrate those areas in some form and to some degree. Good for you—you have a base from which to strengthen. Those who scored one or none: these are areas that you may want to develop, based on relationships and situations you encounter.

LEADING	PERFORMING	ACHIEVING	GIVING	KNOWING	CREATING	BELIEVING	SELF-SUSTAINING
❏ 1	❏ 2	❏ 3	❏ 4	❏ 5	❏ 6	❏ 7	❏ 8
❏ 9	❏ 10	❏ 11	❏ 12	❏ 13	❏ 14	❏ 15	❏ 16
❏ 17	❏ 18	❏ 19	❏ 20	❏ 21	❏ 22	❏ 23	❏ 24
❏ 25	❏ 26	❏ 27	❏ 28	❏ 29	❏ 30	❏ 31	❏ 32
❏ 33	❏ 34	❏ 35	❏ 36	❏ 37	❏ 38	❏ 39	❏ 40
❏ 41	❏ 42	❏ 43	❏ 44	❏ 45	❏ 46	❏ 47	❏ 48
❏ 49	❏ 50	❏ 51	❏ 52	❏ 53	❏ 54	❏ 55	❏ 56

Scores:

Superpower Quiz

Please circle any of the following statements that you feel describe you and how you approach life. There are no right or wrong answers. Please answer as honestly as possible. Select all that apply.

1. I enjoy leading meetings.

2. I've been told that I'm the life of the party.

3. I love setting goals and working to achieve and/or exceed them.

4. I enjoy helping others with no expectation of return.

5. I enjoy gathering and analyzing information before making a decision or forming an opinion.

6. I am really good at coming up with new ideas.

7. I am a calming force in groups.

8. In group settings, I don't feel like I have to prove myself or impress anyone.

9. In group settings, others look to me to take charge.

10. I enjoy meeting new people.

11. I get even more motivated when I am challenged—I love healthy competition.

12. I am a good listener. People often come to me to vent.

13. I live by the motto "knowledge is power."

14. I think often about what the future will look like.

15. I expect good things will come and things will get better, even in the toughest of times.

16. I rarely feel embarrassed.

17. I get energy from giving a speech or presentation.

18. I don't mind being seated next to a stranger at a dinner party—I was born to charm!

19.   I believe practice makes perfect.

20.   I enjoy putting time and thought into buying the perfect gift.

21.   I consider myself a logical and rational person.

22.   I enjoy any creative activity.

23.   I believe everything happens for a reason; if it doesn't happen, it wasn't meant to be.

24.   I do what I want without worrying about what others will think.

25.   I've been told that I am a great coach.

26.   I care whether or not people like me.

27.   I've been known to continue on and/or endure, regardless of setbacks.

28.   If a friend is sick, I'm the first to show up to help.

29.   I enjoy a good to-do list. I can create a spreadsheet for almost any occasion!

30.   I get excited about "firsts"—experiencing or doing something never done before.

31.   Even in tough times, I'm very hopeful about the future.

32.   I'm comfortable in my own skin.

33.   I take charge in planning outings for my friends.

34.   I'm great at telling stories; I love being asked to give a toast!

35.   I'm always measuring how I'm doing, especially to improve.

36.   I've been told that I can be too nice (almost to the point where I feel taken for granted!).

37.   I'm not comfortable making decisions without all the available information.

38.   I believe in things before I can see them.

39.   When I face a setback, I give myself to the universe and/or something greater than me.

40. I don't feel intimidated or threatened by others.

41. I've been told that I like to have things my way too often.

42. I've been told that I can be overwhelming.

43. I can be stubborn and don't know when to let go.

44. I get a lot of satisfaction out of helping others be successful.

45. I enjoy learning new things.

46. I have been told that I am not practical and/or am too much of a dreamer.

47. I practice gratitude (versus worrying about what I can't control).

48. I don't feel the need to explain myself.

49. I'm good at persuading people to participate or contribute to a project or cause.

50. I enjoy being the center of attention.

51. My accomplishments are a big part of who I am.

52. I often feel responsible for the happiness of others.

53. I am a very curious person.

54. I have a really powerful imagination.

55. I usually see the best in every situation and other people.

56. I rarely compare myself to others.

Getting Your Results

Check the boxes next to the numbered questions that you circled. Add up the number of checked boxes in each column. If you have four or more checked boxes for one of the traits, congrats, you've found your superpower(s)! Eighty percent of the women we surveyed score highly in at least one superpower. This is where you feel most comfortable and capable; you already know how to express these forms of confidence naturally. On average, people have two superpowers in which they are strongest. For those of you who had two or three checked boxes, you already demonstrate those areas in some form and to some degree. Good for you—you have a base from which to strengthen. Those who scored one or none: these are areas that you may want to develop, based on relationships and situations you encounter.

LEADING	PERFORMING	ACHIEVING	GIVING	KNOWING	CREATING	BELIEVING	SELF-SUSTAINING
❑ 1	❑ 2	❑ 3	❑ 4	❑ 5	❑ 6	❑ 7	❑ 8
❑ 9	❑ 10	❑ 11	❑ 12	❑ 13	❑ 14	❑ 15	❑ 16
❑ 17	❑ 18	❑ 19	❑ 20	❑ 21	❑ 22	❑ 23	❑ 24
❑ 25	❑ 26	❑ 27	❑ 28	❑ 29	❑ 30	❑ 31	❑ 32
❑ 33	❑ 34	❑ 35	❑ 36	❑ 37	❑ 38	❑ 39	❑ 40
❑ 41	❑ 42	❑ 43	❑ 44	❑ 45	❑ 46	❑ 47	❑ 48
❑ 49	❑ 50	❑ 51	❑ 52	❑ 53	❑ 54	❑ 55	❑ 56

Scores:

Superpower Quiz

Please circle any of the following statements that you feel describe you and how you approach life. There are no right or wrong answers. Please answer as honestly as possible. Select all that apply.

1. I enjoy leading meetings.

2. I've been told that I'm the life of the party.

3. I love setting goals and working to achieve and/or exceed them.

4. I enjoy helping others with no expectation of return.

5. I enjoy gathering and analyzing information before making a decision or forming an opinion.

6. I am really good at coming up with new ideas.

7. I am a calming force in groups.

8. In group settings, I don't feel like I have to prove myself or impress anyone.

9. In group settings, others look to me to take charge.

10. I enjoy meeting new people.

11. I get even more motivated when I am challenged—I love healthy competition.

12. I am a good listener. People often come to me to vent.

13. I live by the motto "knowledge is power."

14. I think often about what the future will look like.

15. I expect good things will come and things will get better, even in the toughest of times.

16. I rarely feel embarrassed.

17. I get energy from giving a speech or presentation.

18. I don't mind being seated next to a stranger at a dinner party—I was born to charm!

19. I believe practice makes perfect.

20. I enjoy putting time and thought into buying the perfect gift.

21. I consider myself a logical and rational person.

22. I enjoy any creative activity.

23. I believe everything happens for a reason; if it doesn't happen, it wasn't meant to be.

24. I do what I want without worrying about what others will think.

25. I've been told that I am a great coach.

26. I care whether or not people like me.

27. I've been known to continue on and/or endure, regardless of setbacks.

28. If a friend is sick, I'm the first to show up to help.

29. I enjoy a good to-do list. I can create a spreadsheet for almost any occasion!

30. I get excited about "firsts"—experiencing or doing something never done before.

31. Even in tough times, I'm very hopeful about the future.

32. I'm comfortable in my own skin.

33. I take charge in planning outings for my friends.

34. I'm great at telling stories; I love being asked to give a toast!

35. I'm always measuring how I'm doing, especially to improve.

36. I've been told that I can be too nice (almost to the point where I feel taken for granted!).

37. I'm not comfortable making decisions without all the available information.

38. I believe in things before I can see them.

39. When I face a setback, I give myself to the universe and/or something greater than me.

40. I don't feel intimidated or threatened by others.

41. I've been told that I like to have things my way too often.

42. I've been told that I can be overwhelming.

43. I can be stubborn and don't know when to let go.

44. I get a lot of satisfaction out of helping others be successful.

45. I enjoy learning new things.

46. I have been told that I am not practical and/or am too much of a
      dreamer.

47. I practice gratitude (versus worrying about what I can't control).

48. I don't feel the need to explain myself.

49. I'm good at persuading people to participate or contribute to a
      project or cause.

50. I enjoy being the center of attention.

51. My accomplishments are a big part of who I am.

52. I often feel responsible for the happiness of others.

53. I am a very curious person.

54. I have a really powerful imagination.

55. I usually see the best in every situation and other people.

56. I rarely compare myself to others.

Getting Your Results

Check the boxes next to the numbered questions that you circled. Add up the number of checked boxes in each column. If you have four or more checked boxes for one of the traits, congrats, you've found your super-power(s)! Eighty percent of the women we surveyed score highly in at least one superpower. This is where you feel most comfortable and capable; you already know how to express these forms of confidence naturally. On average, people have two superpowers in which they are strongest. For those of you who had two or three checked boxes, you already demonstrate those areas in some form and to some degree. Good for you—you have a base from which to strengthen. Those who scored one or none: these are areas that you may want to develop, based on relationships and situations you encounter.

LEADING	PERFORMING	ACHIEVING	GIVING	KNOWING	CREATING	BELIEVING	SELF-SUSTAINING
❑ 1	❑ 2	❑ 3	❑ 4	❑ 5	❑ 6	❑ 7	❑ 8
❑ 9	❑ 10	❑ 11	❑ 12	❑ 13	❑ 14	❑ 15	❑ 16
❑ 17	❑ 18	❑ 19	❑ 20	❑ 21	❑ 22	❑ 23	❑ 24
❑ 25	❑ 26	❑ 27	❑ 28	❑ 29	❑ 30	❑ 31	❑ 32
❑ 33	❑ 34	❑ 35	❑ 36	❑ 37	❑ 38	❑ 39	❑ 40
❑ 41	❑ 42	❑ 43	❑ 44	❑ 45	❑ 46	❑ 47	❑ 48
❑ 49	❑ 50	❑ 51	❑ 52	❑ 53	❑ 54	❑ 55	❑ 56

Scores:

ENDNOTES

Introduction

1. Orgad, Shani, and Rosalind Clair Gill. *Confidence Culture*. Durham, NC: Duke University Press, 2022.

Chapter 1

1. Klein, Ezra. "The Subtle, Sexist Whispering Campaign against Janet Yellen." *The Washington Post*, July 19, 2013. washingtonpost.com/news/wonk/wp/2013/07/19/the-subtle-sexist-whispering-campaign-against-janet-yellen.

2. Goldberg, Emma. "A Two Year, 50-Million Person Experiment in Changing How We Work." *The New York Times*, March 10, 2022. nytimes.com/2022/03/10/business/remote-work-office-life.html.

3. "Manipulating Brain Activity to Boost Confidence." *ScienceDaily*, December 15, 2016, sciencedaily.com/releases/2016/12/161215085902.htm.

4. *Women in the Workplace 2022*, LeanIn.org and McKinsey & Company, womenintheworkplace.com.

Chapter 2

1. Fox, Kate. "Mirror, Mirror: A Summary of Research Findings on Body Image." Social Issues Research Centre, 1997. sirc.org/publik/mirror.html.

2. Simpson, Alison. "Majority of Women Struggle with Self-Eteem Issues." We Are the City, March 8, 2021. wearethecity.com majority-of-women-struggle-with-self-esteem-issues.

3. "Social Comparison Theory." *Psychology Today*, n.d. psychologytoday.com/us/basics/social-comparison-theory.

4. Kay, Katty, and Claire Shipman. "The Confidence Gap." *The Atlantic*, May 2014, theatlantic.com/magazine/archive/2014/05/the-confidence-gap/359815.

5. Zenger, Jack. "The Confidence Gap in Men and Women: Why It Matters and How to Overcome It." *Forbes*, April 8, 2018. forbes.com/sites/jackzenger/2018/04/08/the-confidence-gap-in-men-and-women-why-it-matters-and-how-to-overcome-it/?sh=733ca5963bfa.

6. Purushothaman, Deepa, Lisen Stromberg, and Lisa Kaplowitz. "5 Harmful Ways Women Feel They Must Adapt in Corporate America." *Harvard Business Review,* October 31, 2022. hbr.org/2022/10/5-harmful-ways-women-feel-they-must-adapt-in-corporate-america.

7. Shipman and Kay, "The Confidence Gap," May, 2014

8. Simpson. "Majority of Women Struggle with Self-Esteem Issues."

9. Brooks, Arthur C. "How to Want Less." *The Atlantic*, February 8, 2022. theatlantic.com/magazine/archive/2022/03/why-we-are-never-satisfied-happiness/621304.

10. Salam, Maya. "Does 'Having It All' Mean Doing It All?" *The New York Times*, December 7, 2018. nytimes.com/2018/12/07/business/michelle-obama-women-having-it-all.html

11. Tulshyan, Ruchika, and Jodi-Ann Burey. "Stop Telling Women They Have Imposter Syndrome." *Harvard Business Review*, February 11, 2021. hbr. org/2021/02/stop-telling-women-they-have-imposter-syndrome.

12. *Women in the Workplace 2021*: The Full Report. Lean In, 2021. leanin.org/women-in-the-workplace/2021.

13. Mattison, Ben. "Women Aren't Promoted Because Managers Underestimate Their Potential." *Yale Insights*, September 17, 2022. insights.som.yale.edu/insights/women-arent-promoted-because-managers-underestimate-their-potential.

14. Benson, Alan, Danielle Li, and Kelly Shue. "'Potential' and the Gender Promotion Gap." June 22, 2022

Chapter 4

1. In our quantitative survey, respondents were asked: "Here is a list of situations that people often face in life. Whether you have experienced this situation or can imagine what it would be like, please tell us how capable or comfortable you feel about being able to handle this situation. Please rate on a scale from 1 to 5, where 1 = Not at all comfortable or capable and 5 = Extremely capable or comfortable." The results reflect the top two box percentages (4 or 5).

2. Sivers, Derek. "First Follower: Leadership Lessons from a Dancing Guy," February 11, 2010. sive.rs/ff.

3. Mayo, Margarita. "To Seem Confident, Women Have to Be Seen as Warm." *Harvard Business Review*, July 8, 2016. hbr.org/2016/07/to-seem-confident-women-have-to-be-seen-as-warm.

4. Conant, Douglas R. "Secrets of Positive Feedback." *Harvard Business Review*, February 16, 2011. hbr.org/2011/02/secrets-of-positive-feedback.

5. Duncan, Rodger Dean. "Your Life Story May Say a Lot about Your Leadership." *Forbes*, March 5, 2020. forbes.com/sites/rodgerdeanduncan/2020/03/05/your-life-story-may-say-a-lot-about-your-leadership/?sh=6377d8737827.

6. Antonakis, John, Marika Fenley, and Sue Liechti. "Learning Charisma." *Harvard Business Review*, June 7, 2012. hbr.org/2012/06/learning-charisma-2.

7. Cable, Dan. "How Humble Leadership Really Works." *Harvard Business Review*, April 23, 2018. hbr.org/2018/04/how-humble-leadership-really-works.

8. Brzezinski, Mika. *Know Your Value: Women, Money and Getting What You're Worth.* New York: Hachette, 2012, 2018.

9. Johnson, Stephen. "'Zuckerbergism': Why the Young Founder Myth Is a Trap for Entrepreneurs." Big Think, December 10, 2019. bigthink.com/the-present/young-entrepreneurs.

10. Herrmann, Ned. "What Is the Function of the Various Brainwaves?" *Scientific American*, December 22, 1997. scientificamerican.com/article/what-is-the-function-of-t-1997-12-22.

11. Gerdeman, Dina. "Clayton Christensen: The Theory of Jobs to Be Done." HBS Working Knowledge, October 3, 2016. hbswk.hbs.edu/item/clay-christensen-the-theory-of-jobs-to-be-done.

12. Emmons, Robert A., and Michael E. McCullough. (2003). "Counting Blessings versus Burdens: An Experimental Investigation of Gratitude and Subjective Well-Being in Daily Life." *Journal of Personality and Social Psychology* 84, no. 2: 377–89. doi.org/10.1037/0022-3514.84.2.377.

13. Maltby, Anna. "Mika Brzezinski Speaks: How Getting Fired Saved My Career." Marie Claire (blog). marieclaire.com/career-advice/tips/a5776/mika-brzezinski-interview/

14. Satisfaction was defined as top 2 box (6 or 7) overall on these questions: How satisfied are you with your personal life on the following dimensions? How satisfied are you with your work on the following dimensions? How satisfied were you with that last job on the following dimensions? (Please rate on a scale from 1 to 7, where 1 = Not at all satisfied and 7 = Extremely satisfied.)

15. Chamorro-Premuzic, Tomas. "Why Do So Many Incompetent Men Become Leaders?" *Harvard Business Review*, August 22, 2013. hbr.org/2013/08/why-do-so-many-incompetent-men.

16. Eagly, Alice H., and Blair T. Johnson. "Gender and Leadership Style: A Meta-Analysis." OpenCommons@UConn, January 1, 1990. opencommons.uconn.edu/chip_docs/11.

17. Dixon-Fyle, Sundiatu, Kevin Dolan, Dame Vivian Hunt, and Sara Prince. "Diversity Wins: How Inclusion Matters." McKinsey & Company, May 19, 2020. mckinsey.com/featured-insights/diversity-and-inclusion/diversity-wins-how-inclusion-matters.

18. "Covid-19 Pandemic Disproportionately Affected Women in the Americas." Pan American Health Organization, March 8, 2022. paho.org/en/news/8-3-2022-covid-19-pandemic-disproportionately-affected-women-americas.

19. Madgavkar, Anu, Olivia White, Mekala Krishnan, Deepa Mahajan, and Xavier Azcue. "Covid-19 and Gender Equality: Countering the Regressive Effects."

McKinsey & Company, July 15, 2020. mckinsey.com/featured-insights/future-of-work/covid-19-and-gender-equality-countering-the-regressive-effects.

Chapter 5

1. Jung, C. J. "Story." In *Aion: Researches into the Phenomenology of the Self,* vol. 9, Part 2, 2nd ed., *The Collected Works of C.G. Jung.* Princeton, NJ: Princeton University Press, 1968.

2. Castrillon, Caroline. "How Women Can Stop Apologizing and Take Their Power Back." *Forbes*, July 14, 2019. forbes.com/sites/carolinecastrillon/2019/07/14/how-women-can-stop-apologizing-and-take-their-power-back/?sh=24ad67a24ce6.

3. May, Cindi. "The Advantages of Not Saying You Are Sorry." *Scientific American*, July 2, 2013. scientificamerican.com/article/advantages-of-not-saying-you-are-sorry.

4. Hall, John. "Stop Saying 'I'm Sorry.' Research Says It Makes Others Think Less of You—Here's What Successful People Do Instead." CNBC, June 8, 2020. cnbc.com/2019/04/16/saying-im-sorry-can-make-people-think-poorly-of-you-research-heres-what-successful-people-do-instead.html.

5. Mohr, Tara Sophia. "Helping an Employee Overcome Their Self-Doubt." *Harvard Business Review*, October 1, 2015. hbr.org/2015/10/helping-an-employee-overcome-their-self-doubt.

Chapter 6

1. Bernhard, Meg. "What If There's No Such Thing as Closure?" *The New York Times*, December 15, 2021. nytimes.com/2021/12/15/magazine/grieving-loss-closure.html.

2. Ericsson, K. A., R. T. Krampe, and C. Tesch-Römer. (1993). "The Role of Deliberate Practice in the Acquisition of Expert Performance." *Psychological Review*, 100(3): 363–406.

3. University at Buffalo. "Study Confirms: Whatever Doesn't Kill Us Can Make Us Stronger." ScienceDaily, October 15, 2010. sciencedaily.com/releases/2010/10/101015125645.htm.

Chapter 7

1. Gu, Yumeng, J. M. Ocampo, S. B. Algoe, and C. Oveis. (2022). "Gratitude Expressions Improve Teammates' Cardiovascular Stress Responses." *Journal of Experimental Psychology.* General 151(12): 3281–91. pubmed.ncbi.nlm.nih.gov/35708951.

2. Holt-Lunstad, J., T. B. Smith, M. Baker, T. Harris, and D. Stephenson. (2015). "Loneliness and Social Isolation as Risk Factors for Mortality: A Meta-Analytic Review." *Perspectives on Psychological Science* 10(2): 227–37.

3. Ayers, Keith. "Trust Is the Key to High Performing Organisations: Here's How to Build It." Intégro.integro.com.au/trust-is-the-key-to-high-performing-organisations-heres-how-to-build-it.

4. Wallace, David Foster. "This Is Water" commencement speech. fs.blog/david-foster-wallace-this-is-water.

5. Taylor, S. E., L. C. Klein, B. P. Lewis, T. L. Gruenewald, R. A. Gurung, and J. A. Updegraff. (2000). "Biobehavioral Responses to Stress in Females: Tend-and-Befriend, Not Fight-or-Flight." *Psychological Review* 107(3): 411–29. pubmed.ncbi. nlm.nih.gov/10941275.

6. Fuller, Kristen. "The Importance of Female Friendships among Women." *Psychology Today*, August 16, 2018. psychologytoday.com/us/blog/happiness-is-state-mind/201808/the-importance-female-friendships-among-women.

7. Perel, Esther, and Mary Alice Miller. "In Long-Term Relationships, When Do You Find Yourself Most Drawn to Your Partner?" Esther Perel (blog), 2021.estherperel. com/blog/when-are-you-drawn-to-your-partner-in-long-term-relationships.

8. Russo, Marcello, Gabriele Morandin, and Massimo Bergami. "What You Need to Build a Good Relationship with Your New Boss." *Harvard Business Review*, September 2, 2021. hbr.org/2021/09/what-you-need-to-build-a-good-relationship-with-your-new-boss.

9. Layard, Lord Richard, and Tera Allas. "Happiness and Work: An Interview with Lord Richard Layard." McKinsey & Company, July 1, 2019. mckinsey.com/ featured-insights/leadership/happiness-and-work-an-interview-with-lord-richard-layard.

10. Abbajay, Mary. "What to Do When You Have a Bad Boss." *Harvard Business Review*, September 7, 2018. hbr.org/2018/09/what-to-do-when-you-have-a-bad-boss.

Chapter 8

1. Greenfield, Rebecca. "Sheryl Sandberg's 'Lean In' Missed What Most Women Needed." Bloomberg, June 3, 2022. bloomberg.com/news/articles/2022-06-03/ sheryl-sandberg-s-lean-in-missed-what-women-wanted.

2. Ibarra, Herminia, Robin J. Ely, and Deborah M. Kolb. "Women Rising: The Unseen Barriers." *Harvard Business Review*, September 2013. hbr.org/2013/09/ women-rising-the-unseen-barriers.

3. Celeste, Sofia. "Hadley Gamble on Social Change, Sleep Deprivation and How She's Still Mastering the Dynamics of a Region in Constant Evolution." *Harper's Bazaar Arabia*, July 12, 2022.harpersbazaararabia.com/hbanews/hadley-gamble-interview-bazaar.

4. Savin-Williams, Ritch C. "Toxic Femininity." *Psychology Today*, August 28, 2019. psychologytoday.com/us/blog/sex-sexuality-and-romance/201908/toxic-femininity.

5. Ibid.

6. Reality Check Team. "Queen Bees: Do Women Hinder the Progress of Other Women?" BBC, January 4, 2018. bbc.com/news/uk-41165076.

7. Cooper, Marianne. "Why Women (Sometimes) Don't Help Other Women." *The Atlantic*, June 23, 2016. theatlantic.com/business/archive/2016/06/queen-bee/ 488144.

8. Bradley, Richard. "The Education of Shelley Zalis." *Worth*, April 25, 2019. worth .com/the-education-of-shelley-zalis.

9. Uzzi, Brian. "Research: Men and Women Need Different Kinds of Networks to Succeed." *Harvard Business Review,* February 25, 2019. hbr.org/2019/02/research-men-and-women-need-different-kinds-of-networks-to-succeed.

10. Women's Earnings: The Pay Gap (Quick Take) Mar 11, 2022. catalyst.org/research/buying-power/

11. *Women in the Workplace 2021: The Full Report.* Lean In, 2021. leanin.org/women-in-the-workplace/2021.

12. *The P&G Blog. P&G Honors Asian American and Pacific Islander Heritage Month—Through Action* us.pg.com/blogs/pg-releases-the-name-aapimonth-2022/

13. Fraga, Juli. "The Opposite of Schadenfreude is Freudenfreude. Here's how to cultivate it." *The New York Times,* November 25, 2022. nytimes.com/2022/11/25/well/mind/schadenfreude-freudenfreude.html.

INDEX

ACKNOWLEDGMENTS

Early on in my career, one of my mentors said to me, "No one is born a leader; you learn how to lead from those you admire." When I reflect on these words, I am reminded of the debt of gratitude I owe to the many who have taken the time to teach me. In creating this record of those to whom I am grateful, I am in awe of the beautiful butterfly effect that these extraordinary people have had on my life.

Thank you, Mom (媽媽, 謝謝妳) for lighting the 24 hour per day/365 days per year candle in the temple for me and for ending every conversation with "you will success" (妳會成功的). You make the disappointments easier to bear, and the victories feel sweeter. A tremendous thanks to my brother, who is my role model for what it means to have a strong sense of purpose, who is never afraid to speak his mind and step up in the service of what is right, and who is willing to stand shoulder-to-shoulder with me during the toughest of times. I love you, Thomas. Thank you to my father for all your sacrifices to make sure I had an abundance of opportunities and for being my first public speaking coach, calmly waiting in the wings to make sure I felt strong and capable in any arena.

It's fun to launch a company; it's so much harder to run a company. These pages cannot contain the amount of regard I have for the people I work with every day (Aruk, we are doing it!), the teammates who have been a part of the Gravitas story at different stages (Lyn, Kathy, Deborah, Sus, Henry, Holly, Amy, Michele, Stephanie, Romy, Olivia), and the angels who invested in us before we even had a website. My deepest thanks to Sam Roberson for being with me from the very start and for always believing in me. Cabin Kim, thank you for the Tweezerman pep talk, helping me catch the glass balls, and reminding me that zombies regenerate. I spend more time at work than I do anywhere else, and I am lucky to be in it with my New York City Garment District family and our overseas production teams (thank you, Nancy & Jason!). Through our work, I get to feel the joy of serving our community of customers who inspired this book. Thank you to the women who have believed in us from the start, who shared their stories with us, and who have worn Gravitas proudly. The woman makes the dress; thank you for owning your moment in our pieces and making them shine.

This book is a testament to my literary agent Andrea (Andy) Barzvi's foresight and expert direction (thank you, Margot, for connecting us!). Andy, I felt your gravitas in our very first meeting when you shared your philosophy: if a book makes a difference in your life, you know it will for others. That personal belief has powered me through this process. You brought the incomparable Kathryn Huck into my life as my collaborator and the outstanding Melody Guy into my orbit as my editor. Kathy, thank you for believing in this work, teaching me, being my toughest sounding board, and standing by me on an hourly and daily basis professionally ("I need to record this," 2 A.M. track change sessions, talk-Lisa-down-from-the-ledge and explain-why-that-is-corny moments) and personally (Goo Goo Dolls & Palm Beach, dating horror story debriefs, "what's the real dream" conversations). I look forward to our lifetime of friendship and collaboration. Melody, thank you for your calm, fun, and kind presence in bringing this book to the world. When Andy said I could call you on your personal mobile to accept the offer, I knew we were meant to create something truly special together. Thank you for your supportive and steady hand, your savvy edits that always made the manuscript better, and for always saying "yes" when I asked if you could talk for 15 minutes. We are in this together.

I pinch myself every time I reflect on how the Hay House team has given me this opportunity to amplify the work I do and make a difference in people's lives. Here's to Diane Thomas, who welcomed me warmly into the Hay House family with our very first e-mail exchange. Thank you to Tricia Breidenthal and Shubhani Sarkar for creating the cover design I've always dreamed of and am so proud to have on my bookshelf, and to Claudine Mansour who seamlessly wove together words and charts into a beautiful visual journey. I'm deeply grateful to everyone who has had their fingerprints on this effort: Reid Tracy, Margarete Nielsen, Patty Gift, Betsy Beier, Arya-Mehr Oveissi (thanks for letting me copy you on every edit!), Lindsay McGinty, Pip Davidson, Rylie Walsh, Lizzi Marshall, Nusrah Javed, Diane Hill, John Tintera, Celeste Johnson, Lisa Bernier, Kathleen Reed, Danielle Monaco, Steve Morris, Michele Ayala, and Carrie Wellbaum.

Having an idea and then turning it into a book rooted in insight is only possible because of my mentor and dear friend Sally Dancer. Two decades ago, Sally, you met me as a McKinsey business analyst and took me under your wing, sitting together behind two-way glass mirrors in focus groups and sifting through piles of binders filled with customer survey data. Fast forward, you've had my back at every step of the Gravitas journey (including our Florentine adventure). Thank you for leading the qualitative and quantitative research in your distinctive way, from data table to actionability. Every hypothesis, Excel sheet, and takeaway carries the mark of your brilliance.

Telling the story of my company—and having it mean something in the world—is possible because of Leading Authorities (LAI). Only Rainey Foster would order a Gravitas wardrobe online before we had even met in person, and once we did meet, I knew I had found a kindred spirit. Lauren Wolf, I treasure our friendship (you, Olivia, and I share the cowgirl spirit) and your never-failing support (you raised your hand to take me on from day 1). Katherine Bentley, thank you for seeing something in me, championing my work, and being my thought partner (special thanks to Phoebe & George for the hugs). Matt Jones, thank you for believing in my entrepreneurial journey and supporting my team and me when we most needed it. Thank you to all the incredible program consultants who tirelessly create opportunities (to name a few and in alphabetical order . . . Amaron, Andrew, Brooke, Debbie, Helena, Jacquelyn, James, Jeannette, Jeff, Jonathan, Judy, Katy, Lisa M., Lisa R., Lucinda, Maeve, Megan, Mike, Mimi, Ned, my "brother" Tom) and to the entire LAI team who has helped us amplify our message (Kate,

Haley, Ron, Tim, Darrion). Because of LAI, I've had the opportunity to meet incredible people across the world who inspired this book.

If best friend is a tier and not a title, then I am blessed with the most talented and spirited group anyone could ask for: Alex Rethore (your insights and contributions were invaluable to the content of this book, and thank you for helping when I most needed it); Anh Nguyen (our calls filled with laughter and support buoy me); Anna Kaiser (so lucky to be in this together, and thank you for making me stronger in every way possible); Hana Chang (I treasure your wit and compassion); Mark Ellwood (thank you for really meaning it when you ask, "how are you, darling?"); Marybeth Coleman (your joy and presence lights up all the things); Tekla Back (BFF extraordinaire who reminds me of what matters and who is my chosen sister); Yoshiko Inoue (what would I have done if we didn't live three blocks from each other?). And to Jane Park, thank you for seeing me without judgment, for finding ways to make my life better (especially when the pinholes in the sheets of paper are not aligned), for being the Amy to my Tina (or is it the other way around? Either way, they're just waiting for us to be their BFFs too.), and for reading and editing every single line of this manuscript. I am never alone on this journey because your belief in me gives me the courage to keep going.

When you feel belonging, you can do your best work. I'm grateful to all the people who have embraced me: Dana Cowin (thank you for your mentorship, advice, unwavering support—I hope Angela Lucy and the tarot cards were at least directionally right!); Jim Greenfield and Ene Riisna for giving me a second home filled with love and learning (Ene, thank you for all your thoughtful edits to the manuscript); Ashley Taylor Bronczek (thank you for opening your doors at every turn to support me and for always including me in the fun); Marcia Davies and Elaine Howard (thank you for walking the talk of sisterhood); Vicky Nguyen (so happy that an on-stage West Coast meetup would turn into an East Coast friendship); my Yale Asian alumni women's group (Xiaoyan, thank you for creating a space for us to grow together); my AKS crew (dancing it out with you all like I'm a retired K-pop girl band member is the most joyful moment of every day); my McKinsey mentors, teammates, and clients around the world (there's no better place to "grow up" and I am grateful for the continued support). Here's to all the places that gave me table space, an outlet, and Wi-Fi to write this book (Remi43, Yale Club of New York City, the Met and the MoMA, Cheryl Houser's enchanted forest) and the doormen in my building who I celebrated with after I completed a chapter.

If you ever receive a note from me, I always sign "With gratitude," because gratitude and gravitas are intimately connected; there isn't one without the other. In recognizing those who teach us and support us, we help them see the best in themselves and pay forward a shared sense of belief in one another that fortifies us all.

With gratitude,
Lisa

ABOUT THE AUTHOR

Lisa Sun grew up in California, the daughter of Taiwanese immigrant parents. She overachieved at a young age, graduating from high school two years early and funding her Yale education with six part-time jobs, scholarships, and financial aid. After more than a decade as a consultant at McKinsey & Company, she took a solo trip around the world and decided to start her own clothing line, Gravitas, that promotes body positivity, inclusion, and self-confidence. Six weeks after its launch in 2013, Gravitas was featured in *O, The Oprah Magazine*, *People*, and the *Today* show. The business has taken off since, and includes among its activities a commitment to AAPI causes and New York City's Garment District. Often called the "dress whisperer," Lisa is also a highly sought-after public speaker who likes to impart her hard-won knowledge on gravitas and how to best harness it to other women.

To learn more about Lisa, and Gravitas, visit GravitasNewYork.com and follow @LisaLSun and @GravitasNewYork.

We hope you enjoyed this Hay House book. If you'd like to receive our online catalog featuring additional information on Hay House books and products, or if you'd like to find out more about the Hay Foundation, please contact:

Hay House, Inc., P.O. Box 5100, Carlsbad, CA 92018-5100
(760) 431-7695 or (800) 654-5126
(760) 431-6948 (fax) or (800) 650-5115 (fax)
www.hayhouse.com® • www.hayfoundation.org

———

Published in Australia by: Hay House Australia Pty. Ltd.,
18/36 Ralph St., Alexandria NSW 2015
Phone: 612-9669-4299 • *Fax:* 612-9669-4144
www.hayhouse.com.au

Published in the United Kingdom by: Hay House UK, Ltd.,
The Sixth Floor, Watson House, 54 Baker Street, London W1U 7BU
Phone: +44 (0)20 3927 7290 • *Fax:* +44 (0)20 3927 7291
www.hayhouse.co.uk

Published in India by: Hay House Publishers India,
Muskaan Complex, Plot No. 3, B-2, Vasant Kunj, New Delhi 110 070
Phone: 91-11-4176-1620 • *Fax:* 91-11-4176-1630
www.hayhouse.co.in

———

Access New Knowledge.
Anytime. Anywhere.